Praise for the Book

"Ulf's experiences are applied pragmatically to where the world is today and headed in the future. The methods and systems described in the book will help any group accelerate improves and maintain data and privacy practices."

—Brian Albertson, CRISC, CDPSE, ITIL, VP of Operations for ISACA
Atlanta Chapter, IT Risk Management Execution Led, State Farm

"Ulf Mattssons's book will help distill the complexities of privacy into a concise, compact, easy-to-follow desktop reference. As privacy becomes more important to a company's operational well-being and survival, with GDPR and other privacy-related fines heading upwards to the millions and sometimes billions of dollars, security leaders, especially in small and midsized firms, are finding their swim lanes getting broader, encompassing privacy as an area of responsibility. This book will help navigate, identify gaps and provide practical examples and ideas for building a sustainable and essential privacy framework for any organization."

—Wei Tschang, CISSP, CIPP/US, CISA, CISM, CGEIT, First VP for ISACA
New York Metropolitan Chapter, Head of Information Security, Cadwalader,
Wickersham, & Taft LLP

"Ulf Mattson, whose security insights I have cherished for years, has written the book that C-levels need to read. Data's value to an enterprise is well known, but Ulf explores how it's also a danger. It's a danger to the business in the hands of a cyberthief, it's a danger to the business if it disappears (accidentally or maliciously), it's a danger to business operations if it can't be effectively managed, analyzed, stored and retrieved and it's absolutely a danger to an enterprise when it hurts customers, which is what new data privacy laws are all about. Is data friend or foe? Frustratingly, it's both. Read this book to know how to control data and stop it from controlling you."

—Evan Schuman, Computerworld weekly columnist, Moderator for
MIT Sloan Management Review events, Member, Internet Press Guild

"Information and its usage is a massive component of the digital economy, something Ulf discusses extensively in this book. For privacy professionals looking to understand the complexities of applications at scale in this age, this book provides excellent (if not terrifying) diagrams of how modern systems work. APIs and distributed systems create value together, but that creates unique problems for those of us tasked with protecting the data driving that value. For cybersecurity professionals who want to understand more of what risk and privacy leaders are looking to solve for, this book provides crucial insight into the minds of privacy professionals as they work to apply legal and regulatory frameworks to daily operations."

—Branden R. Williams, DBA, CISSP, CISM

Controlling Privacy and the Use of Data Assets

The book will review how new and old privacy-preserving techniques can provide practical protection for data in transit, use, and rest. We will position techniques like Data Integrity and Ledger and will provide practical lessons in Data Integrity, Trust, and data's business utility.

Based on a good understanding of new and old technologies, emerging trends, and a broad experience from many projects in this domain, this book will provide a unique context about the WHY (requirements and drivers), WHAT (what to do), and HOW (how to implement), as well as reviewing the current state and major forces representing challenges or driving change, what you should be trying to achieve and how you can do it, including discussions of different options. We will also discuss WHERE (in systems) and WHEN (roadmap). Unlike other general or academic texts, this book is being written to offer practical general advice, outline actionable strategies, and include templates for immediate use. It contains diagrams needed to describe the topics and Use Cases and presents current real-world issues and technological mitigation strategies. The inclusion of the risks to both owners and custodians provides a strong case for why people should care.

This book reflects the perspective of a Chief Technology Officer (CTO) and Chief Security Strategist (CSS). The Author has worked in and with startups and some of the largest organizations in the world, and this book is intended for board members, senior decision-makers, and global government policy officials—CISOs, CSOs, CPOs, CTOs, auditors, consultants, investors, and other people interested in data privacy and security. The Author also embeds a business perspective, answering the question of why this an important topic for the board, audit committee, and senior management regarding achieving business objectives, strategies, and goals and applying the risk appetite and tolerance.

The focus is on Technical Visionary Leaders, including CTO, Chief Data Officer, Chief Privacy Officer, EVP/SVP/VP of Technology, Analytics, Data Architect, Chief Information Officer, EVP/SVP/VP of I.T., Chief Information Security Officer (CISO), Chief Risk Officer, Chief Compliance Officer, Chief Security Officer (CSO), EVP/SVP/VP of Security, Risk Compliance, and Governance. It can also be interesting reading for privacy regulators, especially those in developed nations with specialist privacy oversight agencies (government departments) across their jurisdictions (e.g., federal and state levels).

Security, Audit and Leadership Series

*Series Editor: Dan Swanson, Dan Swanson and Associates, Ltd.,
Winnipeg, Manitoba, Canada.*

The *Security, Audit and Leadership Series* publishes leading-edge books on critical subjects facing security and audit executives as well as business leaders. Key topics addressed include Leadership, Cybersecurity, Security Leadership, Privacy, Strategic Risk Management, Auditing IT, Audit Management and Leadership

Agile Audit Transformation and Beyond
Toby DeRoche

Mind the Tech Gap: Addressing the Conflicts between IT and Security Teams
Nikki Robinson

CyRM^{SM}: Mastering the Management of Cybersecurity
David X Martin

The Auditor's Guide to Blockchain Technology: Architecture, Use Cases, Security and Assurance
Shaun Aghili

Artificial Intelligence Perspective for Smart Cities
Vahap Tecim and Sezer Bozkus Kahyaoglu

Teaching Cybersecurity: A Handbook for Teaching the Cybersecurity Body of Knowledge in a Conventional Classroom
Daniel Shoemaker, Ken Sigler and Tamara Shoemaker

Cognitive Risk
James Bone and Jessie H Lee

Privacy in Practice: Establish and Operationalize a Holistic Data Privacy Program
Alan Tangsss

Leading the Digital Workforce
Jeff Brown

Controlling Privacy and the Use of Data Assets V II: What is the New World Currency – Data or Trust?
Ulf Mattsson

*Security Risk Management – The Driving Force for Operational Resilience:
The Firefighting Paradox*
Jim Seaman and Michael Gioia

For more information about this series, please visit: https://www.routledge.com/Internal-Audit-and-IT-Audit/book-series/CRCINTAUDITA

Controlling Privacy and the Use of Data Assets

of Data Assets

Volume 2

What is the New World Currency – Data or Trust?

Ulf Mattsson

CRC Press
Taylor & Francis Group
Boca Raton London New York

CRC Press is an imprint of the
Taylor & Francis Group, an **informa** business

First edition published 2024
by CRC Press
2385 Executive Center Drive, Suite 320, Boca Raton, FL 33431

and by CRC Press
4 Park Square, Milton Park, Abingdon, Oxon, OX14 4RN

© 2024 Ulf Mattsson

CRC Press is an imprint of Taylor & Francis Group, LLC

Library of Congress Cataloging-in-Publication Data
Names: Mattsson, Ulf, author.
Title: Controlling privacy and the use of data assets : what is the new
world currency - data or trust? / Ulf Mattsson.
Description: First edition. | Boca Raton : CRC Press, 2024. | Series:
Security, audit and leadership series | Includes bibliographical
references.
Identifiers: LCCN 2023007091 (print) | LCCN 2023007092 (ebook) | ISBN
9781032185163 (hardback) | ISBN 9781032185187 (paperback) | ISBN
9781003254928 (ebook)
Subjects: LCSH: Data privacy. | Data protection.
Classification: LCC HD30.3815 .M37 2024 (print) | LCC HD30.3815 (ebook) |
DDC 323.44/8--dc23/eng/20230510
LC record available at https://lccn.loc.gov/2023007091
LC ebook record available at https://lccn.loc.gov/2023007092

ISBN: 978-1-032-18516-3 (hbk)
ISBN: 978-1-032-18518-7 (pbk)
ISBN: 978-1-003-25492-8 (ebk)

DOI: 10.1201/9781003254928

Typeset in Times
by SPi Technologies India Pvt Ltd (Straive)

To my love and life partner, Catrine, and our children, Johanna and Markus.
They are the greatest joys of my life.

Contents

SECTION I   Vision and Best Practices

SECTION II   Trust and Hybrid Cloud

SECTION III   Data Quality

Foreword – Ben Rothke, CISSP, CISM, Senior Information Security Manager, Tapad, Inc. New York, NY

I've read countless security books over the last 20 years. After reading tens of thousands of pages of security and privacy text, I think I found what it takes for an excellent information security book. It is the combination of a relevant topic, a knowledgeable author, who is also a capable writer. Some of the books I've read have none of those, many have two, and only a few have all three.

I've known Ulf Mattsson for many years, and he has consistently been able to write excellent content. With a master's degree in physics, he knows that the micro level can significantly impact a system. And with his broad real-world experience at some of the world's largest and most sophisticated companies, he knows what it takes for things to work at the system level.

In 2023, the amount of data seems to expand more quickly than the universe. An average midsize company has more data than those that exist in the Library of Congress. With that much data, firms today deal with multiple competing needs and tensions around their data. Issues, such as access vs. availability, siloed vs. open, and more, require Chief Information Security Officers (CISO) to make decisions that affect all of the data, the liquid gold of the organization.

If they take too aggressive of an approach to data access, overall corporate efficacy can suffer. Too open access to the data, and the company will be on the receiving end of a class action lawsuit. Being able to balance those competing needs requires the steadiness of a tightrope walker.

Most CISOs have to deal with the same tension as tightrope walkers do. And what every tightrope walker has is a pole. They carry these poles during a performance to maintain stability while walking on a narrow rope. It also lowers the center of gravity of the tightrope walker, giving them a greater level of stability.

Ulf has written a book that can be used as a tightrope walker pole for a CISO or anyone tasked with information security management. Terms such as trust, security, privacy, zero-trust, and more are bandied about, often with little guidance on implementing them. Ulf gives the reader everything they need to know to balance the many competing things around data access.

When it comes to security and privacy, the devil is in the details. And this book is heavy on those details. As the details are all the difference between legitimate access and an attacker pilfering the data. For those serious about the topic, this is a broad and deep book written by an author with significant depth and breadth.

The role of a CISO today is to ensure that the CEO's picture is not in the Wall Street Journal due to a data breach. And Ulf's book will help you understand what you have to do in order to do that.

Foreword – Jim Ambrosini, CISA, CRISC, CISSP Cybersecurity Consultant and CISO

"Data is the new oil"—or so we've been told.

For the past 20 years, data has been the key to competitive advantage. Companies that use it effectively have reaped the benefits. This notion has given rise to entire industries and educational programs geared toward the manipulation, analysis, and presentation of data. "BI" or "Business Intelligence" was what we used to call it. Now it's "Data Mining" or "Big Data"—terms that seem more appropriate. But we've hit a bump in the road. Data is only as good as the trust we place in it. How do we trust data in a world with escalating breaches—where it's not a question of "if" a company will get breached, but "when"? As a CISO for several corporations, this is top of mind for me, as well as my clients.

Hence, the new currency—Trust. Data that can be trusted is a prerequisite in all decision-making and transaction processing. The concept of complete trust in data is somewhat of a mythical unicorn—no data can be 100% secure and trusted, right? Or can it?

This is the focus of Ulf Mattson's new book. Volume 1 discussed different forms of access controls and methods to safeguard data. His new book takes the reader through the journey toward Zero Trust. Zero Trust is an IT security model that requires every user and connected device to verify their identity prior to accessing the data. By enforcing Zero Trust architecture, you, essentially, trust no one or no device—until proven otherwise. In this way, you are imbuing trust in the data by ensuring only authorized people or devices have access to it. And yes, it is a journey, not an end state.

I see far too often companies implementing the latest technology or tool promoting "Zero Trust"—but it's not that simple. One of the things I like about this book was how Ulf describes the Zero Trust maturity model as well as tactics for Cloud migrations and network access. He's essentially laid out the roadmap for us. The book flips the script from "Trust and Verify" to "Verify then Trust".

I should spend a minute speaking about the author, Ulf Manson. I came to know Ulf around 2011. I was the President of the ISACA Chapter of New York (ISACA is the largest organization of information security, risk, and audit professionals in the world). The New York Chapter would put on various educational events and conferences, as we were always looking for qualified speakers. Someone recommended Ulf to speak about Data Security—and after that first time, I had him back regularly. Honestly, after each session, I would ask myself "How does this guy know so much about this topic?" I realized the answer—he lives it.

During his career, ULF has been a Chief Security Strategist, Chief Technology Officer, and the founder of Protegrity—a company that specializes in data security. He is also a frequent public speaker on the topic of data trust at numerous conferences and events.

It's fortunate for most of us that Ulf can translate complex technical details into bite-size chunks that are easily understandable. This book is no different and does not disappoint.

I see this book as a reference guide for system engineers, network administrators, consultants, and CISOs. In fact, I am using it right now to dialogue a strategic data security program for one of my clients. It's going to resource that will be referred to for a long time. Zero Trust is the new gold. This book is the treasure map.

Foreword – Jim Ambrosini CISA, CRISC, CISSP Cybersecurity Consultant and CISO

Foreword – Richard Purcell, CEO, Corporate Privacy Group (former Chief Privacy Officer, Microsoft)

In his first volume of *Controlling Privacy and the Use of Data Assets*, Ulf Mattsson described the world's achievement of a technologically significant moment—a world in which data is the "new oil", providing the driving force for economic and social development. He described a number of practices, processes and tools which, when properly and carefully applied, amplify data's accelerant power.

In this succeeding volume, Ulf tackles the logical next question—if data is the driving force, then what is the currency of exchange? As a resource, data is indisputably the foundational element of modern progress, but what is the mechanism for managing the resource? Is it the transportation processes themselves, the data lifecycle of collecting, processing, storing, distributing, and managing the resource? Or is it the confidence that those processes are transparent, fair, reasonable, and designed for broad benefit? In other words, in a world that accepts the dominance of a singular resource, what do we want as the controlling factors that assure its utility to more than the "many chosen few"?

An analogy comes to mind, one that has been decades in the making. The development and application of safety practices for hazardous materials has provided economic, social, and personal benefits through standardized classifications, markings, handling procedures, emergency response measures, storage protocols, and disposal requirements. The next time you see a tanker trailer next to you on the road, look for the placard showing what material and level of handling is on board.

So, why is it, after several decades of information technology, data creation and use, and security breach reporting, that we have not yet undertaken the job of developing similar standards of care for the collection, use, storage, sharing and management of personal data? We have volumes of experience across the globe from engineers, scientists, transportation experts, and others who collaborated with legislative assemblies to develop and promulgate standards to protect the public and private interests in manufacturing, storing, transporting, and disposing of hazardous materials. They have done the heavy lifting already by creating a framework useful for such an undertaking.

In this and his first volume, Ulf Mattsson points the way toward how such an effort could begin to take shape through an understanding and categorization of data types and environments as well as best practices for providing safety protocols to prevent intentional or accidental corruption of the safeguards.

In an age in which Artificial Intelligence and Synthetic Media are quickly becoming the fundamental underpinnings of products and services, such protections are more urgently needed than ever before. Such standards, including the ethical approaches to research, design, development, and deployment of these products and services could mitigate the underlying questions of trust they inherently present. There should never be any doubt in the consumer marketplace as to reality that is experienced or distorted. Our marketplace confidence depends on knowing the distinction; we enjoy fictions today because we know they are fictions and meant to entertain, challenge, and/or stimulate. When those fictional narratives become attempts to distort, though, we have not just a problem but a weakening of our social and economic foundations—disaster lurks.

There is no easy route to global standards, we know. And that is no reason to not take Mr. Mattsson's thoughtful guidance to heart as a good starting point to work the problem. Many have come before us and mapped out the process. Ulf and others are complementing their work by providing us comprehensive and smart inputs to the content—the currency of trust in a data-driven world.

Foreword – Richard Purcell CEO Corporate Privacy Group (former Chief Privacy Officer, Microsoft)

Acknowledgments

This book would not have been possible without the love and support of my wife, Catrine, my son Markus, and my daughter Johanna. They have always been there for me through the ups and downs of taking the leap of faith and moving from Sweden to the United States. It was exciting to build something from the ground up.

This book would have never made it here without my publisher, CRC Press. Especially Dan Swanson. He has been a joy to work with and the person who believed in this book when I pitched him the idea.

Moreover, I'd like to thank members of our team for their help. People on the technology side include Jeffrey Breen, Raul Ortega, Yigal Rozenberg, Nathan Vega, Vic Levy, Clyde Williamson, Joel Kutner, Marco Carmona, Pallavi Suryavanshi, Magnus Sirvio, Anders Lundberg, Thomas Valfridsson, Hans Altsten, Hans Meijer, Tamojit Das, Fredrik Mortberg, and many more.

I'd like to thank members on our business side, including Rick Farnell, Paul Mountford, Alex Vik, Gustav Vik, Paul Mountford, Per Johansson, Gordon Rapkin, Bob Fitzgerald, Ulf Dahl, Jan Johansson, David Morris, RJ Singh, and many more.

Moreover, I'd like to thank members of other organizations, including Elaine, Palmer, Sean Schmit, Kathy Kincaid, Bob Picciano, Tom Parenty, Sandeepan Banerjee, Mary Ann Davidson, Patrick Faith, Malcolm McWhinnie, Bart Preneel, Matt Curtin, and many more.

I would also like to thank all the people who have been involved in reviewing my book.

Last but not least, I want to offer my thanks to all of my readers. I appreciate the faith you are placing in me by reading my book

Thank you all. I am very fortunate to have you all in my life.

About the Author

Ulf Mattsson is a recognized information security and data privacy expert with a strong track record of more than two decades implementing cost-effective data security and privacy controls for global Fortune 500 institutions, including Citigroup, Goldman Sachs, GE Capital, BNY Mellon, AIG, Visa USA, Mastercard Worldwide, American Express, The Coca Cola Company, Wal-Mart, BestBuy, KOHL's, Microsoft, IBM, Informix, Sybase, Teradata, and RSA Security. He is currently the Chief Security Strategist and earlier the Chief Technology Officer at Protegrity, a data security company he co-founded after working 20 years at IBM in software development. Ulf is an inventor of more than 70 issued U.S. patents in data privacy and security.

Ulf is active in the information security industry as a contributor to the development of data privacy and security standards in the Payment Card Industry Data Security Standard (PCI DSS) and American National Standards Institute (ANSI) X9 for the financial industry. He is on the advisory board of directors at PACE University, NY, in the area of cloud security and a frequent speaker at various international events and conferences, including the RSA Conference, and the author of more than 100 in-depth professional articles and papers on data privacy and security, including IBM Journals, IEEE Xplore, ISSA Journal, and ISACA Journal.

Ulf holds a master's in physics in Engineering from Chalmers University of Technology in Sweden.

Introduction

Thank you for taking the time to read my book about protecting your data. This book is about Data Integrity and Trust in Data.

The book will review how new and old privacy-preserving techniques can provide practical protection for data in transit, use, and rest. We will position techniques like Data Integrity and Ledger.

Why do we need this book?

This book will use practical lessons in Data Integrity, and Trust, and data's business utility.

This book is based on a good understanding and experience of new and old technologies, emerging trends, and a broad experience from many projects in this domain. This book will provide unique context about the WHY (requirements and drivers), WHAT (what to do), and HOW (how to implement), and review current state and major forces representing challenges or driving change, what you should be trying to achieve, how do you do it, including discussions of different options. We will also discuss WHERE (in systems) and WHEN (roadmap). Unlike other general or academic texts, this book is being written to offer practical general advice, outline actionable strategies, and include templates for immediate use. The book contains diagrams needed to describe the topics and Use Cases, for example.

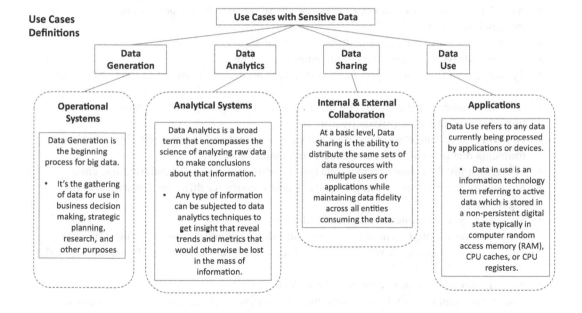

WHO SHOULD READ THIS BOOK?

The book presents current real-world issues and technological mitigation strategies. The inclusions of the risks to both owners and custodians provide a strong case for why people should care.

The book reflects the perspective of a CTO and Chief Security Strategist. I worked in and with startups and some of the largest organizations in the world. The book is for board members, senior decision-makers, and global government policy officials—CISOs, CSOs, CPOs, CTOs, auditors, consultants, investors, and other people interested in data privacy and security. I will also embed a business perspective. Why is this an important topic for the board, audit committee, and senior management regarding achieving business objectives, strategies, and goals and applying the risk appetite and tolerance?

The focus is on Technical Visionary Leaders, including Chief Technology Officer, Chief Data Officer, Chief Privacy Officer, EVP/SVP/VP of Technology, Analytics, Data Architect, Chief Information Officer, EVP/SVP/VP of I.T., Chief Information Security Officer (CISO), Chief Risk Officer, Chief Compliance Officer, Chief Security Officer (CSO), EVP/SVP/VP of Security, Risk Compliance, Governance.

It can also be interesting reading for privacy regulators, especially those in developed nations with specialist privacy oversight agencies (government departments) across their jurisdictions (e.g., federal and state levels).

WHY IS VOLUME 2 OF THIS BOOK NEEDED?

The reader may be interested in different aspects of data privacy and security landscape. This book is discussing perspectives. For example:

- "Trust the User, App, and Data" and how technologies and regulations can address these issues. And the right balance to be found with technologies that can strongly enforce rules and regulations
- Ransomware and other malware are taking different forms of attacking your systems and data
- A roadmap that is addressing different issues
- ABAC (attribute-based access control) or PBAC (policy-based access control) and the journey into zero trust
- Planning for Web 3.0 that can address data ownership
- Planning for issues and benefits of quantum computing
- Synthetic data that can be generated in different ways and measured in terms of risk and utility levels
- Collecting more context in finding privacy issues by evolving ways of scanning applications and implementing privacy by design
- Applying the techniques for different use cases in cloud and increasingly distributed environments that is used by an increasingly distributed workforce
- When to apply these from various data types of different types and different use cases
- Staffing of departments working on privacy and security for different maturity and size of organizations
- Spending on privacy and security across different industries
- Prioritization and alignment of various industry standards and guidance for different regions
- Different types of product vendors that are focusing on various aspects of data privacy and security
- Prescriptive to different use cases and each industry
- You cannot manage what can't measure. Metrics are important for example Zero Trust maturity

HOW TO READ THE BOOK

The Introduction provides a high-level overview, and more technical aspects are discussed in different chapters.

DISCUSSIONS ABOUT TRUST IN USER, APPS, AND DATA

Privacy and security issues and solutions related to User, App, and Data can be found in the different chapters. The Zero Trust chapter (5) discusses users and authorization. Data Quality and Integrity is discussed in separate chapters (8 and 9). Web 3.0 is discussed in Chapter 7. User access is discussed in the ZTA chapter and data confidentiality and integrity aspects are discussed in other chapters: We will focus on the user, data security, web security, and data quality:

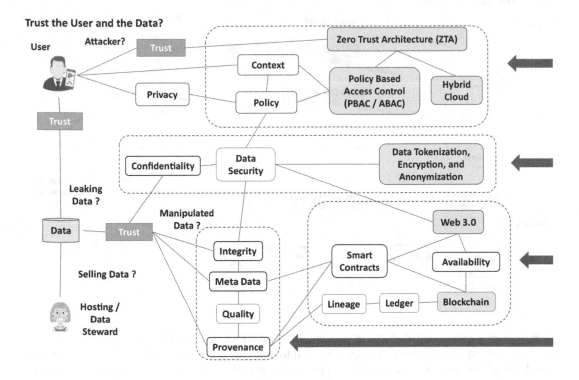

THE FUTURE OF DATA PRIVACY TECHNOLOGIES

This book will discuss how the landscape of data privacy and security is evolving and an online version with different appendices will keep the information up to date:

New risks		
Evolving ransomware and other threats to data	New data privacy regulations	Evolving work force with new work environments
Evolving technologies		

The first book, "Volume I", focused on basic platforms and data protection techniques and a shorter introduction to evolving platforms and data protection techniques.

The theme in this book, "Volume II", is about "The Future of Data Privacy" and talks more about evolving platforms and data protection techniques. A few of the chapters address "Who Owns the New Oil?" and talks about technologies that can help in owning and controlling your private data. It is hard to predict the future but I'm discussing some important technologies that can have great impact.

Additional appendices can be found in the online section. This allows for timely updates.

The different chapters talk about the issues of "Trust the User, App, and Data" and how technologies and regulations can address these issues. The user may not be the real user. Data may be attacked and leaked from data storage. Some hosting is collecting and selling your private data. Different technologies can address the issues of user access and data leakage. Other technologies can address data ownership and issues of data sharing. The right balance could be found with technologies that can strongly enforce rules and regulations may not be strongly enforced:

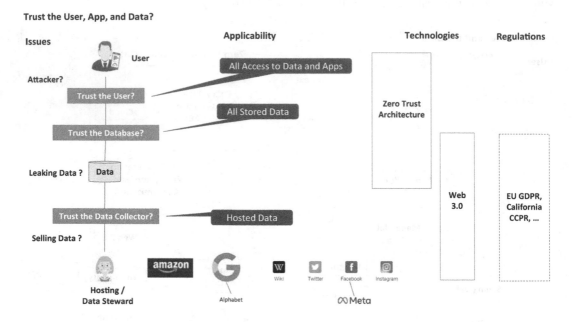

Ransomware and other malware are taking different forms of attacking your systems and data. Education is important, but technology is needed to continuously defend against these attacks. We will discuss how zero trust can create a new perimeter around your critical resources. Attackers may already be in your system and Chapter 1 is discussing that attacks are coming from different directions and how a layered security model can catch attackers at different layers:

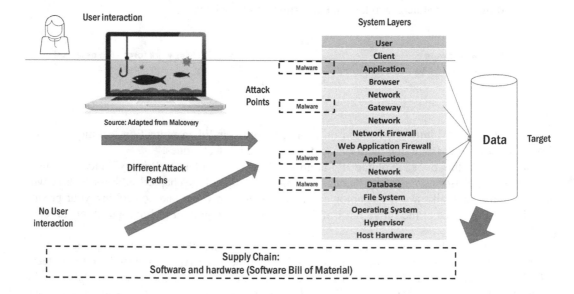

These are drivers for cybersecurity spending according to EY. Top drivers are still risk reduction and regulatory compliance. New initiatives, breach responses, and cost reduction are on the rise:

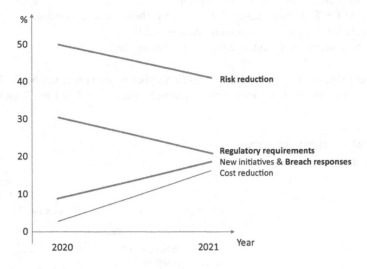

Source: Adapted from EY

REQUIREMENTS, USE CASES, AND BUSINESS VALUES

We will discuss different requirements, use cases, and business values in this book. EY reported that top drivers are still risk reduction, innovation, lower risk, and breach prevention and lower cost for compliance are on the rise. We will review some data sharing use cases with the top requirements and values that also focus on centralized data privacy policy across hybrid cloud, analytics, and ML:

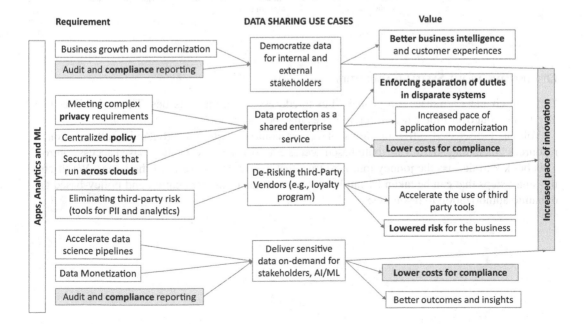

We will discuss some DATA SHARING solutions that enable these data privacy capabilities:

- Anonymization SDKs for Cloud and on-prem.
- Generative AI for Test Data Management with Synthetic data generation.
- Generative AI for AI/ML with Synthetic data generation.
- Data Sharing Patterns and guidance for safely sharing data.

Interest in different solutions and capabilities can be another way to enter the book. A roadmap that is implementing Zero Trust and addressing the discussed issues is outlined in Chapter 3:

Example of a Data Security Roadmap

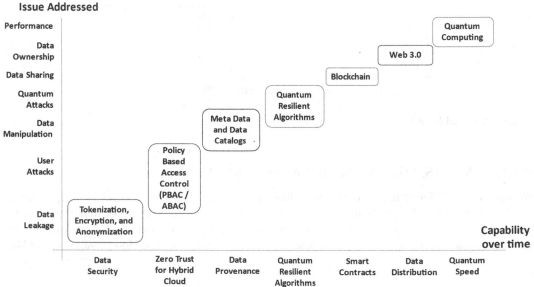

Discussions about System Capabilities

Different chapters are discussing capabilities to address the different issues. The capabilities may also be laid out over time when different issues may be addressed.

Volume I discussed different forms of access control, including "dynamic authorization to resources" including ABAC (attribute-based access control) or PBAC (policy-based access control). This book will discuss the jouney into zero trust that can address several of the issues. We discuss the small steps that can be taken by implementing multifactor authentication and policy-based and dynamic authorization to resources:

Data Roadmap Example

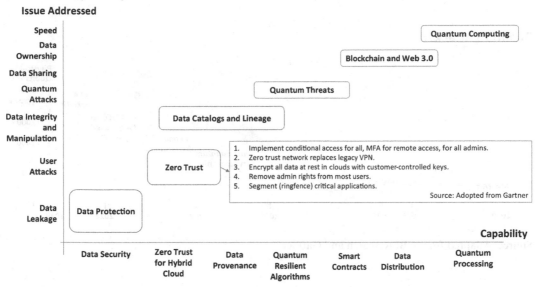

Planning for Web 3.0 can address data ownership is discussed in Chapter 3:

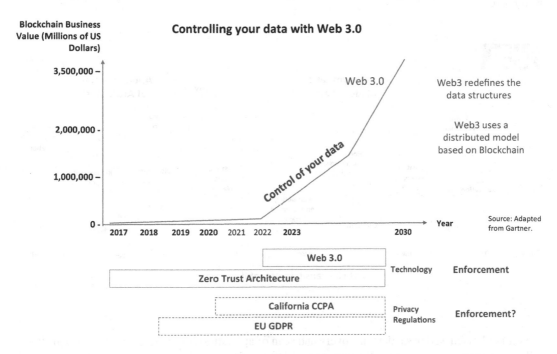

Planning for issues and benefits of quantum computing is discussed in Volume I of this book:

Quantum Attacks?

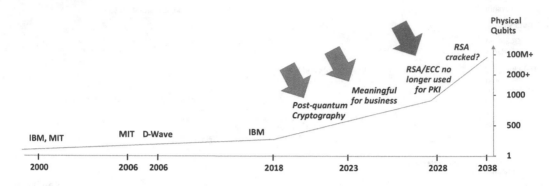

Source: Adapted from CBI Research and Gartner

Volume I discussed different techniques for protecting data. This book will continue the journey into synthetic data. Synthetic data can be generated differently and measured in terms of risk and utility levels:

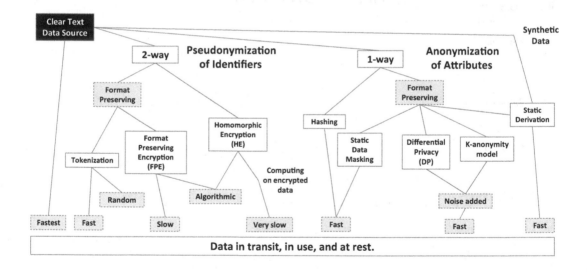

Volume I discussed basic data discovery and scan of applictions to find security issues. This book will continue the journey into collecting more context in finding privacy issues by evolving ways of scaning applications. This can also help in implementing privacy by design:

Privacy by Design vs. Security by Design

Scanning Apps and Data for Issues with Privacy and Security

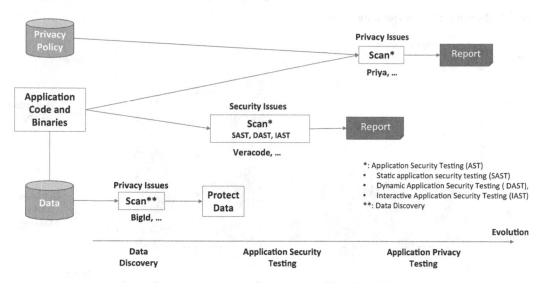

Volume I discussed basic data protection techniques for sensitive data. This book will continue the journey into applying the techniques for different use cases in cloud and increasingly distributed environments that is used by an increasingly distributed workforce:

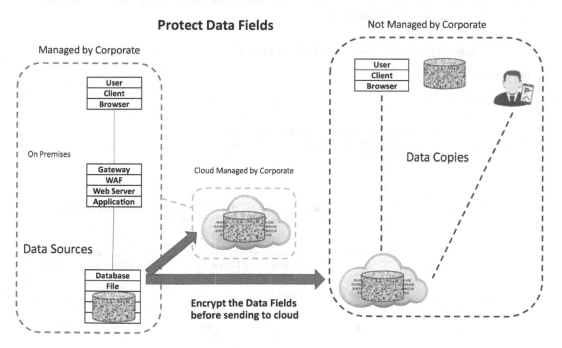

Volume I discussed basic data protection techniques for sensitive data. This book will discuss when to apply these from various data types, different types, and different use cases:

Use of different Techniques for Data Security

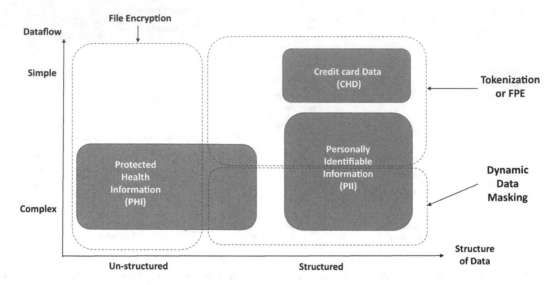

Chapter 3 discusses org structure and staffing of departments working on privacy and security for different maturity and size of organizations:

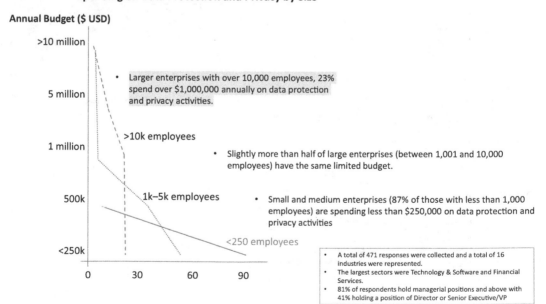

Source: Adapted from CPO Magazine

Chapter 3 discusses spending on privacy and security across different industries:

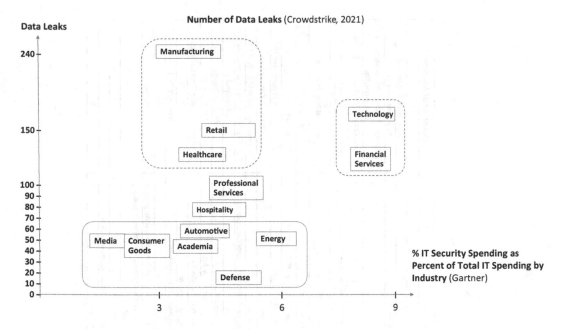

Chapters 2 and 3 discuss prioritization and alignment of various industry standards and guidance for different regions:

Chapters 2 and 3 position different types of product vendors that are focusing on various aspects of data privacy and security. Other vendors are focusing on consulting, emails, smaller devices, networks, or detection and response:

Example of Alignment to Standards and Guidance

Area	Standard, Guidance, or Organization	1-Most Important			Comments	Examples of Alignment
		US	EMEA	APAC		
US National Institute for Standards and Technology	NIST SP 800-207				Zero Trust	Zero Trust Architecture
	NIST SP 800-53				Encrption and Keys	Key states, key lengths
	NIST FIPS 140-2				Encryption	Key storage, PKCS#11 integration, Level 1 encryption lib.
	NIST SP 800-171				Access Control	Access Control (PRAC), Data Security (PR.DS)
Financial Industry Standard	PCI DSS				Payment cards Industry Standard	Encryption
	ANSI X9				Standards for the financial services industry in the U.S.	Tokenization, Encryption
	PKCS				Public Key Cryptography Standard	PKCS #5, #11, #12
Application and Encryption Guidance	Homomorphic.Computing.org				Homomorphic.Computing.org for researchers and industry (IBM, Intel, MS ...)	Future Lattice-based algorithms
	OWASP				The Open Web Application Security Project	Top 10 for API Security and WA
	CSA				Cloud Security Alliance	Quantum Computing
	CMMC 2.0				Required by US Government	Alignment with NIST SP 800-171
International Standards	ISO/IEC 27001				International Standards Organization anf International Electrotechnical Commission	ISO 27001 Annex A, or the core controls
	ISO/IEC 20889				Data De-Identification	k-Anonymity
EU Data Privacy	GDPR				General Data Protection Regulation	EU Data Privacy
US Healthcare	HIPAA				Health Insurance Portability and Accountability Act	Access Control
	IEEE				The Institute of Electrical and Electronics Engineers	Integration with Data Catalogs
User Groups	CCC				The Confidential Computing Consortium	
	ISACA				Information Systems Security Association, 140k members	Journal, COBIT,
	ISSA				Information Systems Security Association	Journal
	IAPP				International Association of Privacy Professionals, comprehensive global information privacy	Journal
	(ISC)2				The International Information System Security Certification Consortium specializes in training and certifications (CISSP ...)	
	IIA				Institute for Internal Auditors	
	BCS				The Chartered Institute for IT, formerly known as the British Computer Society	
	OMG				Object Management Group	

Vendor	Email	Consulting	Devices	Network	Response	Monitor	Identity	Discover	Encrypt	Mask	Features https://www.rsaconference.com/marketplace/search#f:product=[Data%20Security]
A								Discover			discover, manage, protect, sensitive, and personal data a
B						Monitor		Discover			discover & monitor external threats
C								Discover			discover, migrate and govern
D			Devices			Monitor		Discover			discovers all endpoint devices
E						Monitor		Discover			detect and investigate threats to your most sensitive data
F			Devices					Discover			Discover, manage, and automate the lifecycle of SSH keys
G									Encrypt	Mask	CASB, SWG, and ZTNA
H									Encrypt	Mask	field-level protection
I									Encrypt		key management, tokenization, cloud key management, encryption and HSM
J									Encrypt		key management
K										Mask	Activity Monitoring, Database Firewall, Dynamic and Static Data Masking, Discovery

Chapter 3 discusses how solutions are more prescriptive to different use cases and each industry. For example, using protected data in machine learning to address fraud in the financial industry:

Use Case - Reducing Risk with Financial Data

- Anonymization minimized the risk of identification at a bank for credit card approval transactions.
- The bank reduced the **privacy risk from 26% to 8%** and still provided **98% accuracy** compared to the initial **Machine Learning** model used in the analytics.
- Anonymization is a non-reversible method of protection because it can advance data-intensive business applications, such as analytics, by using **differential privacy or k-anonymity**.
- **Pseudonymization** is a reversible approach that can be based on Encryption or tokenization.

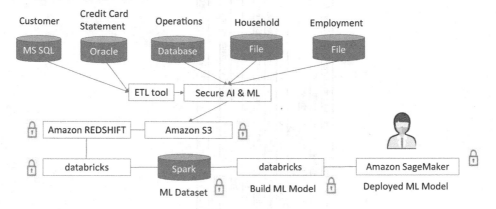

You cannot manage what can't measure. Metrics are important. Chapter 5, for example, discusses Trust maturity:

Zero Trust Maturity Model

Areas

Identity	Device	Environment (NW)	Application	Data
Analytics				
Automation				
Governance				

Maturity Levels

Maturity	Identity	Device	Environment (NW)	Application	Data
Traditional	Password or Mult Factor (MFA)	Simple inventore	Macro segmentaion	Access based on local validation	Static control
Advanced	MFA or some Federation	Data access depends on device posture	Micro perimeters	Access based on central validation	Cloud data encrypted
Optimal	Continous realtime ML analysis	Data access depends on realtime analysis	ML threat protection	Access continuously validated	All data is encrypted

Source: Adapted from CISA.org

Section I

Vision and Best Practices

1 Risks and Threats

INTRODUCTION

In this chapter, we will discuss Risks and Threats and how to Ensure that your data is private and protected in transit, in use, in memory, and at rest. We will discuss Trust and Data Breaches.

We will also discuss how to Prevent Attacks and Recover after Attacks, particularly Ransomware attacks and cloud databases.

Attackers may already be in your system. A multi-layered defense can protect your sensitive data.

A LACK OF TRUST

Trust is important for organizations to beg data-driven:

Trust is holding organizations back from being data-driven

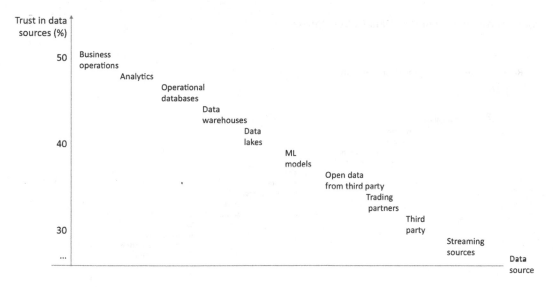

Source: Adapted from IDC

Data powers the future enterprise in a digital-first world.

Digital-first applies to any company, government, or person that is always asking:

"Is there some digital-based capability or enhancement that could improve our lives and desired outcomes?"

A digital-first world requires business change:

98% of organizations are on a digital transformation journey.

Data management is critical to digital transformation:

Organizations with solid data leadership are three times more likely to be well underway with digital transformation.

- 87% of CXOs said being an intelligent enterprise is their top priority.
- 83% of executives have articulated the need to be more data-driven than before the pandemic.

DOI: 10.1201/9781003254928-2

Q: When you make data-driven decisions, what do you expect and demand to know?

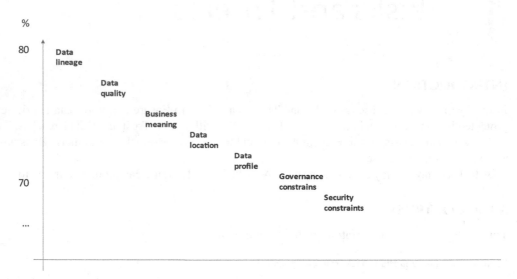

Source: Adapted from IDC Data Culture Survey

Q: Rate how well your organization performs

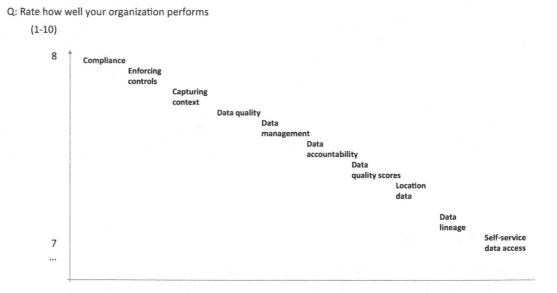

Source: Adapted from IDC Data Culture Survey

DATA PRIVACY

A mature privacy posture can only be achieved by using privacy management, privacy control, and (typically data-centric) security capabilities. Cutting across various disciplines, privacy is much more than a security-only discipline.

On the other hand, SECURITY leaders can proactively facilitate the achievement of Operational goals in analytics and Operational intelligence through data-centric controls like synthetic data or differential privacy. Beyond sanctions, privacy risk mitigation focuses primarily on post-breach financial risks, consumer trust decay, and brand damage.

- According to Gartner, by year-end 2023, 75% of the world's population will have its data covered under modern privacy regulations, up from 25% today.
- Before year-end 2023, more than 80% of companies worldwide will face at least one privacy-focused data protection regulation.
- By 2024, privacy-driven spending on data protection and compliance technology will break through to more than $15 billion worldwide.
- By 2025, 60% of large organizations will use one or more privacy-enhancing computation techniques in analytics, operational intelligence, or cloud computing.

PRIVACY BECOMES MISSION CRITICAL

Privacy has become an Operational imperative and a critical component of customer trust for organizations worldwide.

We will discuss some relevant areas of Data Security:

- Data governance, privacy, and risk, including DSG, DRA, PIA, data breach response, privacy by design (PbD), and financial data risk assessment (FinDRA).
- Data discovery, categorization, and classification of structured and unstructured data, including data classification, cloud native data loss prevention (DLP), file analysis, cloud access security broker (CASB), enterprise digital rights management (EDRM), data access governance (DAG), and multicloud database activity monitoring (Multicloud DAM).
- Data processing and analytics across endpoint, application, or storage layers, including DataOps, DevOps test data management, machine identity management, blockchain for data security, file analysis, and privacy management tools.
- Anonymization, pseudonymization, PEC, and other data protection techniques, including confidential computing, homomorphic encryption, differential privacy, format preserving encryption (FPE), secure multiparty computation (SMPC), zero-knowledge proofs, multi-cloud key management as a service (KMaaS), enterprise key management, EDRM, transport layer security (TLS) decryption platform, cloud data protection gateways, CASB, secure instant communications, and dynamic data masking (DDM).
- Monitoring access, activity, alerting, and auditing of user activity with data, including DAG, multicloud DAM, CASBs, and file analysis.
- Multicloud solutions with multifunctional data security controls, including data security as a service (DSaaS), data security platform, multicloud KmaaS, multicloud DAM.

THE THREAT LANDSCAPE

According to "Protecting Data from Ransomware and other Attacks", attacks continue to increase. The U.S. Secret Service reported that most organizations had adequate data backups. Cyber actors focus more on the exfiltration of sensitive data and threaten to publicize the data unless an additional ransom is paid.

THREAT FOR BUSINESSES

Ransomware gangs are changing. It can be very expensive for some victims, and some ransomware groups are shifting toward smaller targets.

RANSOMWARE

PREVENT ATTACKS

ABAC (attribute-based access control) can dynamically enforce policies based on a wide range of attributes (user attributes, resource attributes, object, environment attributes, etc.) to protect data.

DATA SECURITY FOR HYBRID CLOUD

Create data security policies and rules to protect data at rest and in transit. Use tokenization, anonymization, encryption, and other privacy models that are defined in the INTERNATIONAL DATA PRIVACY STANDARD ISO/IEC 20889. Centrally manage enterprise users and continuously monitor security behavior across hybrid cloud.

DATA BREACHES

INSIDER THREAT

According to several industry studies, insiders have caused 60% of breaches in an organization. Privileged users and third-party developers often have untethered access to some of your most sensitive data. Beyond privileged access management, restricting access to actual data values can help ensure privacy for your company's data, according to "Database and File Encryption Challenges".

SPECTRE-CLASS VULNERABILITIES

Much has been written about the multitude of vulnerabilities and side channel attacks on hardware-based enclave security. While there is promise in the technology, there is also some significant risk. For organizations looking to leverage privacy-preserving analytics and confidential computing, it's important to understand what hardware-independent method can offer.

TRENDS IN DATA BREACHES

North America

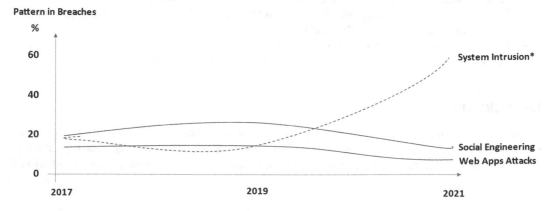

*System Intrusion is also where most of the Ransomware cases reside

Source: Adapted from Verizon DBIR, 2022

Financial Industry

Pattern in Breaches

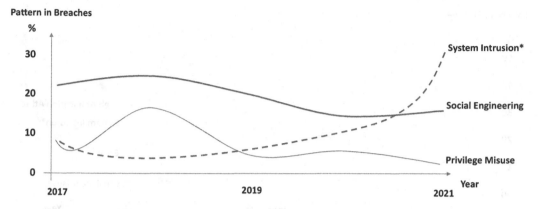

*System Intrusion is also where most of the Ransomware cases reside

Source: Adapted from Verizon DBIR, 2022

Retail Industry

Pattern in Breaches

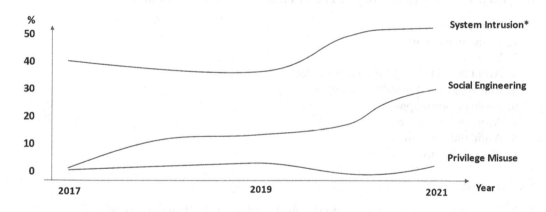

*System Intrusion is also where most of the Ransomware cases reside

Source: Adapted from Verizon DBIR, 2022

Healthcare Industry

Pattern in Breaches

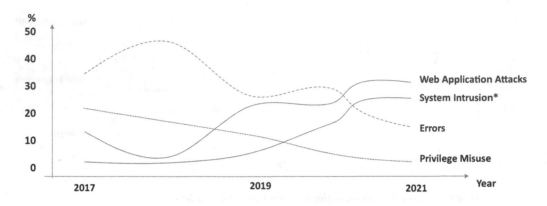

*System Intrusion is also where most of the Ransomware cases reside

Source: Adapted from Verizon DBIR, 2022

Prevent Attacks

Adopted from "NIST IR 8374 Cybersecurity Framework for Ransomware":

1. Maintain antivirus
2. Maintain patching
3. White-list apps
4. Avoid BYOD (Bring Your Own Device)
5. Run with lowest possible privileges
6. Avoid personal apps
7. Avoid unknown files
8. Avoid unknown links
9. Black-list ransomware sites

Ransomware

In 2021, targeted intrusion adversaries continued to adapt to the changing operational opportunities and strategic requirements of technology and world events.

Governments are also adapting. This year, CrowdStrike Intelligence debuted two new adversary animals—WOLF and OCELOT—to label targeted intrusions emanating from Turkey and Colombia, respectively.

Threat Landscape

The CrowdStrike Falcon OverWatch team measures breakout time—the time an adversary takes to move laterally from an initially compromised host to another host within the victim environment. Our analysis of the breakout time for hands-on eCrime intrusion activity in 2021—where such a metric could be derived—revealed an average of just 1 hour 38 minutes.

HACKTIVIST

Ransomware

According to "Ransomware in 2022: We're all screwed", Ransomware is now a primary threat for businesses, and cybersecurity experts believe this criminal enterprise will reach new heights in the future with Colonial Pipeline. JBS. Kaseya and other victims of threat groups, including DarkSide, REvil, and BlackMatter.

According to "Ransomware in 2022: We're all screwed", the "perfect" prospective ransomware victim in the United States will have a minimum annual revenue of $100 million. Ransomware infection—including types like WannaCry, NotPetya, Ryuk, Cerber, and Cryptolocker—can be designed to elicit a blackmail payment from a victim organization.

Ransomware groups may also steal corporate data and threaten to publish or sell this information going after major profitable companies.

Ransomware-as-a-Service (RaaS)

Ransomware-as-a-Service (RaaS)—in which operators will lease out or offer subscriptions to their malware creations to others for a price—is lucrative and difficult to track down and prosecute operators.

Implications for Cyber Insurance

The cyber insurance industry is likely to go mainstream and is a simple cost of doing business. Here are a few options to consider.

The explosion in high-profile ransomware attacks is also potentially going to cause massive shifts in cyber insurance, premiums, and whether or not ransomware incidents will be covered at all.

ONE IN SEVEN RANSOMWARE EXTORTION ATTEMPTS LEAK KEY OPERATIONAL TECH RECORDS

Researchers say that double-extortion ransomware attacks represent a severe risk to operational processes.

Researchers say that one in seven ransomware extortion data leaks reveals business-critical operational technology data.

Ransomware has evolved from barebone encryption and basic demands for payment into something potentially far more severe in recent years.

MISCONFIGURING A CLOUD DATABASE

Misconfiguring a cloud database has leaked more than 14 billion data records as reported by the Breach Level Index, according to "Building Cloud Services for Security".

STEAL DATA DURING HOMOMORPHIC ENCRYPTION

According to "Researchers show they can steal data during homomorphic encryption", homomorphic encryption allows it to steal data even as it is being encrypted.

Homomorphic encryption preserves data privacy but allows users to use the data.

Microsoft, for example, created the SEAL Homomorphic Encryption Library to facilitate research and development on homomorphic encryption by the broader research community.

They found a way to "crack" homomorphic encryption by using that library via a side-channel attack.

CRYPTO CRIME TRENDS

Cryptocurrency usage is growing, according to "Crypto Crime Trends for 2022: Illicit Transaction Activity".

The growth of legitimate cryptocurrency usage far outpaces the growth of criminal usage, according to "Crypto Crime: $14 Billion in Digital Currency Was Stolen".

DEFI HAS CONTINUED TO GROW

Following are the issues with stolen funds:

In 2020, just under $162 million worth of cryptocurrency was stolen from DeFi platforms, which was 31% of the year's total amount stolen.

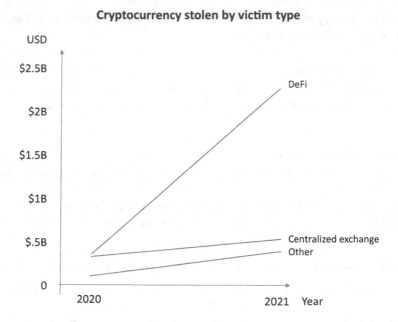

Source: Adapted from https://go.chainalysis.com

DeFi protocols showed the maximum growth by far in usage for money laundering at 1.964%. DeFi is one of the most exciting areas of the broader cryptocurrency ecosystem, presenting tremendous opportunities. But DeFi is unlikely to realize its full potential if the same decentralization that makes it so dynamic also allows for widespread scamming and theft. One way to combat this is better communication—both the private and public sectors have an essential role to play in helping investors.

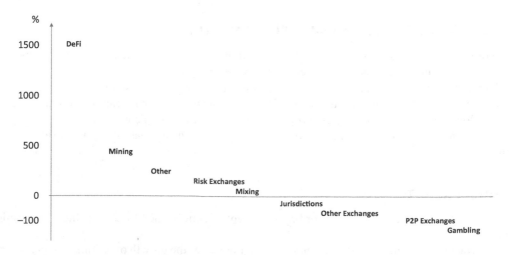

Source: Adapted from https://go.chainalysis.com

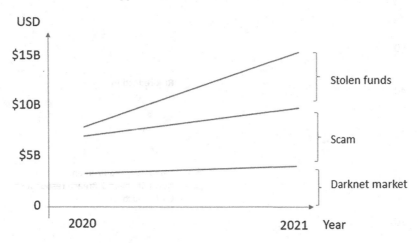

Crypto Crime Trends

Source: Adapted from https://go.chainalysis.com

Transactions involving illicit addresses were 0.15% of cryptocurrency transaction volume. In the last Crypto Crime Report, 0.34% of 2020's cryptocurrency transaction volume was associated with illicit activity—now raised the figure to 0.62%. Law enforcement's ability to combat cryptocurrency-based corruption is also evolving. Criminal abuse heightens the likelihood of restrictions being imposed by governments and, worst of all, victimizes innocent people around the world, according to "Crypto Crime Trends for 2022: Illicit Transaction Activity".

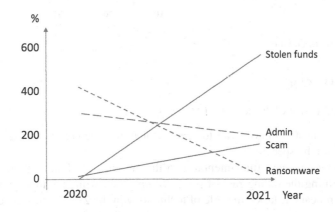

DeFI rise leads to new opportunities in Crypto Crime

Source: Adapted from https://go.chainalysis.com

CHANGING DRIVERS FOR INCREASED CYBERSECURITY SPENDING

RISK REDUCTION IS STILL THE TOP DRIVER

Risks and compliance are still top drivers (from 48% to 42%) and (from 29% to 18%) for increased cybersecurity spending.

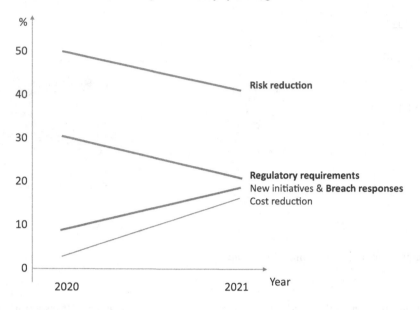

Source: Adapted from EY

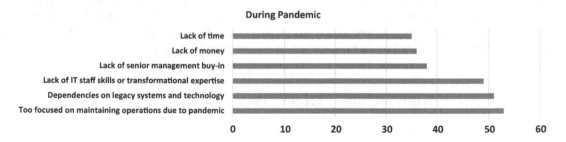

Source: Adapted from Gartner

FUTURE OF THE SOC

FORCES SHAPING MODERN SECURITY OPERATIONS

Automation is the most common way to scale. But is it effective at finding malicious acts as a manual investigation by specialists?

What has changed is more fundamental than the entrance of cloud technology. It's the role of technology in fighting the falling rate of profit. Simply put, while technology in the 20th century helped automate repeatable tasks, the role of technology in the 21st century focuses on the automation of repeatable cognitive processes, in other words—of decisions. Otherwise, automation would take care of the routine tasks, but the amount of non-routine tasks that require thinking would still overwhelm the available human analysts. It is business imperative to make the right decision faster than the competitor, according to "Future of the SOC Forces".

DATA BREACH RESPONSE

Data breach response, augmentation, and the associated disclosure are the set of activities required to assess and potentially notify regulatory authorities. Today, disclosure is mandated by omnibus laws such as the European Union's GDPR or subject/region-specific laws, as is the case with individual U.S. state breach notification legislation.

WHY THIS IS IMPORTANT

Appropriate management of a breach-impacting personal data can substantially reduce fines (as Gartner has observed on multiple occasions) and potentially strengthen ties with affected consumers by demonstrating that the organization is proactively taking ownership of the situation. Inversely, delayed response, limited transparency, and overly legal-language-based communications often elicit regulatory investigations and are paired with reputational damage and customer loss.

NOTES

1. Cloud Security Alliance, https://cloudsecurityalliance.org/group/security-guidance/
2. Cloud Standards Customer Council 2016, Practical Guide to Hybrid Cloud Computing.
3. Cloud Standards Customer Council 2016, Public Cloud Service Agreements: What to Expect and
4. D. Proud-Madruga, "Project Summary for Privacy, Access and Security Services (PASS) Healthcare"
5. FIPS 140-2 Annex A, http://csrc.nist.gov/publications/fips/fips140-2/fips1402annexa.pdf
6. https://www.thecipherbrief.com/column/sponsored-content/crypto-crime-trends-for-2022
7. IHS 2016 Update: The Complexities of Physician Supply and Demand: Projections from 2014 to 2025
8. ISO/IEC 27017 (2015). Code of Practice for Information Security Controls Based on ISO/IEC 27002for Cloud Services. http://www.iso.org/iso/catalogue_detail?csnumber=43757
9. ISO/IEC 27018 (2014). Code of practice for protection of personally identifiable information (PII) in public clouds acting as PII processors. http://www.iso.org/iso/catalogue_detail.htm?csnumber=61498
10. Japan's Updated Pharmaceutical and Medical Device Act https://www.pmda.go.jp/english/bobsguide: Cloud Target Operating Model: Revolution, Evolution or a Bit of Both?
11. https://www.sciencedirect.com/science/article/abs/pii/B9780323898249000057
12. K. Terry, "Why Telemedicine Should Be Integrated With EHRs, ACOs", Inf. Week, 2013.
13. Mckinsey & Company (August, 2016): How tech-enabled consumers are reordering the healthcareland-scape. http://healthcare.mckinsey.com/how-tech-enabled-consumers-are-reordering-healthcarelandscape
14. NIST 800-131 A, http://nvlpubs.nist.gov/nistpubs/SpecialPublications/NIST.SP.800-131Ar1.pdf
15. NIST 800-160, http://csrc.nist.gov/publications/drafts/800-160/sp800_160_second-draft.pdf
16. ONC Health I.T. Certification Program
17. Regulation (E.U.) 2016/679 of the European Parliament and of the Council (2016): E.U. General Data
18. Search Health I.T.: HITECH Act. http://searchhealthit.techtarget.com/definition/HITECH-Act
19. https://www.healthit.gov/isa/
20. U.S. Food & Drug Administration Medical Device Regulation
21. https://www.legislation.gov.uk/ukpga/1998/29/contents
22. https://www.gov.uk/guidance/on-site-access-to-electronic-health-records-by-sponsor-representatives-in-clinical-trials
23. "Building Cloud Services for Security". https://www.rapid7.com/info/3-common-misconfigurations/
24. "CrowdStrike report cites zero trust". https://insidecybersecurity.com/daily-news/crowdstrike-report-cites-zero-trust-tech-upgrades-key-combating-ransomware-threat
25. "CrowdStrike's Annual Threat Report" https://www.benzinga.com/pressreleases/22/02/b25626122/crowdstrikes-annual-threat-report-reveals-uptick-around-ransomware-and-disruptive-operations-expos
26. "Crypto Crime Trends for 2022: Illicit Transaction Activity". https://blog.chainalysis.com/reports/2022-crypto-crime-report-introduction/
27. https://finance.yahoo.com/news/crypto-crime-14-billion-digital-172810251.html?fr=sycsrp_catchall
28. "Database and File Encryption Challenges". https://baffle.io/challenges/
29. "Protecting Data from Ransomware and other Attacks". https://www.globalsecuritymag.com/Protecting-Data-from-Ransomware,20210831,115566.html
30. "Ransomware as a service: Negotiators". https://www.zdnet.com/article/ransomware-as-a-service-negotiators-between-hackers-and-victims-are-now-in-high-demand/
31. "Ransomware gangs are changing their tactics". https://asaniali.org/2022/02/07/ransomware-gangs-are-changing-their-tactics-that-could-prove-very-expensive-for-some-victims/

32. "Ransomware in 2022: We're all screwed" ZDNet. https://www.zdnet.com/article/ransomware-in-2022-were-all-screwed/

33. "Researchers show they can steal data during homomorphic encryption". https://techxplore.com/news/2022-03-homomorphic-encryption.html

34. "Crypto Crime Trends for 2022"

35. "Future of the SOC Forces". https://www2.deloitte.com/content/dam/Deloitte/us/Documents/about-deloitte/us-deloitte-google-cloud-alliance-future-of-the-SOC-whitepaper.pdf

36. 2.0. http://www.cloud-council.org/deliverables/practical-guide-to-cloud-service-agreements.htm

37. "Advisory", CMS, Washington DC, RPRT, Aug. 2016.

38. "Audit Services Conceptual Model". HL7, Ann Arbor, MI OR - HL7, 09-May-2016.

39. Bioinform, p. bbv118, Feb. 2016. http://dx.doi.org/10.1093/bib/bbv118

40. CDNET, Ransomware gangs are changing their tactics. https://www.zdnet.com/article/ransomware-gangs-are-changing-their-tactics-that-could-prove-very-expensive-for-some-victims/

41. Cloud Standards Customer Council 2015, Practical Guide to Cloud Service Level Agreements, Version

42. D. Major, "Million Veteran Program signs up bio analysis firm for hybrid cloud", GCN, Apr. 2016.

43. HIPAA. http://www.hhs.gov/hipaa/

44. http://dx.doi.org/10.1016/j.jss.2013.09.012

45. http://www.cloud-council.org/deliverables/practical-guide-to-hybrid-cloud-computing.htm

2   Opportunities

INTRODUCTION

In this chapter, we will discuss Opportunities and Innovation.

Your ability to utilize enterprise data determines success or failure. Analyzing future trends across technical and nontechnical domains in the business context provides a foundation to generate, evaluate and deliver innovation. Architecture and technology innovation leaders must create and manage processes to facilitate these elements.

With the business context established as a foundation, EA and technology innovation leaders need to examine trends that impact the business and design innovation processes to move ideas from inception to demonstrable business value. Defining these processes ensures the organization is not missing critical stages and can avoid common pitfalls that derail innovation (e.g., the inability to move beyond proof of concept).

INNOVATION

Organizations insufficiently use privacy protection to foster customer trustworthiness, leaving opportunities for increased sales and business value while fostering distrust.

- While expectations for privacy in the workplace may differ from other contexts, employees' right to privacy is also protected. Monitoring must follow legal requirements and be proportionate to the risks assessed.
- Various privacy-enhancing computation (PEC) techniques provide in-use data protection for current use cases, including international data transfers and (multiparty) analytics.
- Privacy laws require adequate data protection during acquisition, storage, and processing of personal data, which creates the need for a coherent data risk assessment.
- The data produced by the Internet of Things (IoT) devices increasingly allows behavior analysis, with opportunities for event and information feedback loops to influence those behaviors. In particular, the unintended consequences of this Internet of Behaviors (IoB) will potentially have a greater impact on a personal and societal level.

According to Gartner:

- By 2023, organizations embedding privacy user experience into the customer experience will enjoy greater trustworthiness and up to 20% more digital revenue than those that don't.
- By 2023, organizations that do not excessively monitor remote working employees will experience up to 15% higher productivity than those that do.
- By 2025, 50% of large organizations will default to PEC for processing data in untrusted environments and multiparty analytics use cases.
- By 2023, over 20% of organizations will use a data risk assessment to identify and manage appropriate privacy controls, despite a lack of guidance from regulators on how to implement it.
- By year-end 2025, multiple IoB systems will elevate the risk of unintended consequences, potentially impacting over half of the world's population.

DOI: 10.1201/9781003254928-3

The demand for processing data, especially in external environments, and performing multiparty data sharing and analytics is rapidly growing. The increasing complexity of analytics engines and architectures mandates a by-design privacy capability rather than a bolt-on approach. Unlike common data-at-rest security controls, PEC protects data in use, thus enabling these use cases while maintaining secrecy or privacy. Each technology provides specific secrecy and privacy guarantees, and some can be combined for greater efficacy. Some PEC techniques are not yet ready for prime-time. PEC varieties may each have limited use cases and are not a panacea for privacy protection.

- The first provides a trusted environment in which sensitive data can be processed or analyzed and includes trusted third parties and hardware-trusted execution environments (also referred to as "confidential computing").
- The second performs processing and analytics in a decentralized manner and includes federated machine learning and privacy-aware machine learning.
- The third transforms data and/or algorithms before, during, or after processing or analytics. This includes differential privacy, homomorphic encryption, secure multiparty computation, zero-knowledge proofs, private set intersection, and private information retrieval.

Privacy-Enhancing Computation (PEC) Techniques

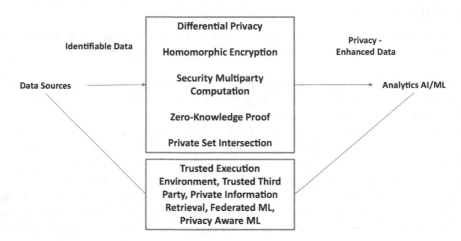

Source: Adapted from Garter

THE INNOVATOR'S DILEMMA

Clayton Christensen's Innovators dilemma concept is a classic management framework. In this seminal book, innovation expert and Harvard Business School Professor Clayton M. Christensen revealed a startling truth: even when the most successful companies can seemingly do everything right, they can lose market leadership. Most companies, Christensen says, will miss out on innovation, according to https://www.stratrix.com/innovators-dilemma/.

COMPANIES OFTEN FALL INTO COMFORTABLE BOXES

When confronted by disruptive technology, companies often fall into comfortable boxes. They talk to their customers, who tell them there's no need to change. They track competitors who they see as not embracing innovation.

Regions across the world and departments across an organization have different requirements for product features. It is important to understand these differences:

	Region 1	Region 2	Dep a	Dep b
Feature 1	Priority 1	Priority 2	Priority 2	Priority 2
Feature 2	Priority 3	Priority 1	Priority 3	Priority 3
...	Priority 2	Priority 3	Priority 1	Priority 1

PRIVACY-PRESERVING TECHNOLOGY (PET) IS EVOLVING

Regulations drive innovation in Pseudonymization and other protection techniques for personal data. In Privacy-Preserving Technology (PET), different approaches are evolving, including Homomorphic Encryption and advanced forms of data Tokenization.

Secure Multi-Party Computation (MPC)

Private multi-party machine learning with MPC

Using MPC, **different parties send encrypted messages to each other**, and obtain the model F(A,B,C) they wanted to **compute without revealing their own private input**, and without the need for a trusted central authority.

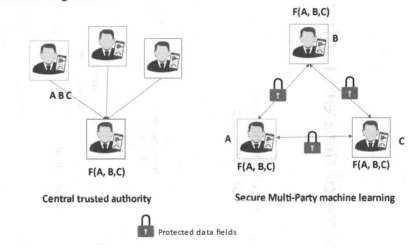

Central trusted authority

Secure Multi-Party machine learning

 Protected data fields

IMPROVE BUSINESS USABILITY

New and special features for data protection may be required for different types of data, including International Unicode, other formats of Dates, and Floating Point.

The new techniques can be faster, more scalable, more transparent to applications, better privacy, lower risk for the data breach, or improve business usability:

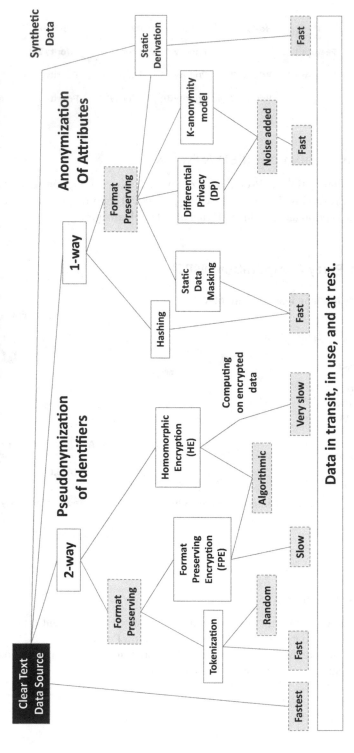

HOW REGULATORY FRAMEWORKS DRIVE TECHNOLOGICAL INNOVATIONS

Regulation can establish fairness and openness but is often viewed as an additional hurdle. To many businesses, these rules require adjustments and additional costs in their operations.

"… openness or competition in product markets provides the necessary conditions for research and innovation", states an OECD paper on regulatory reform and innovation, https://www.oecd.org/sti/inno/2102514.pdf.

Regulation May Not Hinder Innovation

Cryptocurrency exchanges have lacked compliance and U.S. government now implemented the validation of identities. The lack of regulation results in higher risk, and some governments proposed a new licensing regime under their anti-money laundering legislation. This requires all cryptocurrency trading platforms that operate there, or target investors in the city, to apply for an SFC license, according to "How Regulatory Frameworks Drive Technological Innovations". https://www.entrepreneur.com/article/360111.

Finance and technology of decentralization and democratization are not easy. Case in point: Many have already adopted digital assets, but only a few understand fintech technically. Numerous scams border on exit scams, so-called cloud mining operations and the like.

REGULATIONS HELP INNOVATION

Regulations help guide innovation to produce secure solutions and unlikely to be met with local and geopolitical challenges.

GDPR DRIVES NEW PROTECTION TECHNIQUES

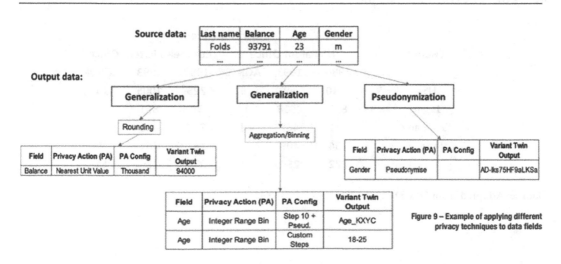

Figure 9 – Example of applying different privacy techniques to data fields

Article 4 (5) GDPR defines Pseudonymization as the processing of personal data without the use of additional information.

OPENNESS OR COMPETITION IN PRODUCT MARKETS PROVIDES INNOVATION

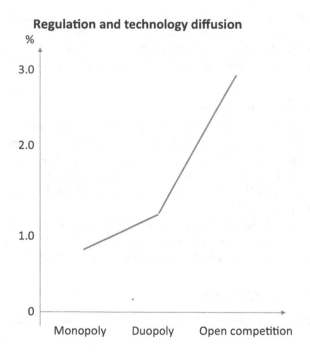

Source: Adapted from OECD, DSTL

INNOVATION IN TELECOMMUNICATION

Country	Growth in patents					
	US Patent Office			European Patent Office		
	1980	1993	AGR %	1980	1993	AGR %
USA	3710	69	5	225	1005	15
Japan	862	4518	14	79	861	24
Germany	341	482	3	224	443	6
France	254	409	4	141	281	7
UK	222	259	1	44	186	14

Source: Adapted from OECD

Growth in Patents

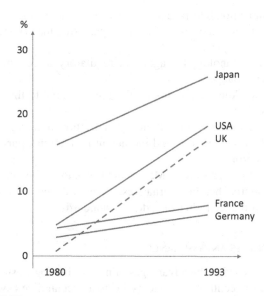

Source: Adapted from OECD

US Patent Filings in the Area of Granular Data Protection

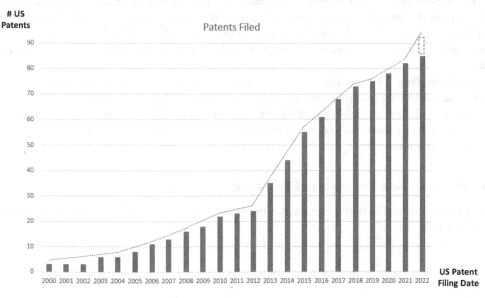

Growth in US Patent Filings in the area of Granular Data Protection (Example from one vendor)

UNDERSTAND REGULATION/TECHNOLOGY LINKAGES AND TECHNOLOGY-DRIVING APPROACHES

OECD of the regulation/innovation interface leads to several general conclusions on how to improve the positive regulatory effects on innovation without jeopardising the original regulatory objectives:

1. Understand regulation/technology linkages. The regulatory process must be ever vigilant to the effects of technical change.
2. Introduce competition. Competition among firms is essential to the innovative process in all economic sectors.
3. Streamline regulations. In economic efficiency and innovation, regulatory reform should seek to remove duplicative, onerous and inefficient regulations, particularly to aid small- and medium-sized enterprises.
4. Use technology-driving approaches. Maximum use should be made of technological-friendly regulatory approaches or alternatives, such as economic instruments, voluntary agreements, and performance rather than design standards.

COMPLIANCE GIVES ENTERPRISES AN ASSURANCE

Many large businesses acknowledge the advantages of new technologies such as blockchain and the benefits of breaking away from centralized systems due to a decentralized system's possible security and legal threats.

The innovation can be a free from the risks associated with money laundering through regulatory compliance.

COMPLEX REGULATION-TECHNOLOGY RELATIONS

Well-thought-out regulation is not adverse to innovation and can even serve as a stimulus. Regulations can be a powerful stimulus to innovation in most fields, ranging from banking to environment to retailing, according to "How Regulatory Frameworks Drive Technological Innovations".

Standardization in compliance mechanisms will encourage the adoption of platforms and solutions.

Regulations help foster competition, and larger companies quickly absorb smaller ones that threaten their dominant positions with their innovative new products and services.

Regulatory frameworks may appear limiting, but they can be viewed from another perspective. This can present opportunities to develop products that do not only address pressing needs through innovative solutions.

INNOVATION AND NEW INITIATIVES IN CYBERSECURITY SPENDING

New opportunities and initiatives are increasing from 9% to 14% as drivers for increased cybersecurity spending.

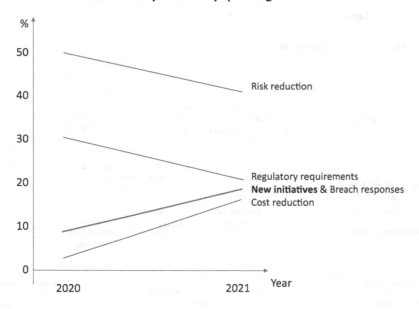

Drivers for increased cybersecurity spending

Source: Adapted from EY

EXAMINING YOUR INNOVATION PORTFOLIO

Impact and Disruption Matrix

	Existing	New
Radical	Transform	Disrupt (higher risk for big reward)
Incremental	Optimize	Extend

INNOVATION STAGES

Basic Innovation Stages

The Innovation Process – Basic Innovation Stages

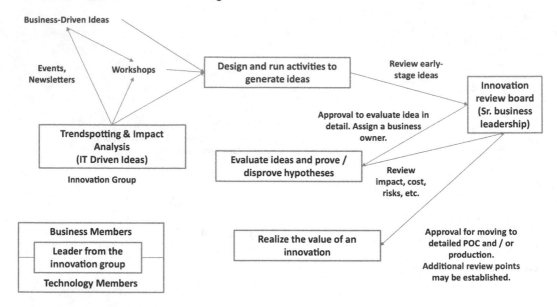

EXPERIMENTAL APPROACHES

Combining Iterative and Experimental Approaches

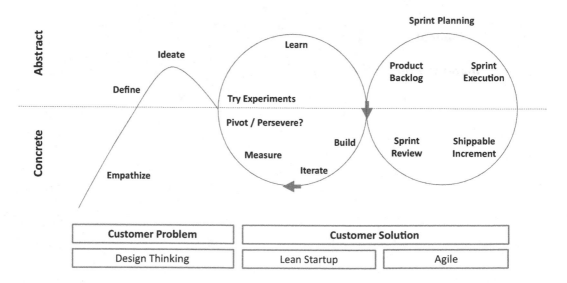

Source: Adapted from Gartner

MANAGING INNOVATION AND EVOLUTION

Product management is often caught between the pressures to innovate new features and the need to evolve products to support existing customers. Product managers must balance innovating and evolving to maintain product success.

INNOVATION MANAGEMENT MATURITY

To improve innovation management maturity, organizations must enhance the innovation process.

Organizations should aim to optimize innovation management capabilities at one level to lay the groundwork for proceeding to the next.

INNOVATION MANAGEMENT MATURITY MODEL

Gartner's Innovation Management Maturity Model assists enterprises in developing and advancing a sustainable innovation management competency. The maturity model is structured into five levels that reflect the status of enterprise-wide innovation management.

The maturity levels are:

1. Reactive
2. Active
3. Defined
4. Performing
5. Pervasive

Summary of innovation management maturity levels and key characteristics:

Combining Iterative and Experimental Approaches

Maturity level				
1. Reactive	2. Active	3. Defined	4. Performing	5. Pervasive
				World-class leader
			Strategic partnerships	Open innovation programs
		Involves external resources	Catalyst teams	Distributed teams
	Teams share best practices	Teams funded	Best in class processes	Pervasive culture
Driven by personality	Locally funded	Processes formalized	Funded at enterprise level	Integral to business activities

Source: Adapted from Gartner

Emphasis on the Six Dimensions

The degree of emphasis on the six dimensions varies in the lower maturity levels.

Specifically, the first three dimensions—strategy and intent, processes and practices, culture and people—require consistently greater attention through all maturity levels, while the three remaining dimensions—organization and infrastructure, partnerships and open innovation, and innovating how we innovate—will require less focus in the lower levels of maturity but significantly more attention by Level 3.

Dimension	Importance to Maturity				
	1. Reactive	2. Active	3. Defined	4. Performing	5. Pervasive
Strategy	High	High	High	High	High
Processes	Medium	High	High	High	High
Culture	Medium	High	High	High	High
Organization	Low	Medium	High	High	High
Infrastructure	Low	Medium	High	High	High
Partnerships	Low	Low	Medium	High	High

Source: Adapted from Gartner

THE OPPORTUNITY

OPPORTUNITIES IN SECURITY

- Security leaders who redefine the cybersecurity function and technology architecture are positioning the business to maintain and increase value in an increasingly agile, distributed, and decentralized environment.
- Organizations that push cybersecurity decision-making out to the business units are improving their security posture, even as a digital scale and complexity increase.
- Security education that emphasizes organizational cultural change and fosters better cyber judgment is the most effective way to avoid social engineering incidents and poor decisions about business technology.
- Security product consolidation and the cybersecurity mesh enable leaders to build a more efficient and integrated security infrastructure for the expanding attack surface.

DATA CATALOGING FOR DATA GOVERNANCE

A global auto manufacturer wants to reimagine its customer outreach, so it looks for ways to improve its analytics insights—and realizes it needs a complete and governed view of all its enterprise data. A global financial services firm seeking to launch new services more rapidly automates its data governance program to expand employee access to key information. These examples show that successful enterprises realize that trusted, governed data represents a key business asset. Organizations can improve the bottom line by finding new ways to leverage data: identifying new product opportunities, optimizing pricing, reducing costs and risks, and improving the customer experience—to name just a few business initiatives.

For any business seeking competitive advantage in data, data governance is critical for business decisions and is trustworthy. It enables you to measure and monitor the quality of your data so that everything from analytics to customer experience initiatives is more successful. And at the same time, an enterprise data governance program promotes regulatory compliance, helps reduce risk, and protects personal and sensitive data.

A successful data governance program enables collaboration between your business and IT stakeholders so that data isn't just IT's responsibility—it's something to be used and governed across your organization.

None of these benefits, however, is possible until you know what data you have, what the quality is, and what systems and processes use it. This is where an enterprise data catalog makes the difference. And not just any data catalog but one that enables agile data governance at scale, with the ability to provide broad visibility across all enterprise-wide data assets and a deep understanding of those assets.

ENTERPRISES ARE COLLECTING MORE DATA, BUT DO THEY KNOW WHAT TO DO WITH IT?

A new survey from Seagate and IDC reveals what challenges enterprises will need to address before they can better leverage the data they're collecting. Enterprise data collection is expected to increase data at a 42.2% annual growth rate, according to "Enterprises are collecting more data".

However, a substantial chunk of data remains unleveraged due to data management and security challenges.

The report says that enterprises want data lakes where new data is taken in, and old data is moved to low-cost disk. The report surveyed more than 1000 respondents globally in North America, Europe, APJ, and China) from different-sized businesses.

WORLDWIDE GLOBAL ENTERPRISE DATA

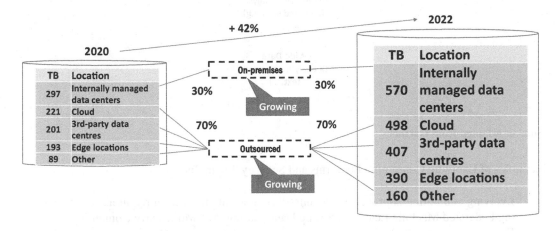

Source: Adapted from Seagate and IDC

Personal data is lucrative and, therefore, vulnerable to cybercrime.

- PHI can sell for several hundreds of USD per record and is often resold to multiple threat actors. Customer PII is the most likely to get exposed or compromised in data breaches, with 80% of data breaches affecting PII records.

The main growth in data collection is used in analytics and the cloud. Organizations collect only 56% of the available data through internal operations. Of this data, 43% went largely unused.

Thirty percent of stored data is in internal data centers, 20% in third-party data centers, 19% in edge locations, 22% in the cloud, and 9% in other locations. This may not change in two years.

Managing data in multi-cloud and hybrid-cloud environments is a top challenge expected over the next two years, and better data management is two-thirds of survey respondents reported security as insufficient.

Enterprises could leverage a well-functioning data architecture, emphasizing DataOps, bringing siloed data systems into a unified entity where DataOps will help with metadata management, data classification, and policy management.

FROM BIG TO SMALL AND WIDE DATA

As companies experience the limitations of big data as a critical enabler of analytics and AI, new approaches known as "small data" and "wide data" are emerging, according to Gartner. The wide data approach leaves behind the reliance on single large, monolithic data sources by enabling the analysis and synergy of various small and large, unstructured and structured data sources. The small data approach is about applying analytical techniques that require less data but still offer useful insights. These include the tailored use of less data-hungry models, such as certain time-series analysis techniques, rather than using more data-hungry deep learning techniques in a one-size-fits-all approach.

According to Gartner, by 2025, 70% of organizations will be compelled to shift their focus from big to small and wide data, providing more context for analytics and making AI less data-hungry.

Source: Adapted from Gartner

Examples of Evolving Computing Platforms and Security Technologies

- Evolving computing approaches may introduce new data protection requirements, including Federated Machine Learning, Secure Data Sharing, and Multi-party Computing.
- Evolving computing platforms may introduce new data platforms and interfaces, including Client/server, Big data and Hadoop, cloud databases, Web3 storage models, and data sharing/segmentation:

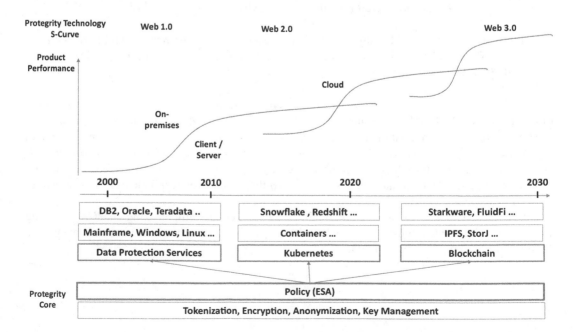

Technology S-Curves for Data Protection Techniques

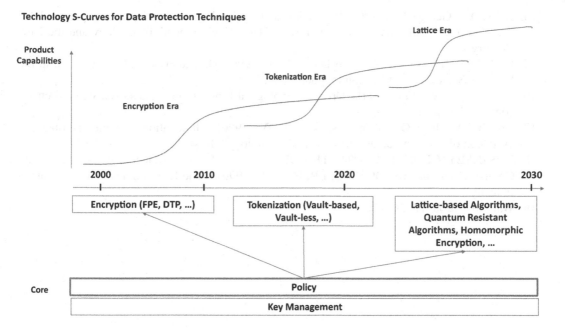

NOTES

1. https://www.zdnet.com/article/enterprises-are-collecting-more-data-but-do-they-know-what-to-do-with-it/
2. "Enterprises are collecting more data, but". https://www.zdnet.com/article/enterprises-are-collecting-more-data-but-do-they-know-what-to-do-with-it/
3. https://www.oecd.org/sti/inno/2102514.pdf
4. https://www.sciencedirect.com/science/article/pii/S0267364918300153#:~:text=Article%20 4%20%285%29%20GDPR%20defines%20pseudonymisation%20as%20the,attributed%20 to%20an%20identified%20or%20identifiable%20natural%20person
5. "Why small and wide data matters – Technology Decisions" https://www.technologydecisions. com.au/content/it-management/article/why-small-and-wide-data-matters-216930801
6. https://www.gartner.com/doc/3906956?plc=ddc
7. https://www.entrepreneur.com/article/360111#:~:text=Regulations%20help%20guide%20 innovation%20to%20produce%20solutions%20that,to%20be%20met%20with%20local%20 and%20geopolitical%20challenges
8. BAILY, Martin Neil (1993), Competition, Regulation and Efficiency in Service Industries, Brookings Papers in Microeconomics 2.
9. "Enterprises are collecting more data" https://www.zdnet.com/article/enterprises-are-collecting-more-data-but-do-they-know-what-to-do-with-it/
10. COHEN, Wesley M., Richard R. NELSON and John WALSH (1996), Appropriability Conditions and Why Firms Patent and Why they Do Not in the American Manufacturing Sector, paper prepared for the OECD Conference on New S&T Indicators for the Knowledge-Based Economy, Paris, 19–21 June.
11. ECAA (1994), White Paper on Restructuring, European Car Assembly Association.
12. EUROPEAN COMMISSION (1995), Green Paper on Innovation.
13. ERNST & YOUNG (1994), Biotechnology's Economic Impact in Europe: A Survey of its Role in Competitiveness.

14. HEATON, George R. (1990), Regulation and Technological Change, paper prepared for the WRI and OECD Symposium on Toward 2000: Environment, Technology and the New Century.

15. HOJ, Jens, Toshiyasu KATO and Dirk PILAT (1996), Deregulation and Privatisation in the Services Sector, OECD Economic Studies, No. 25.

16. "How Regulatory Frameworks Drive Technological Innovations". https://www.entrepreneur.com/article/360111

17. LANJOUW, Jean Olson and Ashoka MODY (1996), "Innovation and the International Diffusion of Environmentally Responsive Technology", Research Policy, No. 25.

18. McKINSEY GLOBAL INSTITUTE (1992), Service Sector Productivity, McKinsey and Company, Washington, DC. MILLER, Henry I. (1996), "The EU Hobbles Its Own Biotech Industry".

19. Wall Street Journal, 26 July.

3 Best Practices

INTRODUCTION

In this chapter, we will discuss best practices for analytics on real-time data and data increasingly stored in the cloud. We will discuss the growing need for data privacy, and security is demanding better techniques to protect data and solutions. Data risks, privacy regulations, and threats are evolving, and we will discuss this changing landscape. This chapter is divided into sections about data growth, privacy, threats, trust, security, products, and changing privacy laws.

Traditional data-at-rest encryption is not a sufficient control for creating data confidentiality and privacy, especially in third-party data processing and data sharing scenarios. In addition to adding existing field-level transformation approaches, such as data masking, organizations should look into emerging techniques: differential privacy, SMPC, homomorphic encryption, and hardware security for key management.

USE CASES

Use Cases Definitions

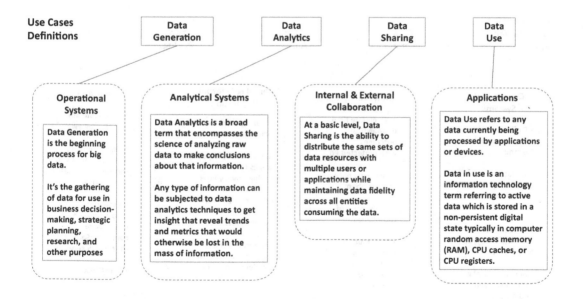

Use Cases Definitions

Data Generation

Operational Systems

Data Generation is the beginning process for big data.

It's the gathering of data for use in business decision-making, strategic planning, research, and other purposes

Data Analytics

Analytical Systems

Data Analytics is a broad term that encompasses the science of analyzing raw data to make conclusions about that information.

Any type of information can be subjected to data analytics techniques to get insight that reveal trends and metrics that would otherwise be lost in the mass of information.

Data Sharing

Internal & External Collaboration

At a basic level, Data Sharing is the ability to distribute the same sets of data resources with multiple users or applications while maintaining data fidelity across all entities consuming the data.

Data Use

Applications

Data Use refers to any data currently being processed by applications or devices.

Data in use is an information technology term referring to active data which is stored in a non-persistent digital state typically in computer random access memory (RAM), CPU caches, or CPU registers.

DOI: 10.1201/9781003254928-4

Use Cases Common Challenges

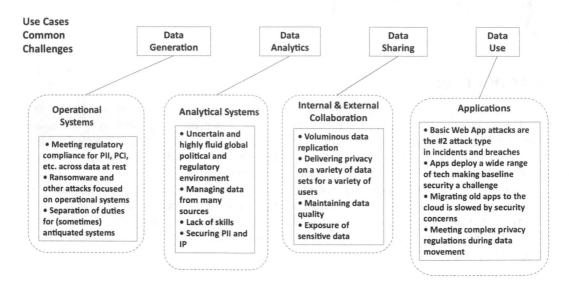

Use Cases Common Challenges

Data Generation

Data Analytics

Data Sharing

Data Use

Operational Systems
- Meeting regulatory compliance for PII, PCI, etc. across data at rest
- Ransomware and other attacks focused on operational systems
- Separation of duties for (sometimes) antiquated systems

Analytical Systems
- Uncertain and highly fluid global political and regulatory environment
- Managing data from many sources
- Lack of skills
- Securing PII and IP

Internal & External Collaboration
- Voluminous data replication
- Delivering privacy on a variety of data sets for a variety of users
- Maintaining data quality
- Exposure of sensitive data

Applications
- Basic Web App attacks are the #2 attack type in incidents and breaches
- Apps deploy a wide range of tech making baseline security a challenge
- Migrating old apps to the cloud is slowed by security concerns
- Meeting complex privacy regulations during data movement

Use Cases Business Value Add

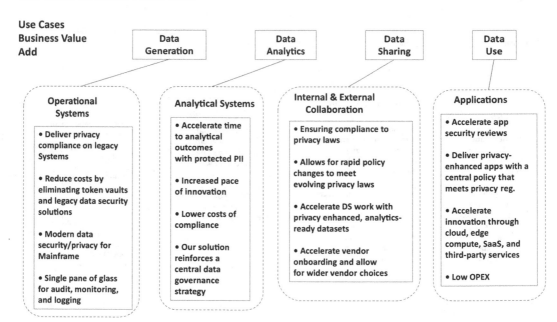

Use Cases Business Value Add

Data Generation

Data Analytics

Data Sharing

Data Use

Operational Systems
- Deliver privacy compliance on legacy Systems
- Reduce costs by eliminating token vaults and legacy data security solutions
- Modern data security/privacy for Mainframe
- Single pane of glass for audit, monitoring, and logging

Analytical Systems
- Accelerate time to analytical outcomes with protected PII
- Increased pace of innovation
- Lower costs of compliance
- Our solution reinforces a central data governance strategy

Internal & External Collaboration
- Ensuring compliance to privacy laws
- Allows for rapid policy changes to meet evolving privacy laws
- Accelerate DS work with privacy enhanced, analytics-ready datasets
- Accelerate vendor onboarding and allow for wider vendor choices

Applications
- Accelerate app security reviews
- Deliver privacy-enhanced apps with a central policy that meets privacy reg.
- Accelerate innovation through cloud, edge compute, SaaS, and third-party services
- Low OPEX

Use Cases Technical Value Add

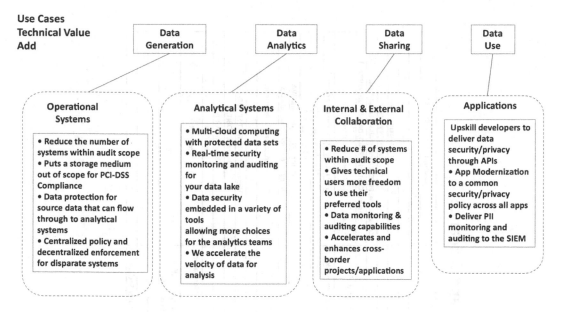

THE FUTURE OF DATA PRIVACY

The book's theme is "The Future of Data Privacy", and it talks about evolving platforms and data protection techniques.

A few chapters address "Who Owns the New Oil?" and talk about technologies that can help in owning and controlling your private data.

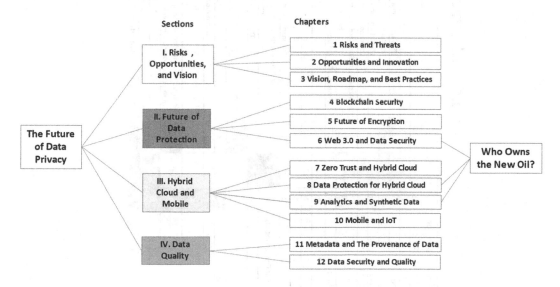

EXAMPLE OF SIMPLE STEPS TO FIND A PROTECT DATA

WHAT REGULATIONS AND GUIDANCE DO YOU NEED TO IMPLEMENT?

Example of Alignment to Standards and Guidance

Standard, Guidance, or Organization	1-Most Important			Comments	Examples of Alignment
	US	EMEA	APAC		
PCI DSS	1	1	1	Payment cards Industry Standard	Encryption
NIST SP 800-207	1	1	1	US National Institute for Standards and Technology	Zero Trust Architecture
NIST SP 800-53	1	1	1	US National Institute for Standards and Technology	Key states, key lengths
NIST FIPS 140-2	1	1	1	US National Institute for Standards and Technology	Key storage, PKCS#11 integration, Level 1 encryption lib.
NIST SP 800-171	1	1	2	US National Institute for Standards and Technology	Access Control (PR.AC), Data Security (PR.DS)
ANSI X9	1	2	3	The Accredited Standards Committee X9 (ASC X9, Inc.) developing standards for the financial services industry in the U.S.	Tokenization, Encryption
ISO/IEC 27001	3	1	3	International Standards Organization anf International Electrotechnical Commission	ISO 27001 Annex A, or the core controls
CSA	2	2	2	Cloud Security Alliance	Quantum Computing
PKCS	2	2	2	Public Key Cryptography Standard	PKCS #5, #11, #12
OWASP	2	3	2	The Open Web Application Security Project	Top 10 for API Security and WA
IEEE	2	3	2	The Institute of Electrical and Electronics Engineers	Integration with Data Catalogs
Homomorphic.Computing.org	2	4	2	Homomorphic.Computing.org brings together researchers with practitioners and industry (IBM, Intel, MS ...)	Future Lattice-based algorithms
CCC	2	4	3	The Confidential Computing Consortium	
CMMC 2.0	2	2	4	Required by US Government	Alignment with NIST SP 800-171
ISACA	3	3	4	Information Systems Security Association, 140k members	Journal, COBIT,
ISO/IEC 20889	4	2	3	Data De-identification	k-Anonymity
ISSA	4	3	3	Information Systems Security Association	Journal
IAPP	4	3	3	International Association of Privacy Professionals, comprehensive global information privacy	Journal
(ISC)2	4	3	4	The International Information System Security Certification Consortium, or (ISC)², is a non-profit organization which specializes in training and certifications (CISSP ...)	
OMG	4	4	3	Object Management Group	
IIA	4	4	4	Institute for Internal Auditors	
BCS	5	5	4	The Chartered Institute for IT, formerly known as the British Computer Society	

FOR EXAMPLE, FOR GDPR, THESE STEPS TO IMPLEMENT DATA SECURITY COULD BE FOLLOWED

GDPR Security Requirements Framework

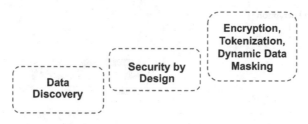

Source: Adapted from IBM

I START TO SCAN DATA STORES AND APPLICATIONS FOR DATA THAT NEED TO BE PROTECTED

Privacy by Design vs. Security by Design
Scanning Apps and Data for Issues with Privacy and Security

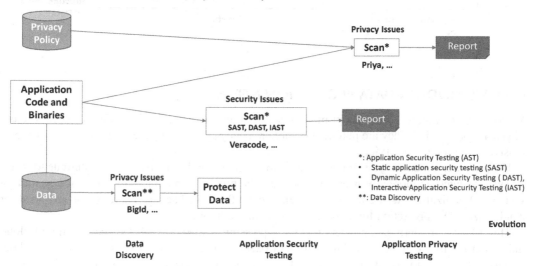

I Chose a Protection Technique for Different Types of Data

Use of different Techniques for Data Security

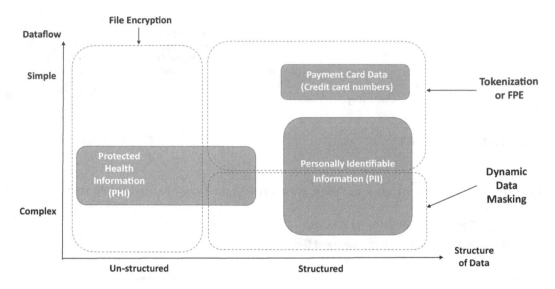

TODAY'S MODERN DATA PROTECTION NEEDS

As organizations aggressively adopt modern services and new applications, data protection challenges are on the rise. They are putting pressure on legacy systems and the desire for more comprehensive data protection services.

Unfortunately, many organizations are still struggling to get legacy backups to continue to work. As systems become more advanced and complex, the pressure on aging data protection is starting to show. Organizations desire more from their backup than just backup. There is a strong need for standardized data protection for all data across all environments.

The need for modern data protection is more pressing than ever. With the acceleration of cloud and modern delivery practices and the reality of backup and restoration issues with legacy backup, modern data protection is essential. But what is it, according to the organizations that really need it?

According to the 3000 global organizations that took part in the research, integrated data protection and security (35%), cloud workload portability (36%), and the ability to make disaster recovery via a cloud service (DRaaS) (38%) top the list.

Collectively, the research shows that modern data protection needs to support the vast diversity of organizations' IT platforms (cloud, SaaS, virtual, physical), make data safe, accessible, and usable for purposes such as DevOps and analytics, and ultimately enable consistent and unified data protection. To enable consistent and unified data protection for hybrid cloud is among the top four needs (34%):

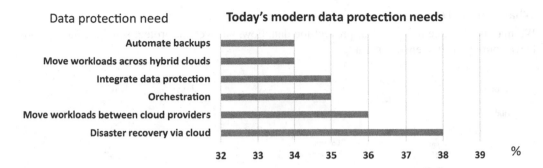

Source: Adapted from Gartner

TRENDS IN CONTROL OF DATA

Over time, more data is exposed in an environment that may not be in our corporate control. We may have:

- Contracted providers of SaaS and other services in the cloud.
- Outsourced testing of applications.
- Individuals that are storing data locally or using services from providers that are not contracted by corporate.

MORE DATA IS OUTSIDE CORPORATE CONTROL

This data may be regulated or exposed to attacks:

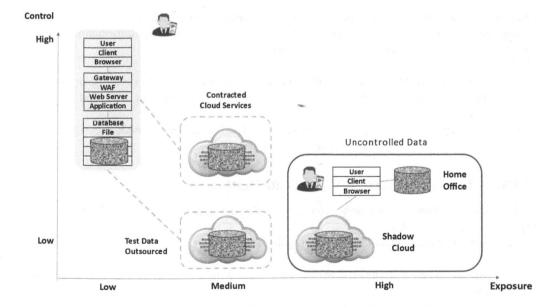

What Can We Do?

We may not be able to control or prevent the data flow, but we can protect sensitive data before it leaves our controlled environment:

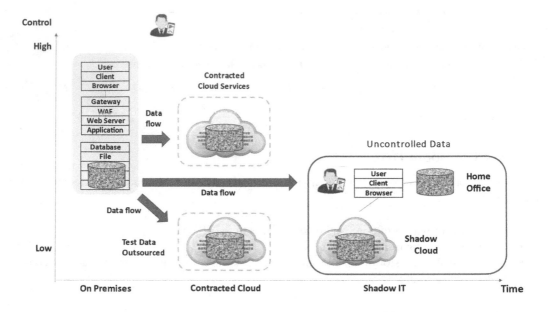

DATA-AT-REST ENCRYPTION ONLY DOES NOT PROVIDE ENOUGH PROTECTION FROM DATA THEFT

Organizations are increasingly concerned about data security in several scenarios, including collecting and retaining sensitive personal information; processing personal information in external environments, such as the cloud; and sharing information.

- Data-at-rest encryption only, as commonly implemented, does not provide strong protection from data theft and privacy disclosures. It is unable to secure data in use and data sharing scenarios.
- Several privacy-preserving and privacy-enhanced techniques can provide security for data in use and data sharing, but none universally cover all use cases.

TRENDS IN DATA PROTECTION INTEGRATION

Major implementations of data protection in networks and data management infrastructures have evolved in steps since 2000.

These are some major Data Protection integration trends:

- Implementations of granular data protection started in 2000 with several major database vendors.
- Tokenization was introduced to PCI DSS and the payment systems industry to provide a higher level of security control, flexibility, and application transparency. Tokenization was increasingly used for PII data to provide a higher level of security control and separation of duties.
- Integration into networks with CASB solutions followed that.
- They were later followed by integration with data discovery tools and database catalogs.

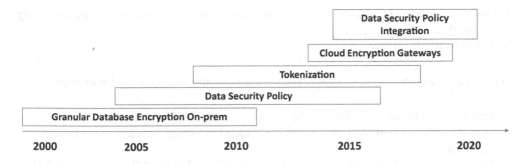

Source: Protegrity

Automation of integration and policy management followed these milestones. We will discuss this more in separate chapters in this volume.

CONFLUENCE OF DATA SECURITY CONTROLS

Amalgamation of more comprehensive Data Security Platforms (DSP):

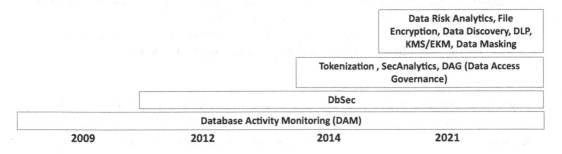

Source: Adapted from Gartner, 2021

DSP FUTURE STATE

This will be DSP Future State according to Gartner:

1. Consistent visibility on (sensitive) data, policies, and applicable regulations.
2. High levels of integration and simplified deployment.
3. Ease of administration via a consolidated policy.
4. Democratized access to secure data thoroughly.
5. Roles move from being focused on a single product or technology to multidimensional.
6. Data stores for AI, like data lakes, will increase in importance.
7. Complex administration using disparate products no API integration.
8. Rudimentary or nonexistent sensitive-data visibility and control.
9. Lack of hybrid cloud capabilities. DSPs that are partially still not ready for cloud or solutions that lack support for on-premises data stores.
10. Very long planning and implementation cycles. Eventually, it delivers only part of what was envisioned.
11. Immature privacy-enhanced computation technologies (PECT).
12. Not all vendors address the full set of required DSP capabilities.
13. Pattern-driven data discovery capabilities without considering the context.

14. Frustrating amount of false positives making it hard to understand what is really happening to your data.
15. Separate and siloed teams.

We will discuss a number of these areas in the separate chapters of this book, for example:

- Area #1: Sensitive-data visibility and control is a critical capability of DSP.
- Area #2: The use of API integration and cloud-delivered services will increase in importance.
- Area #3: The DSP management control plane is decoupled from data types and control objects, allowing centralized administration. The administrative interface will allow data security policy to be managed from a single console.
- Area #4: DSPs are available as stand-alone tools and cloud-based service offerings. Cloud-based offerings will make most of the DSP security objects available via low threshold API integration.
- Area #10: Clients must bring complex (product) architectures and processes in place before they can configure the first policies or reports.
- Area #11: Established vendors frequently do not have the adoption of PECT on the roadmaps of their DSP.
- Area #12: Some DSP offerings only focus on adapting traditional product platforms rather than entirely replatforming their data security capabilities.
- Area #13: Data discovery rarely makes use of AI/ML support to do semantic analysis to find out what something really is. For example, a newspaper article's dateline. Each data type will need the appropriate level of protection.

Relevant Data Security Concepts Where DSPs Are Becoming the Central Dominant Force:

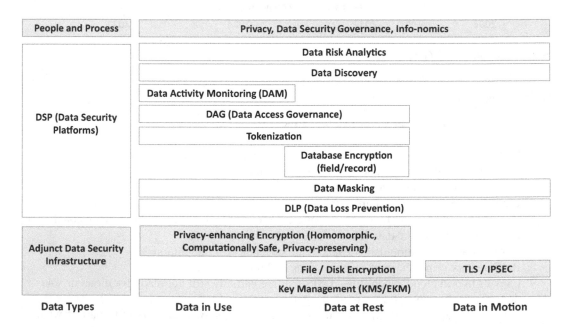

Source: Adapted from Gartner, 2021

CYBERSECURITY MESH

By 2024, organizations adopting a cybersecurity mesh architecture will reduce the financial impact of individual security incidents by an average of 90%, according to Gartner.

The cybersecurity mesh architecture concept is evolving and gaining popularity as a technical approach, driven by bundled vendor offerings and new emerging standards. Although not exclusively offered on an "as a service" basis, the transition to the cybersecurity mesh approach has also made cloud delivery the preferred approach for most cybersecurity technologies.

Existing security and identity architectures approaches are siloed and work in isolation from each other. This makes challenging a zero-trust architecture—where context and (near) real-time events drive an adaptive security posture. A cybersecurity mesh architecture (CSMA) helps provide a common, integrated security structure and posture to secure all assets, whether they're on-premises, in data centers, or in the cloud.

CSMA creates and leverages interoperable connections between stand-alone security tools to promote composability and a consistent security posture. This allows these tools to share and leverage security intelligence and apply a dynamic policy model that is based on the current state of assets.

API MANAGEMENT

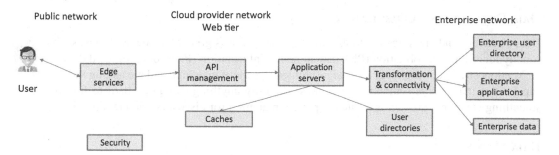

Source: Adapted from Object Management Group

API Management Runtime Flow:

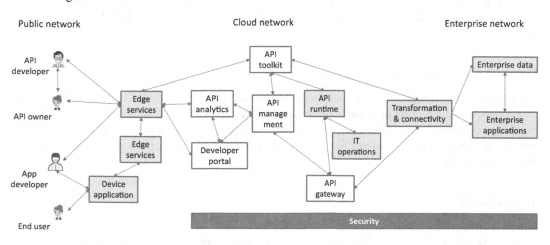

Source: Adapted from Object Management Group

People and Process

Data Security Governance (DSG)

DSG refers to a subset of information governance that deals specifically with protecting corporate data (in both structured databases and unstructured file-based forms) through defined data policies and processes, and implemented via technologies that are by and large drawn from DSPs.

Privacy

Privacy compliance, and its accompanying architecture requirements, has become a predominant driver for many elements of data security in Gartner inquiry. Privacy and related regulations require a data protection impact assessment and usually avoid specifying specific data security controls.

Infonomics

Enabling the secure and lawful monetization data is a competitive differentiator for leading organizations.

For example, an emergent product category is data exchange vendors with a data sharing platform and services that companies can license—allowing them to operate their own secure closed-ecosystem data sharing, containing only approved participants.

Data Discovery and Classification

Data discovery and classification tools may use alternate, less granular categorizations, such as personally identifiable information (PII), patient health information (PHI), or credit card data.

Vendors strive to move away from algorithmically pattern matching and are adding AI/ML-based capabilities that enable semantic capabilities—literally anything. It can be hard to find out what something is when a product is limited to pattern matching for discovery and classification.

Data Masking

Data masking transforms data or deidentifies data, allowing processing to be in a compliant fashion. DSPs may have a dedicated capability or as part of the tokenization capabilities. It can be applied as a separate step.

Static data masking (SDM) creates a deidentified copy of a dataset.

Dynamic data masking (DDM) is essentially a form of access control. DDM protects data in use only.

Database Encryption (Field/Record)

Field-level encryption (FLE) can protect individual fields and documents with all key management, encryption, and decryption operations occurring exclusively outside the database server. With FLE enabled, a compromised administrator or user obtaining access to the database, the underlying file-system, or server memory contents (e.g., via scraping or process inspection) will only see unreadable encrypted data.

Tokenization

Tokenization and format-preserving encryption (FPE) protect a data field by replacing its value with a substitute when it is loaded into an application or data store. This protects data at rest, as well as data in subsequent use. If an application or user needs the real data value, the substitute can be transformed back because the algorithms are designed to be reversible. The algorithms are designed to provide unique and consistent mapping between the real value and the token, where referential integrity is maintained.

Tokenization is useful for many use cases besides Payment Card Industry Data Security Standard (PCI DSS). Vendors are responding by amalgamating adjunct features such as discovery and monitoring into comprehensive DSPs rather than specialist products that are tied to single use cases.

FULL DISK ENCRYPTION

Full-disk encryption (FDE) software encrypts the complete contents of an endpoint's storage device, which is typically the full hard disk, including the operating system. The only files excluded from encryption are the ones needed for the actual booting of the system. FDE is the most important protection against loss of sensitive data through endpoint/device loss.

FILE ENCRYPTION

In some cases, individual files or folders on an endpoint need to be protected from unauthorized user access. Just because multiple users have authorized access to an endpoint does not mean that they are all authorized to decrypt the files stored there. For example, administrators need remote and local access to employee devices for troubleshooting and maintenance purposes. However, administrators are not authorized to decrypt sensitive employee files and should not be able to do so.

ENTERPRISE KEY MANAGEMENT (EKM) AND SECRET MANAGEMENT

Managing keys and secrets, such as credentials needed to programmatically authenticate to an API, is vital to maintaining security and availability. It is especially critical for data-at-rest encryption, such as TDE, database field level encryption or tokenization, where the loss of keys make data inaccessible. With encryption being ever more pervasive, the number of keys and secrets is rapidly growing, and the number of systems and applications that use encryption become more diverse.

PRIVACY-ENHANCING COMPUTATION (PEC) TECHNIQUES

PEC techniques comprise several protection methods or devices that protect data in use. Hostile environments could be clouds or data ecosystems, requiring secure data processing and data analytics.

SPENDING ON DATA PROTECTION

A worldwide headcount of 5000 employees appears to be the point when organizations begin to ramp up their spending on data protection and privacy.

A vast majority of small and medium enterprises (87% of those with less than 1000 employees) spend less than $250,000 on data protection and privacy activities.

More than half of large enterprises (between 1001 and 10,000 employees) have the same limited budget. Of the larger enterprises with over 10,000 employees, 23% spend over $1,000,000 annually on data protection and privacy activities.

Budgets increase for bigger enterprises, and 94% of enterprises with less than 5000 employees are still operating with a budget of less than $500,000, according to the CPO Magazine study.

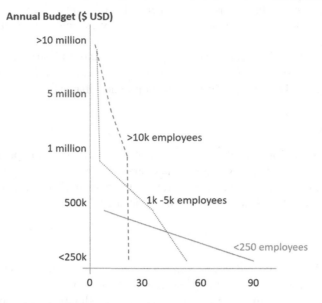

Spending on Data Protection and Privacy by Size

Source: Adapted from CPO Magazine

More work is required, and presumably, more resources are needed in the early stages; spending goes up only as the data protection and privacy program matures.

Though one might assume that organizations at an early stage would be among the biggest spenders in getting new programs established, 87% spend less than $500,000 on their data protection and privacy.

Spending patterns do not necessarily increase significantly until a company is mature. Just 40% of the organizations in the Early to Late Middle stages are spending more than $250,000 annually.

Organizations in the early stages of maturity have more work to do, but tend to spend less due to budget and resource challenges rather than a lack of desire or awareness.

Spending increases consistently correlate with maturity increases. This is likely due to establishing a privacy-aware culture and increased executive support.

Organizations are generally not focusing on deploying supporting technologies and solutions until they are in the mature stages.

In the early and middle stages, organizations place a greatest emphasis (26%) on building a privacy-aware culture as a foundation. There is enhanced governance goal of data processing activities, according to the CPO Magazine study:

- A total of 471 responses were collected, and 16 industries were represented. The largest sectors were Technology & Software and Financial Services.

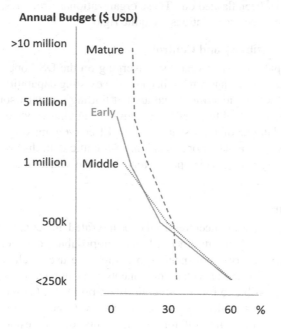

Spending on Data Protection and Privacy by Maturity

Annual Budget ($ USD)

Source: Adapted from CPO Magazine

HOW TO ENHANCE MATURITY

- Enhance governance of data processing activities
- Build privacy-aware culture in your organization
- Improve compliance management processes
- Deploy supporting technologies and solutions
- Train and Upskill Team Members

CURRENT STATE

Security tools running in a silo and different vendors, for example, for data discovery, data masking, tokenization, DAM, multicloud DAM functions, are handled by separate teams, and roles for each data security control have created a complex and unmanageable collection of vendors, product architectures, and consoles. Locking away your data rather than securing it well enough to make it an asset class ready to multiply its wealth through commercialized digital markets.

GAP ANALYSIS AND INTERDEPENDENCIES

Supporting DSPs and the ever-evolving data security, compliance and data sharing needs require that SRM leaders shed the familiar 10% incrementalism. The most significant gaps that will inhibit DSP migration include:

Organizational Silos and Existing Investments

The status quo of siloed data security is simply not scalable and does not support the pace of digital business. A DSP implementation requires a coordinated and cohesive approach across data security teams, compliance staff, and data scientists. This is an easier problem for midsize enterprises, as separate roles may not have been flashed out. These organizational structures, budgeting processes, and responsibilities within large organizations are quite rigid.

Semantic Sensitive-data Visibility and Control

This is a high-priority capability. Most vendors converging on the DSP opportunity have data discovery capability. However, large gaps remain because the existing capabilities examine data stores for metadata only or well-known identifiers, and are not finding out what something really is. For example, if a data classification tool finds a date, then it does not know whether it is a date of birth, a transaction date, or the dateline of a newspaper article. Effectively making data discovery useless in complex environments such as large organizations. Semantic data discovery must be delivered natively by the DSP offering and provide options for where the sensitive data is protected, such as data masking or tokenization.

Composable Architecture

Monolithic and virtual appliance architectures need to be migrated into composable DSPs. Individual controls are deployed where they are most needed, in a composable, scalable, flexible, and resilient manner—rather than every security tool running in a silo. The use of cloud-delivered DSPs and data security as a service (DSaaS) provided components may impact adoption for some regions and verticals. While it is possible to use a DSP entirely on-premises, Gartner observes that cloud-based deployment models can significantly reduce complexity, Capex and make more data security controls available. Every enterprise has different requirements for data residency and compliance.

Paradigm Shift from Need-to-Know to Need-to-Share

Traditionally, organizations have had a limited view of how they can help business leaders commercialize data, focused on the perceived data security and compliance obstacles. All too often best practices, security policies, or regulations seem to mandate that you lock your data away, limiting access to employees that need to know. Innovative approaches to data security, such as DSP and data ecosystem governance, are required. Although awareness of the value of data is growing, these CDOs and CIOs rarely have the data security knowledge or experience to have their data secured for virtually any use case.

STREAMLINE YOUR CURRENT DATA-CENTRIC SECURITY ARCHITECTURE

Streamline your current data-centric security architecture and overcome known pain points and obstacles. Form a joint D&A, compliance, and security team to develop a three-year roadmap for DSP transformation of your entire data supply chain.

- Demonstrate greater return value by enabling data processing and sharing use cases that have not been possible (yet).
- Engage with D&A leaders to identify where traditional data security hinders the organization to improve data's value. Develop a pragmatic and common vision to enable "good enough" data security and data utility for all silos and use cases.

Start with advanced controls. DSPs focusing on advanced controls generally have broader coverage than those focusing on traditional control. For example, DSPs that offer tokenization or (field-level) encryption capabilities frequently include data masking (as a post processing step for the token), cell level authorization, and database activity monitoring. In contrast, DSPs that focus on DAM rarely include advanced controls.

Evaluate single vendor offerings, ideally including DAM and PECT.

- Prioritize the consolidation of DSP architectures that consolidate several components into, for example, API-based approaches, cloud services or at a minimum, single agents. Set a goal to replace 90% of stand-alone data security controls.
- Capitalize on external expectations. External expectations, for example, compliance requirements or legislation, are opportunities to accelerate DSP deployment for the data (stores) in scope of the compliance requirement or legislation at hand.

Identify data security capabilities that are not fit for purpose in your environment.
Examples are data security controls that

- Form control silos, stand-alone products that do not integrate well with your remaining controls or products.
- Are data security products that do not deliver the anticipated value and have evolved into checkbox controls rather than actively contributing to data security goals. Selected examples are:
  - DAM implementations do not give you insight into what happens on your databases because they deliver several thousands of non-relevant log entries per minute.
  - Automated data classification tools that constantly misclassify or mislabel your data to the extent that no one takes the data classifications seriously anymore.
  - Data classification tools that do not classify data because the implementation required so many components and dependencies that it has never been finished.

DATA SECURITY STATE

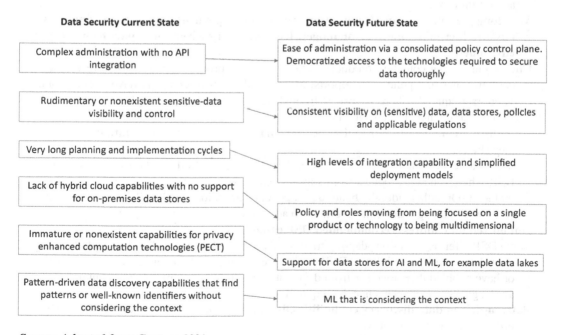

Source: Adapted from Gartner, 2021

Data Security Current State

1. Complex administration using disparate products that frequently have no API integration.
2. Rudimentary or nonexistent sensitive-data visibility and control.
3. Lack of hybrid cloud capabilities. DSPs are partially still not ready for cloud or solutions that lack support for on-premises data stores.
4. Very long planning and implementation cycles. The implementation of a new data security product takes one year or longer. Eventually, it delivers only part of what was envisioned.
5. Immature or nonexistent capabilities for privacy enhanced computation technologies (PECT).
6. Not all vendors address the full DSP capabilities.
7. Pattern-driven data discovery capabilities find patterns or well-known identifiers without considering the context.

Complex administration using disparate products that frequently have no API integration.

Data security products' APIs expose some functionality, but are used mostly for integration or user experience connectivity, and act as veneers on otherwise still siloed controls.

Rudimentary or nonexistent sensitive-data visibility and control.

Some offer data discovery capabilities, others partner, while others offer only basic data discovery based on, for example, the column metadata of relational databases. Very few offer sensitive data discovery across data silos and locations, such as on-premises data stores and the cloud.

Lack of hybrid cloud capabilities. DSPs that are partially still not ready for cloud or solutions that lack support for on-premises data stores.

Many products lack consistent support for hybrid cloud architectures. Products' line support is handled either in the public cloud or via on-premises data centers. Data centers are rare for products that can consistently support data security in public clouds, private clouds, and on-premises.

Very long planning and implementation cycles. The implementation of a new data security product takes one year or longer. Eventually, it delivers only part of what was envisioned.

Clients must bring complex (product) architectures and processes in place before they can configure the first policies or reports. Meaningful proof of concepts have become rare. Vendors frequently shore up prices through feature licenses or complex licensing constructs that no mere mortal can understand.

Immature or nonexistent capabilities for privacy-enhanced computation technologies (PECT).

Established vendors frequently do not have the adoption of PECT on the roadmaps of their DSP, whereas newer products from startup companies frequently have PECT capabilities included. On either side, the benefits, scope, and limitations of PECT are not communicated well making it difficult for clients to adopt them.

Not all vendors address recommended DSP capabilities.

Some DSP offerings focus on adapting traditional product platforms rather than replatforming their data security capabilities. DSPs sometimes provide only a partial set of capabilities or have cobbled them together from different acquisitions; multiple control centers, appliances, gateways, or agents may be required.

Pattern-driven data discovery capabilities find patterns or well-known identifiers without considering the context.

Data discovery rarely uses AI/ML support to do semantic analysis to find out what something is. For example, depending on the context, a date can be a date of birth, a transaction date, or a newspaper article's dateline. Each data type will need the appropriate level of protection.

Frustrating amount of false positives make it nearly impossible to understand what is happening to your data.

Since DAM was conceived as a stand-alone technology, the created audit trails remain mostly false positives. No one can really reconstruct what happens to your data by looking at these logs. This contributes to the poor breach detection rate in organizations.

Separate and siloed teams responsible for each data security capability.

Product specialists with vendor training and certifications for any data security control are working without much interfacing. Gartner finds that clients frequently entertain redundant data security capabilities, for example, multiple data catalogs or multiple data masking capabilities. While many data security and privacy decisions have enterprise-wide impact, they are rarely based on the insights of cross-functional teams.

DATA SECURITY FUTURE STATE

1. Consistent visibility on (sensitive) data, data stores, policies, and applicable regulations.
2. High levels of integration capability and simplified deployment models.
3. Ease of administration via a policy control plane.
4. Democratized access to the technologies required to secure data thoroughly.
5. Roles move from being focused on a single product or technology to multidimensional.
6. Data stores for AI and ML, for example data lakes, will increase in importance.

Consistent visibility on (sensitive) data, data stores, policies, and applicable regulations.

Sensitive-data visibility of DSP. This is enabled using a consistent overview of data silos, data security policies, controls, and applicable regulations. The best DSPs will have semantic capabilities for data classification—judging what something is rather than relying on pre-configured identifiers.

High levels of integration capability and simplified deployment models.

The use of API integration and cloud-delivered services will increase in importance. DSP provides several integration options with popular data stores, such as API, agent software, or network gateways. Customers can choose the DSP implementation architecture that is least/noninvasive in their environment. Customers can position enforcement points as close to data assets as possible. This will maximize protection while minimizing user impact.

Ease of administration via a consolidated policy control plane.

The DSP management control plane is decoupled from data types and control objects, allowing centralized administration. The administrative interface will allow data security policy to be managed from a single console and applied regardless of the data silo or the required control objective. AI and ML will be integral to automating policy creation. Full API enablement allows automation and integration with existing processes and tools.

Democratized access to the technologies required to secure data thoroughly.

DSPs are available as stand-alone tools and cloud-based service offerings. Cloud-based offerings will make most of the DSP security objects available via low-threshold API integration, making best-in-class data security controls achievable and affordable for many.

Roles move from being focused on a single product or technology to be multidimensional.

DSP engineers and administrators live at the intersection of securing data and sharing data. The primary roles of DSP engineers are to secure data well enough so that it can be used as required (without compromising security), instead of locking data away by maintaining a single product-driven data security control.

Data stores for AI and ML, for example data lakes, will increase in importance.

The use of identifiable and regulated data for AI model training raises security and compliance concerns around personal data usage and the potential negative effects in production deployments. Gartner expects DSPs to make an essential contribution to the mitigation of those. For example, providing data security for next-generation use cases, enabling migration to public clouds, and providing scalable and reliable controls that can support immense data volumes.

DATA SILOS

No single product or single vendor product portfolio can support all data silos and data security functionality, but some promising multicloud developments are emerging at the InnovationTrigger stage. More specifically, there is no "single pane of glass" solution for data security. Disparate vendor products rarely integrate or share policies and apply proprietary techniques for the same security controls. This results in challenges when applying consistent security policies across these disparate controls. It drives the urgency for new product innovations and methods to orchestrate these policies and controls across all data security, identity access management (IAM), privacy, and application management consoles. Therefore, it is relevant to use DSG, DRA, FinDRA, and/or PIA to create a framework that addresses these product shortcomings by identifying gaps and inconsistencies in how policies are implemented and orchestrated across the deployed product portfolio.

THE CONVERGENCE IS CONTINUING

Data classification sees innovations and integrations across most data governance and security markets.

- New anonymization and pseudonymization technologies are emerging and integrating through EKM and KMaaS.
- Integration of data monitoring and protection techniques are emerging across new technologies such as DSaaS, DSP, and multicloud DAM.
- DSG, DRA, FinDRA, PIA, and data breach response processes are increasingly needed to implement consistent policies, especially through data residency impacts and new privacy laws.

DATA LINEAGE, PROVENANCE, AND CATALOGS

Catalogs

Digital transformation is paramount across industries, and it seems obvious then that data should be carefully maintained and developed. But is it?

This study by BARC explores the difficulties:

Key findings include, according to "LEVERAGE YOUR DATA":

1. Everyone agrees that data use is too difficult.
2. Leveraging data requires transparency. A data catalog can deliver that.
3. Data catalogs require input from business people.
4. Usability of data starts where data is collected.

Organizations everywhere are awash in data, and the right people in an organization may not get access to this data, according to "LEVERAGE YOUR DATA".

BEST-IN-CLASS COMPANIES

Best-in-class companies do a better job of addressing business-related data challenges:

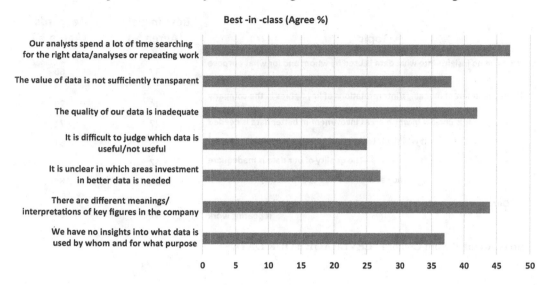

Source: Adapted from Collibra "LEVERAGE YOUR DATA"

Laggard companies do a less good job of addressing the business-related data challenges:

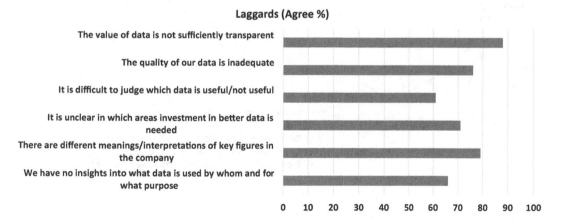

Source: Adapted from Collibra "LEVERAGE YOUR DATA"

Best-in-class companies vs. Laggard companies of addressing the business-related data challenges:

Topic	Best-in-class (Agree %)	Laggards (Agree %)
We have no insights into what data is used by whom and for what purpose	37	66
There are different meanings/interpretations of key figures in the company	44	79
It is unclear in which areas investment in better data is needed	27	71
It is difficult to judge which data is useful/not useful	25	61
The quality of our data is inadequate	42	76
The value of data is not sufficiently transparent	38	88
Our analysts spend a lot of time searching for the right data/analyses or repeating work	47	88

Source: Adapted from Collibra "LEVERAGE YOUR DATA"

Effective approaches are known in theory but rarely applied in practice:

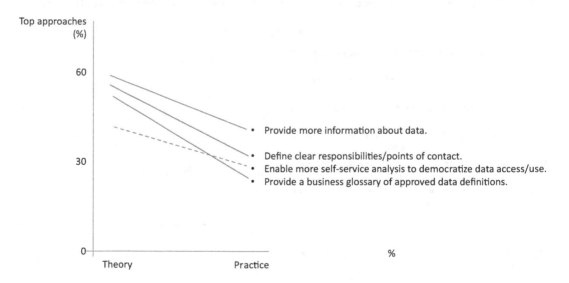

Source: Adapted from Collibra

Data democratization requires a new deal on how data is handled across the enterprise

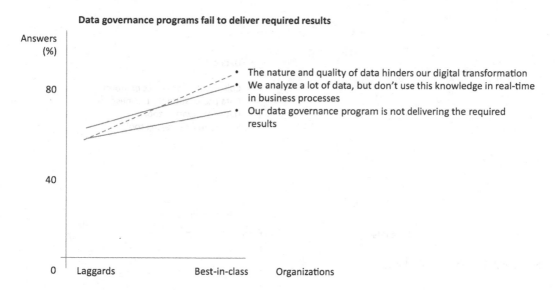

Data governance programs fail to deliver required results

Source: Adapted from Collibra

Architecture plays an important role in the transition to a data-driven enterprise:

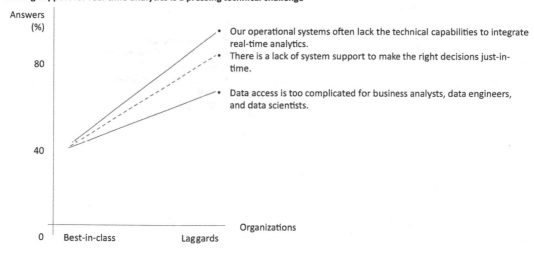

Lacking support for real-time analytics is a pressing technical challenge

Source: Adapted from Collibra

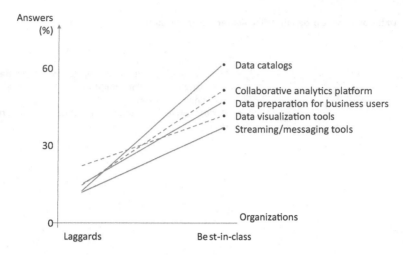

Notable technology approaches of best-in-class companies

Source: Adapted from Collibra

Enabling self-service without neglecting data governance is key:

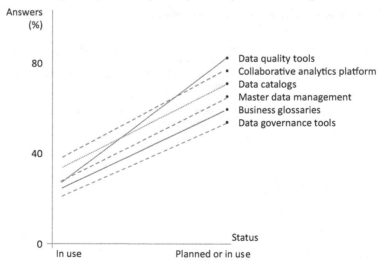

Which technologies do you currently use or plan to improve the handling of data?

Source: Adapted from Collibra

Which conceptual architectural measures have you implemented or plan to improve data handling

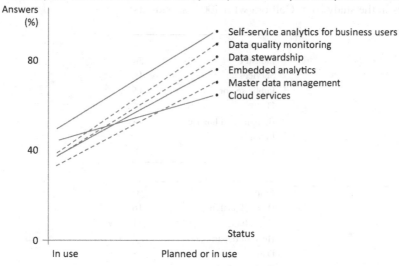

Source: Adapted from Collibra

Enabling a data-driven enterprise requires a fundamental cultural change by the executive level:

Laggards are not yet addressing their data problems in a targeted manner

top three approaches of laggards to improve the handling of data

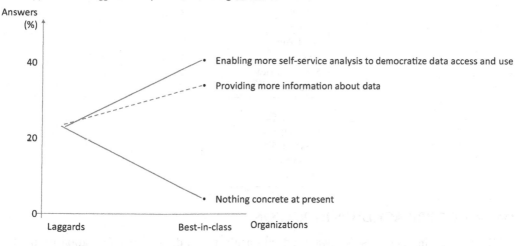

Source: Adapted from Collibra

Demographics

Demographics in the study from Collibra with 400 respondents:

Sector	%
Industry	24
Services	19
Public sector	16
IT	16
Banking and finance	14
Retail	8
Other	3

Role	%
Head of analytics	16
Consultant	11
Head of department	8
Data Architect	8
Business analyst	7
Power user	6
Head of IT	5
User of analytics	5
Board level	5
Data engineer	4
Developer	4

Region	%
Europe	64
North America	24
APAC	6
South America	3
Other	2

Company size	%
Less than 500	31
500 to 5000	32
More than 5000	37

IMPACT OF PRIVACY LAWS BY REGION

BARC is a leading enterprise software industry analyst firm delivering information to more than 1000 customers each year. For over 20 years, BARC analysts have combined market, product, and implementation expertise to advise companies and evaluate BI, Data Management, ECM, CRM, and ERP products according to "BARC".

Percentage saying positive impact

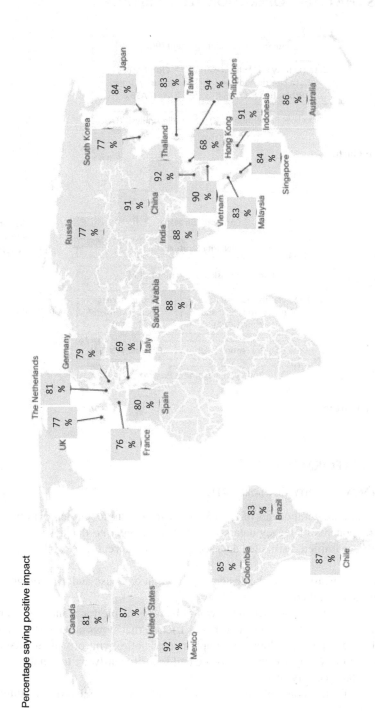

Source: Adapted from CISCO Privacy Benchmark Study

TECHNOLOGIES THAT HELP OPERATIONALIZE PRIVACY

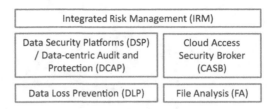

Source: Adapted from Gartner

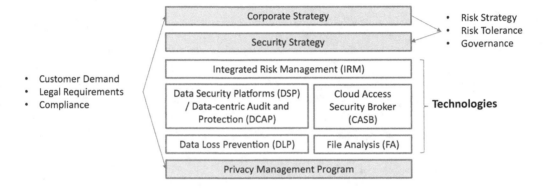

Source: Adapted from Gartner

CONVERGING PLATFORMS

HYPERCONVERGED DATA SECURITY PLATFORM (HDSP)

HDSP merges the traditional components of Data Security into a single, unified platform.

It replaces the components of legacy data security, that is, separate database security and file storage security, with one unified distributed data security system, creating a highly scalable hybrid data security center.

In a traditional legacy infrastructure, the design requires that database and file storage security be individually configured and linked.

In this structure, a dedicated IT security team would be responsible for managing a single component, which becomes costly and complex and creates friction that slows down business initiatives.

HDSP is using cloud computing technologies implemented entirely in software to enable clusters of database security and file storage security software and security hardware to reliably and predictably power enterprise data security services.

Ultimately, HDSP is far more flexible, maneuverable, and scalable, delivering a simple, speedy deployment model.

PRIVACY IMPACT ASSESSMENT

Organizations worldwide struggle to implement detailed regulatory requirements for maturing privacy laws. However, while focusing on privacy-proofing existing personal data processing activities, compliance in operations is negatively affected by projects. Every project related to the processing of personal data either introduces a new processing activity or at least applies different technology to existing processes, which may cause risk and attack surfaces to change considerably. Privacy oversights at project completion will result in a never-ending stream of compliance remediation actions when insufficiently addressed. Such bolt-on measures are costly and make system and application infrastructures increasingly complicated, which, in turn, is security's greatest challenge. Possibly worse, they add to the meantime privacy risk in between project completion and final remediation. Security and risk management (SRM) leaders can prevent this by including a few key concepts before and during the project. Examples include establishing a proper retention scheme and purposeful processing, enforcing the following granular access and deletion controls, and integrating with a customer self-service portal where privacy rights can be exercised.

Many application and system architectures lack privacy capabilities by design, which leads to unnecessary storage of personal data, adding privacy risk and liability.

- Failure to demonstrate during business as usual (BAU) that personal data is only used as intended and within (legal) restrictions leads to compliance and transparency gaps.
- Bolting on privacy measures after project completion increases system and infrastructure complexity, cost, the feeling of project failure, and privacy risk.

Make a Quick-Scan Impact Assessment Mandatory at Every Project Initiation Organizations do not exist to maintain personal data; they maintain personal data to exist. This means that personal data serves a purpose (use Gartner's "Toolkit: Assess Your Personal Data Processing Activities" as a basis for the quick scan). While ensuring compliance in existing operations, SRM leaders are often confronted with innovations and ongoing development in IT projects. Those projects could be in development or already live and operational (see Figure). This throws the organization into a vicious cycle of new gaps and endless remediation. But with a few strategic changes in project management rules, SRM leaders can become enablers by substantially elevating their level of support for the business in every area where personal data is processed.

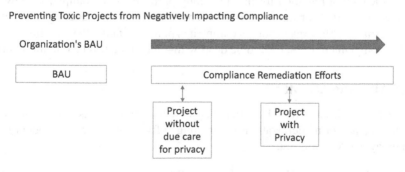

Preventing Toxic Projects from Negatively Impacting Compliance

Source: Adapted from Gartner

First, ensure there is a good grasp of what personal data will be processed after the project goes live in BAU, including what purpose that data serves and how long it must be kept. For that, it's important to consider: The process scope in project management is the project at hand. Every processing activity has one or more goals or "purposes". Examples include executing a contract with an individual (employee or customer), handling a complaint, abiding by other regulatory requirements, etc. In short, visualize a sheet with columns and rows as shown in the Figure.

- The amount of data processed and its sensitivity ("can we do with less?")
- Possible pseudonymization measures ("does it have to be directly identifiable?") Determining who is the business process owner and working together to shape the business process, establishing the purposes for processing, and setting retention periods in connection to the purposes
- Using the resulting information to dictate the personal data life cycle, handle subject rights, instruct data processors, and monitor for potential misuse of the data:

Quick Assessment

Source: Adapted from Gartner

The processing purposes fill the column headers in the sheet. Subsequently, for every purpose, business process owners, with the aid of SRM leaders, must explain what types of personal data are necessarily processed to achieve that purpose. The personal data records fill the rows. The result is a cross-connection between rows and columns. Some cells are empty, indicating there is no need for a specific data type to achieve that column's purpose. Other cells contain a cross-reference, indicating the necessary usage of such data. Next, retention periods must be added because once a purpose is achieved, the data is obsolete for that purpose. Although many retention periods may be a given (e.g., derived from legal requirements), others may have to be justified internally. SRM leaders should urge business process owners to obtain the regulatory requirements from legal counsel and to add justification of retention for the remaining purposes. For example, tax law may dictate a five-year retention period for financial transactions. For complaint handling, there usually is no legal period determined. The organization's complaints policy—stating the maximum period of time within which a complaint must be filed to be dealt with—then dictates the retention period.

LIFE CYCLE API MANAGEMENT

According to Gartner, demand for APIs, fueled by new business models, application development trends, and the urgency of modernization, is directing software engineering leaders to the diverse market with many vendors offering:

- API life cycle stages: Not all vendors support all four stages
  For example, some vendors do not offer an API gateway but support integrating a few third-party gateways to which customers must purchase or subscribe. Some vendors provide nominal developer portals and offer weaker support for the development of APIs. Customers must review this aspect in light of the critical capabilities (described in the companion Critical Capabilities for Full Life Cycle API Management) to ensure alignment with their organization's API management needs.

- Multicloud API management: Cloud vendors (such as AWS, Microsoft [Azure], and Google) and their native offerings deeply influence vendor choices for prospective buyers. Cloud API gateways provide strong operational capabilities and access to serverless and other cloud-native services. These gateways are attractive for many organizations (and essential for some). However, customers who adopt these offerings often need to procure multiple API management solutions to support on-premises and/or multi-cloud scenarios. Although vendors have improved their capabilities, no one vendor provides strong support for both multi-cloud and multiproduct API management.

LIFE CYCLE APPLICATION PROGRAMMING INTERFACE (API) MANAGEMENT

Gartner defines the full life cycle application programming interface (API) management market as the market for software that supports all stages of an API's life cycle, namely planning and design, implementation and testing, deployment and operation, and versioning and retirement.

Central to the full life cycle, API management offerings' capabilities are supported in the following functional areas:

- Developer portals: A self-service catalog of APIs for enabling, marketing to, and governing ecosystems of developers who produce and consume APIs.
- API gateways: Runtime management, security, and usage monitoring for APIs.
- API design and development: A meaningful developer experience and tools for designing and building APIs and for API-enablement of existing systems.
- API testing: From basic mock testing to advanced functional, performance, and security testing of APIs.

ENCRYPTING AND LINKING TRANSACTIONS

A proposed new standard from Object Management Group, Linked Encrypted Transaction Streams (LETS), would define methods for encrypting and linking transactions into ordered structures (streams) with control over who can access that information. Blockchain, Distributed Ledger Technology, IPFS, distributed file systems and other Distributed Immutable Data Objects (DIDO) ecosystems would all benefit from improved business workflows and IoT data access control via contextual messaging within this class of distributed messaging applications.

The Object Management Group is creating this standard that would exist independent of any underlying Blockchain or Distributed Ledger protocol. In particular, the RFP solicits specifications for the following:

- Linking methods for arranging transactions into ordered structures, or "streams".
- Methods for applying encryption and digital signing to transaction elements, transaction streams, or parts of transaction streams
- Optionally methods for extending the semantics of the relationships among messages in linked transaction streams

A STRATEGIC ROADMAP FOR DATA SECURITY PLATFORMS

Gartner's 2023 strategic roadmap for Data Security Platforms includes four different segments:

1. Broad-spectrum DSPs (bDSPs)—which provide strong consolidation for structured data in databases located in the cloud. Gartner inquiry volume for bDSP with tokenization capabilities has increased by more than 100% year-over year.

2. Data security posture management (DSPM), which offers posture management and data discovery across silos.
3. Data loss prevention (DLP)
4. Data access governance (DAG) products

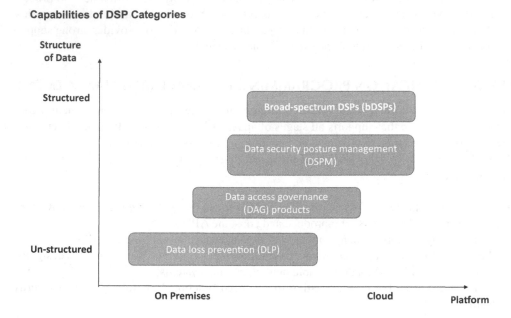

Capabilities of DSP Categories

Source: Adapted from Gartner

According to Gartner's 2023 strategic roadmap for Data Security Platforms, consolidate vendors and cut complexity and costs as contracts renew. For example, database activity monitoring, data masking, data discovery, data encryption, or data access governance products are good candidates for consolidation into bDSPs or DSPM.

- Actively engage with initiatives for data lakes, artificial intelligence (AI), and machine learning (ML) use cases. The aim should be to integrate a data security platform into the scope of project planning.
- Plan to implement a bDSP that covers cloud-based, next-generation data stores as a part of your multiyear consolidation efforts.

By 2025, 30% of enterprises will have adopted bDSP, up from less than 10% in 2021, due to the increasing demand for higher levels of data security and the rapid increase in product capabilities. According to Gartner's 2023 strategic roadmap for Data Security Platforms:

- Include data security in your zero-trust initiative. The data security capabilities pertaining to zero trust are data discovery and cataloging, data access management, data encryption, and data governance. These are part of the consolidated features offered by bDSP. For structured data, DSPM offers most of these capabilities.
- Start with advanced controls. bDSPs that focus on advanced controls generally have broader coverage than DSPs focusing on a single traditional control. For example, bDSPs that offer tokenization or field-level encryption capabilities frequently include data masking (as a postprocessing step for the token), cell-level authorization, and database activity monitoring.

SUMMARY

We discussed Best Practices for analytics on real-time data and data increasingly stored in the cloud and adding existing field-level transformation approaches, such as data masking; organizations should look to emerging techniques: differential privacy, SMPC, homomorphic encryption, and hardware security for key management.

NOTES

1. LEVERAGE YOUR DATA. https://www.collibra.com/wp-content/uploads/Leverage-your-data_Collibra.pdf
2. Gartner's 2023 strategic roadmap for Data Security Platforms. https://www.gartner.com/document/4018989
3. CMS Sensitive Information is defined in the Risk Management Handbook (RMH) Volume I Chapter 10 (https://www.cms.gov/ResearchStatistics-Data-and-Systems/CMS-Information-Technology/InformationSecurity/Downloads/RMH_VI_10_Terms_Defs_Acronyms.pdf) and subject to Executive Order 13556, Controlled Unclassified Information (https://www.white house.gov/the-press-office/2010/11/04/executiveorder-13556-controlled-unclassified-information).
4. HHS Standard for Encryption of Computing Devices and Information (HHS-OCIO-2016-0005): https://www.cms.gov/Research-Statistics-Dataand-Systems/CMS-Information-Technology/InformationSecurity/Info-Security-Library-Items/HHS-Standard-for-Encryption-of-ComputingDevices-and-Information
5. CMS Acceptable Risk Safeguards (ARS) version 3.1: https://www.cms.gov/Research-Statistics-Data-and-Systems/CMS-InformationTechnology/InformationSecurity/Info-Security-Library-Items/ARS-31-Publication 4 CMS ARS 3.1 SC-08 (Transmission Confidentiality and Integrity) and SC-28 (Protection of Information at Rest).
6. HHS, "Standard for Encryption of Computing Devices and Information," HHS-OCIO-2016-0005, December 14, 2016 10 CMS Acceptable Risk Safeguards (ARS) version 3.1: https://www.cms.gov/Research-Statistics-Data-and-Systems/CMS-InformationTechnology/InformationSecurity/Info-Security-Library-Items/ARS-31-Publication 11 CMS Information Systems Security and Privacy Policy (IS2P2) version 2.0: https://www.cms.gov/Research-Statistics-Data-andSystems/CMS-Information-Technology/InformationSecurity/Info-Security-Library-Items/CMS-Information-Systems-Security-and-PrivacyPolicy-IS2P2 12 As CMS encryption policy is linked to protecting sensitive information, it's important to understand the terms Sensitive Information, PII, and
7. Sensitive PII. See Appendix 1 for definitions. 13 Federal Information Processing Standard (FIPS) 140-2 specification: https://csrc.nist.gov/publications/detail/fips/140/2/final 14 Federal Information Processing Standard (FIPS) 140-3 specification https://csrc.nist.gov/publications/detail/fips/140/3/final
8. https://www.datamation.com/security/90-percent-cybersecurity-pros-data-privacy-business-imperative/?utm_campaign=Oktopost-General+industry+News&utm_content=Oktopost-LinkedIn&utm_medium=social&utm_source=LinkedIn
9. BARC. https://www.datamation.com/security/90-percent-cybersecurity-pros-data-privacy-business-imperative/?utm_campaign=Oktopost-General+industry+News&utm_content=Oktopost-LinkedIn&utm_medium=social&utm_source=LinkedIn
10. https://www.collibra.com/us/en/download/leverage-your-data?utm_source=bing&utm_medium=Paid&utm_campaign=NA-WP-Search-NB-General-Catalog-BARC&utm_content=BARC-Leverage-Your-Data&utm_term=data%20catalog&_bk=data%20catalog&_bt=&_bm=p&_bn=o&msclkid=03bebcbf039415e7b04ddd258711ceb3

4 Vision and Roadmap

INTRODUCTION

In this chapter, we will discuss planning for the future of data privacy and how to measure my zero trust mature, and how to I plan for Web 3.0 and Quantum Computing.

What issues do I need to address?

Example of a Data Security Roadmap

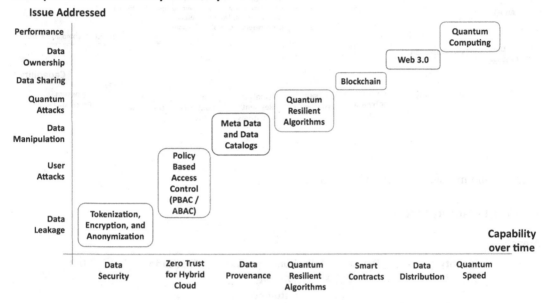

For example, what can be the first steps for Zero Trust?

Data Roadmap Example

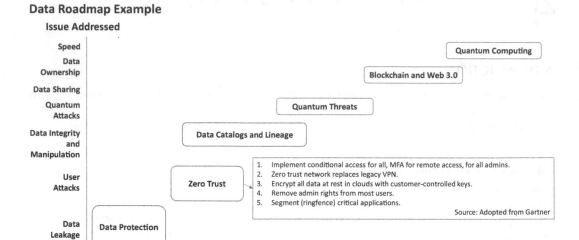

How can i measure my zero trust mature?

Zero Trust Maturity Model

Areas

Identity	Device	Environment (NW)	Application	Data
Analytics				
Automation				
Governance				

Maturity Levels

Maturity	Identity	Device	Environment (NW)	Application	Data
Traditional	Password or Mult Factor (MFA)	Simple inventore	Macro segmentaion	Access based on local validation	Static control
Advanced	MFA or some Federation	Data access depends on device posture	Micro perimeters	Access based on central validation	Cloud data encrypted
Optimal	Continous realtime ML analysis	Data access depends on realtime analysis	ML threat protection	Access continously validated	All data is encrypted

Source: Adapted from CISA.org

For example, when should i plan for Web 3.0?

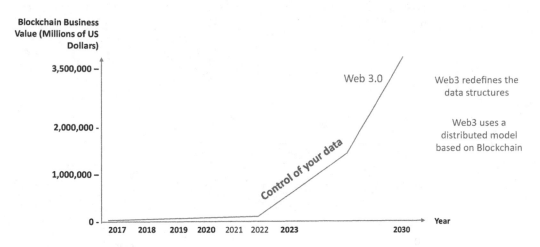

Controlling your data with Web 3.0

Source: Adapted from Gartner

For example, when should i plan for Quantum Computing?

Quantum Attacks?

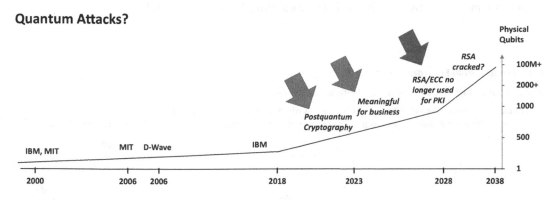

Source: Adapted from CBI Research and Gartner

DATA GROWTH

We may need to find more effective ways to control data privacy and security for the growing amount of data stored.

ESTIMATED TERABYTES OF DATA WORLDWIDE, 2019–2024

This IDC study presents a five-year forecast for the worldwide Global DataSphere market, according to "Worldwide Global DataSphere Forecast, 2021–2025: The World".

"Growth of the Global DataSphere is driven more by the data that we consume and analyze than what we create", according to Dave Reinsel, senior vice president, IDC's Global DataSphere. "Instead of hindering growth, the COVID-19 pandemic accelerated it, creating a surge in video-based content consumption and disrupting the Global DataSphere growth trend, especially in 2020 and 2021".

This is the IDC Worldwide Global Datasphere Forecast 2020–2024:

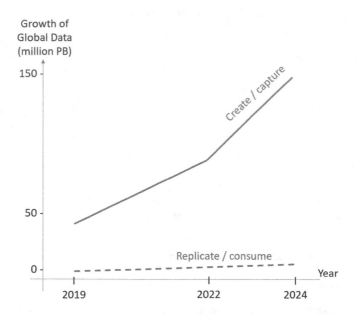

Source: Adapted from IDC Worldwide Global Datasphere Forecast 2020–2024

Worldwide Global Enterprise Data

Personal data is lucrative and therefore vulnerable to cybercrime.

- PHI can sell for hundreds of dollars per record and is often resold to multiple threat actors
- Customer PII is most likely to get exposed or compromised in data breaches, with 80% of data breaches affecting PII records

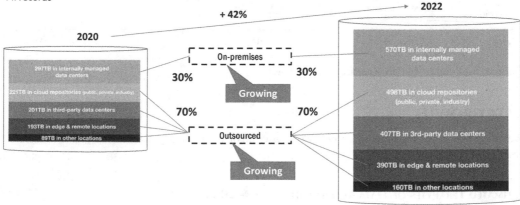

Source: Adapted from Seagate and IDC, https://www.zdnet.com/article/enterprises-are-collecting-more-data-but-do-they-know-what-to-do-with-it/

REFRAMING SECURITY

REFRAMING THE SECURITY PRACTICE

The dramatic changes in scope, scale, and complexity of the modern digital organization have obsoleted the centralized approach to cybersecurity control. New cybersecurity leaders are being placed in different parts of the organization to decentralize security decisions.

Business technologists are making significant IT decisions, and social engineering continues to grow as a source of successful attack. For these and other reasons, traditional approaches to security awareness training are becoming embarrassingly ineffective. Distributing security responsibility requires reconsidering and refocusing security awareness programs to enable more sophisticated security thinking. Progressive security and risk management (SRM) leaders are investing heavily in security behavior and culture programs fostering new ways of thinking and embedding new behaviors to help secure the organization.

RETHINKING TECHNOLOGY

Gartner clients increasingly express frustration with the operational complexity of the modern security stack. Given the human capital constraints, efficient cybersecurity remains out of reach for the majority of organizations. As such, there is an increased desire to consolidate security products into multifunction solutions addressing a broad set of related challenges, such as securing "hybrid work" or "cloud workloads". Across a range of security domains, integration capabilities such as secure access service edge (SASE) and extended detection and response (XDR) are leading to enhanced product integration.

TECHNOLOGIES THAT HELP OPERATIONALIZE PRIVACY

ALthough numerous useful technologies are available for SRM leaders to consider, a lack of insight into the available markets with overlapping functions slows down operational readiness, according to Gartner.

The required tooling must span the capabilities of discovery, mapping, classification, access controls, tokenization/encryption/pseudonymization or anonymization, and end-of-life controls. Integrated risk management (IRM) sets the outline of what is needed. The other markets of cloud access security broker (CASB), data security platforms (DSP), data-centric audit and protection (DCAP), data loss prevention (DLP), and file analysis (FA) bring the specific technologies to create cohesion between data security control and privacy. DSP is discussed in a separate chapter.

This is an illustration with DSP that evolved from DCAP

Technologies That Help Operationalize Privacy

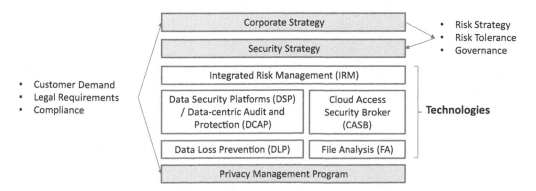

Source: Adapted from Gartner

ENTERPRISE LOW-CODE APPLICATION PLATFORMS

According to Gartner, organizations are increasingly adopting LCAPs to enable fusion team development with IT and business to quickly deliver new solutions and modernize business capabilities.

By 2025, 70% of new applications developed by enterprises will use low-code or no-code technologies, up from less than 25% in 2020.

SUMMARY

We discussed planning for the future of data privacy and how to measure my zero trust mature, and how to I plan for Web 3.0 and Quantum Computing.

NOTES

1. LEVERAGE YOUR DATA, https://www.collibra.com/wp-content/uploads/Leverage-your-data_Collibra.pdf
2. HHS Standard for Encryption of Computing Devices and Information (HHS-OCIO-2016-0005): https://www.cms.gov/Research-Statistics-Dataand-Systems/CMS-Information-Technology/InformationSecurity/Info-Security-Library-Items/HHS-Standard-for-Encryption-of-ComputingDevices-and-Information;
3. CMS Acceptable Risk Safeguards (ARS) version 3.1: https://www.cms.gov/Research-Statistics-Data-and-Systems/CMS-InformationTechnology/InformationSecurity/Info-Security-Library-Items/ARS-31-Publication 4 CMS ARS 3.1 SC-08 (Transmission Confidentiality and Integrity) and SC-28 (Protection of Information at Rest).
4. https://www.datamation.com/security/90-percent-cybersecurity-pros-data-privacy-business-imperative/?utm_campaign=Oktopost-General+industry+News&utm_content=Oktopost-LinkedIn&utm_medium=social&utm_source=LinkedIn
5. BARC. https://www.datamation.com/security/90-percent-cybersecurity-pros-data-privacy-business-imperative/?utm_campaign=Oktopost-General+industry+News&utm_content=Oktopost-LinkedIn&utm_medium=social&utm_source=LinkedIn
6. https://www.collibra.com/us/en/download/leverage-your-data?utm_source=bing&utm_medium=Paid&utm_campaign=NA-WP-Search-NB-General-Catalog-BARC&utm_content=BARC-Leverage-Your-Data&utm_term=data%20catalog&_bk=data%20catalog&_bt=&_bm=p&_bn=o&msclkid=03bebcbf039415e7b04ddd258711ceb3

Section II

Trust and Hybrid Cloud

5 Zero Trust and Hybrid Cloud

INTRODUCTION

I discussed this with John Kindervag when he worked at Forrester Research around 2010. He asked why traditional security controls are not effective. He said that network segmentation I to static, and when the attacker is let inside the network segment, we are no longer tracking what resources the attacker is accessing. We need to change from "trust and verify" to "verify and then trust".

We will also discuss that another security aspect is Zero-knowledge proof, which means you actually are in possession of knowledge without sharing the secret. Zero Trust and zero knowledge and how they are different. So, you can convince someone that you have a secret without disclosing the secret.

WHAT IS ZERO TRUST?

Zero trust provides an idea designed to enforce dynamic, least privilege per-request access validations in information systems and services.

- Zero Trust Network Access (ZTNA) augments traditional VPN.
- Zero Trust Architecture (ZTA) was created before remote working became popular and organizations' traditional perimeter-based security models broke up.

ZTA IS A SECURITY PLAN

ZT is moving to a data-centric approach based on fine-grained security controls. ZT covers users, systems, data, and assets. ZT can be dynamic and can change over time. Implementing a ZTA is non-trivial. ZT enforcement requires security policies that provide context for each data resource request.

ZT may require a change in philosophy and culture of security. The road to ZT can take years.

Transitioning to Zero Trust:
1. Identify Actors
2. Identify Assets
3. Identify Key Processes
4. Formulating Policies
5. Identifying Candidate Solutions.
6. Initial Deployment and Monitoring.

DOI: 10.1201/9781003254928-7

Zero Trust Components

PDP

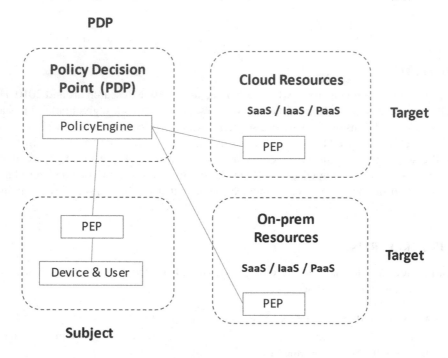

Source: Adapted from RSA365

ZT NETWORK ACCESS (SOFTWARE DEFINED PERIMETER)

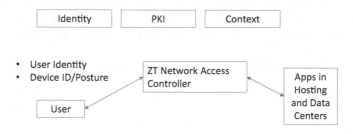

Source: Adapted from Gartner

SECURE ACCESS SERVICE EDGE (SASE)

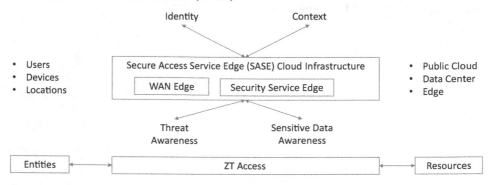

Source: Adapted from Gartner

SECURE ACCESS SERVICE EDGE (DETAILS)

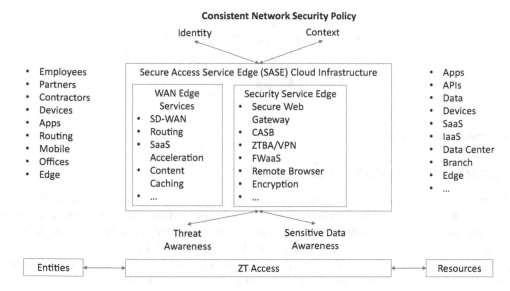

Source: Adapted from Gartner

POSITIONING OF ZTA

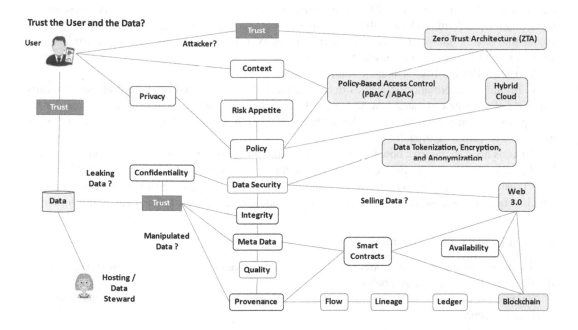

ZERO TRUST ARCHITECTURE

www.manageengine.com/ad360

TRADITIONAL PERIMETER SHORTCOMINGS

Traditional security methods classify everything (users, devices, and applications) inside the corporate network as trustworthy. These security models use technologies such as virtual private networks (VPNs) and network access control (NAC) to verify users' credentials outside the network before granting access. With the proliferation of remote work, the new enterprise architecture is redefining the perimeter. Data is stored outside of corporate walls, and users access enterprise applications through various types of devices from locations outside the corporate network.

The Zero Trust model is a response to the fact that the perimeter-based security model doesn't work—innumerable data breaches have occurred because hackers got past corporate firewalls and were able to move through internal business-critical systems easily.

Organizations realize the importance of implementing a comprehensive cybersecurity framework to survive in the future. According to a survey conducted by virtual private networking firm NetMotion Software, more than 70% of organizations are considering adopting a Zero Trust model following the pandemic and the shift to extensive remote work. The 2020 Zero Trust Progress Report shows that nearly one-third of cybersecurity experts expressed interest in applying Zero Trust to address hybrid IT security concerns.

Zero Trust Powers Digital Transformation

As digital transformation strategies diversify, the risk of privileged credential abuse increases multifold. Forrester estimates that 80% of data breaches are caused by privileged access abuse. Enterprises urgently need to replace their legacy identity management approaches with a "never trust, always verify" approach.

IT teams need to improve how they're protecting the most privileged access credentials by granting the just-enough, just-in-time privilege. Of the many cybersecurity frameworks available today, Zero Trust is the most effective, enabling IT to grant the least privilege access to users upon verifying who is requesting access, the context of the request, and the sensitivity of the access environment.

Steps to Build a Zero Trust Model

NIST lists out a few conceptual guidelines that the design and deployment of a Zero Trust Architecture should align with (summarized below):

You need not comply with all of these tenets. Pick and choose the ones that will make your network more secure.

Tenets of Zero Trust Architecture

Consider the Entire Enterprise Private Network Insecure

This requires actions such as authenticating all communications and encrypting network traffic before assets are granted access to enterprise-owned resources.

With bring your own device (BYOD) policies in place, not all enterprise resources are on enterprise-owned infrastructure. Similarly, not all devices on the enterprise network are owned by the enterprise.

Remote subjects should not trust the local (i.e., non-enterprise-owned) network. All connection requests should be authenticated and authorized, and all network traffic should be monitored securely.

Assets and workflows migrating from enterprise on-premises data centers to non-enterprise cloud instances should follow access policies and maintain proper security posture.

Identify the places where the identities need to interact with the resources and control the level of access provided at various levels of interaction.

LOGICAL COMPONENTS OF ZERO TRUST ARCHITECTURE

Here are a few logical points an enterprise implementing a Zero Trust Architecture should consider for network connectivity:

SHORTCOMINGS IDENTITY SECURITY CURRENT STATE

The functioning of these components is enabled by several local and external data sources that work together to make access decisions. These include continuous diagnostics and mitigation (CDM) systems, compliance systems, threat intelligence programs, data access policies, identity management systems, and security information and event management (SIEM) systems. According to NIST, the several logical components that make up a Zero Trust system can be categorized into three levels:

Policy

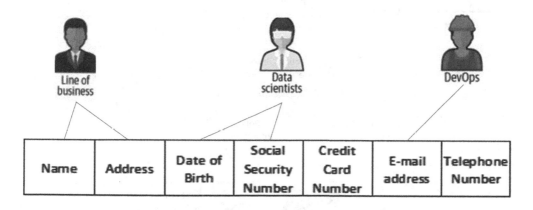

Policy Engine (PE)

The component is charged with deciding who gets access to the enterprise's resources and who doesn't. Further, it makes the access decision based on several factors and let the Policy Administrator (PA) execute it.

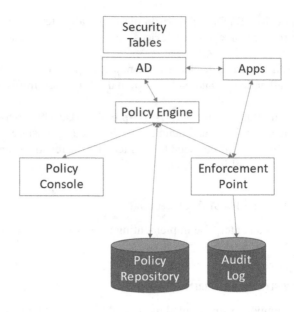

Policy Administrator (PA)

This component is in charge of enabling, monitoring, and eventually terminating connections between a subject and an enterprise resource.

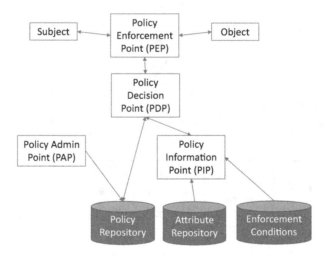

Role-Based Policy Enforcement

Policy-Based Enforcement

Policy-Based Access Control (PBAC)/Attribute-Based Access Control (ABAC)

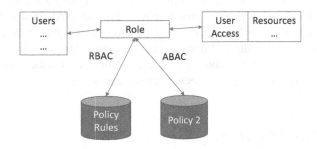

SHORTCOMINGS IDENTITY SECURITY CURRENT STATE

It's essential that organizations are equipped to monitor their entire IT environment for signs of malicious activity. While external attackers first need to penetrate the network before they can find the information they seek, malicious insiders already know where all the valuable data is and how to access it.

A Zero Trust environment utilizes automated security operations as a method of staying ahead of such security threats. Therefore, security analytics plays a crucial role in implementing a solid Zero Trust model.

With automations and machine learning, you can generate risk scores for potential threats as they occur. Based on these scores, automated workflows can be triggered to respond to these risks, allowing organizations to mitigate legitimate threats quickly and effectively.

Organizations need to align themselves with the current cybersecurity landscape by leveraging machine learning (ML) models and user-behavior analytics (UBA) to predict, detect, and prevent insider threats, access abuse, and cyber-fraud. ML-based behavior analytics can extract context from big data, so there's no dependency on traditional rule-based security controls that are often offered by SIEM systems.

Organizations can continuously monitor behavior and dynamically calculate risk scores for real-time responses to anomalies. Unfortunately, cyber threats are becoming increasingly advanced, and the speed at which threats should be detected and eliminated has to be machine-speed. Security analytics rely on algorithms to provide in-depth analysis that otherwise cannot be achieved through manual processes.

DRIVERS

Users, applications, and enterprise data are everywhere. Old data center-centric security architectures/products need adjustment. SASE offerings are the necessary adjustment.

SECURE ACCESS SERVICE EDGE (SASE)

Secure access service edge (SASE) delivers multiple converged network and security as service capabilities, such as SD-WAN, SWG, CASB, NGFW, and zero trust network access (ZTNA). SASE supports branch office, remote worker, and on-premises general internet security use cases. SASE is delivered as a service and enables zero trust access based on the identity of the device or entity, combined with real-time context and security and compliance policies.

Why This Is Important

SASE is a key enabler of modern digital business transformation, including work from anywhere and the adoption of edge computing and cloud-delivered applications. It increases visibility, agility, resilience, and security. SASE also dramatically simplifies the delivery and operation of critical network and network security services mainly via a cloud-delivered model. SASE can reduce the number of vendors required for secure access from four to six today to one to two over the next several years.

SASE is driven by enterprise digital business transformation: the adoption of cloud-based services by distributed and mobile workforces, edge computing and business continuity plans that must include flexible, anywhere, anytime, secure remote access, and use of the internet and cloud services, according to Gartner.

FIREWALL AS A SERVICE (FWaaS)

Firewall as a service (FWaaS) is a multifunction security gateway delivered as a cloud-based service, often intended to protect small branch offices and mobile users. FWaaS can provide simpler, more flexible architecture using centralized policy management, multiple enterprise firewall features and traffic tunneling to partially or fully move security inspections to a cloud infrastructure. Why This Is Important The uptick in remote work, and growing adoption of SD-WAN and hybrid WAN architectures are increasing interest in using FWaaS. We anticipate that this trend will continue. FWaaS offerings are of varying levels of maturity. Organizations considering FWaaS should conduct extensive proofs of concept or limit the scope of an initial production deployment.

CLOUD WEB APPLICATION AND API PROTECTION (WAAP)

Organizations moving critical web applications to the public cloud frequently select cloud WAAP solutions from WAF, CDN, or infrastructure-as-a-service (IaaS) providers to shield these applications. These solutions can be delivered and managed more flexibly than a traditional virtual appliance due to their ability to be easily deployed. Cloud WAAP roadmaps are dynamic and continue to improve their detection capabilities and the maturity of their management and monitoring consoles.

SOVEREIGN CLOUD

Sovereign cloud provides cloud services within a single geography meeting data residency and legislative requirements. Sovereign cloud helps ensure that data remains free from external jurisdiction control and provides protection from foreign legislatively enforced access. Countries engage a sovereign cloud to achieve digital and data sovereignty to provide rules and legal requirements to apply data protection controls, residency requirements, protectionism, and intelligence gathering.

Why This Is Important

The importance of digital sovereignty has risen in step with growing discord within global economics, protecting intellectual property, expanding privacy legislation and the desire to be more self-sufficient due to the dominance of a small number of large Chinese and American technology and service providers.

ZERO TRUST IS THE FIRST STEP TO GARTNER'S CARTA

Block/allow security solutions don't allow enough contextual decision-making and real-time security evaluation—they cannot simply block user access to corporate networks because the user is not located within the organization's four walls.

Building on the idea of Zero Trust, Gartner's Continuous Adaptive Risk and Trust Assessment (CARTA) strategy is specially designed for continuous adaptation that goes beyond basic allow or deny models to provide contextually relevant access. In this model, all systems and devices are considered potentially compromised, and their behaviors are continuously assessed for risk and Trust.

Gartner notes that Zero Trust is the first step on the road to the CARTA framework, where observations continue after logins and logins are reassessed regularly. In this way, Trust can be initially established upon authentication but can also be revoked based on the pattern of behavior.

Both CARTA and Zero Trust support real-time assessments and monitoring. CARTA's additional security measures not only reduce the risk of a breach but also improve attack containment in case a hacker does manage to gain network access.

CARTA Takes the Zero Trust Idea Further by Introducing:

- Continuous monitoring, assessment, discovery, and risk mitigation
- Contextual access control
- Continuous device visibility
- Automated device control
- Dynamic risk assessments and responses

SHORTCOMINGS IDENTITY SECURITY CURRENT STATE STEPS TO BUILD GARTNER'S CARTA

NIST warns that the Zero Trust Architecture is not a single off-the-shelf product. It's comprised of a set of principles that operate thematically. There are six key steps to follow before implementation.

Migrating to a Zero Trust environment is a strategic exercise that does not require an outright replacement of existing infrastructure or security frameworks. Instead, it's a journey that involves practicing Zero Trust principles and processes and then moving toward technology solutions and workflows.

POLICY

Example of Storing Policy in GIT:

Example of Storing Policy on Blockchain:

Example of Policy and Reporting:

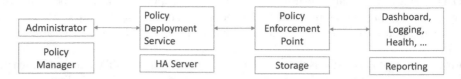

OPEN POLICY AGENT

Open Policy Agent, or OPA, is an open source, general purpose policy engine. OPA decouples policy decisions from other responsibilities of an application.

OPA enables unified, context-aware policy enforcement across the entire stack.

User

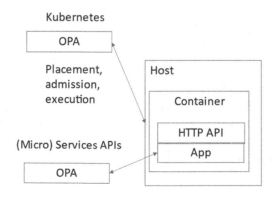

Source: Adapted from CNCF

OPA generates policy decisions by evaluating the query input against policies and data, not limited to simple yes/no or allow/deny answers. Like query inputs, your policies can generate arbitrary structured data as output.

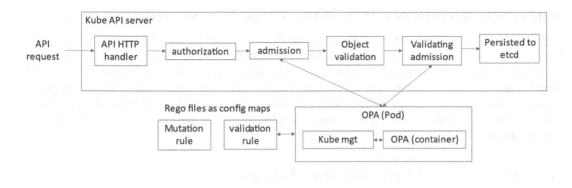

NSTAC, ZERO TRUST, AND NIST 800-207

NIST 800-207 really has nothing to do with Zero Trust and is an identity document.

NSTAC subcommittee report section 1.1 has a short history of Zero Trust.

Words like "strategy" are better to describe ZT (as you'll see in the NSTAC document), rather than "architecture".

NSTAC makes 24 recommendations, nine of them key, in the report to foster a culture of Zero Trust according to CISA. The scope of zero Trust can be large and all-encompassing, so breaking the process into smaller and more manageable components is important.

Faster adoption of cloud services and the promise of cloud services to enable zero trust implementation is appropriately acknowledged in EO 14028:

Improving the Nation's Cybersecurity, 70, which includes several requirements and provisions to accelerate federal agencies' movement to secure cloud services.

Cloud-based architectures enable enterprises to:

1. More easily identify their DAAS; know where they are and who is accessing them; and restrict access according to their policies (i.e., define and monitor their protect surfaces).
2. Facilitate mapping transaction flows as well as implementing access controls and user and application segmentation.
3. Continuously inspect and log all traffic to identify anomalous activity and create and enforce policies, accordingly.

MICROSEGMENTATION IS ESSENTIAL FOR ZERO TRUST PRIVATE NETWORKS

More than a decade after Forrester first defined the Zero Trust (ZT) Model for information security, most of the operational domains of Zero Trust have matured quickly. The exception is the private network: Applying Zero Trust principles remains the most difficult domain. The private network needs microsegmentation the most; it is still far too flat and is the happy home of insecure printers and unsuspecting users easily lured into ransomware situations by cybercriminals. Therefore, this evaluation focuses on solutions for private networks and excludes public cloud and container environments.

REMOTE WORKFORCE SECURITY AND EASE OF USE

As legacy technology becomes outdated and less effective, improved technical capabilities powering the future of work will dictate which providers will lead the pack. Vendors that can provide a secure remote workforce, Zero Trust mission completion, and easy-to-use technology position themselves to successfully deliver true Zero Trust to their customers.

ZERO TRUST MATURITY MODEL

The Zero Trust Maturity Model represents a gradient of implementation across five distinct pillars, where minor advancements can be made over time toward optimization.

Identity	Device	Environment (NW)	Application	Data
		Analytics		
		Automation		
		Governance		

Source: Adapted from CISA.org

ZERO TRUST MATURITY MODEL USING THREE STAGES

Zero Trust Maturity Model gradient can be described using three stages, with increasing levels of protection, detail, and complexity for adoption, as outlined below. The following descriptions of each stage were used to identify maturity for each zero trust technology pillar and to provide consistency across the maturity model:

- Traditional – manual configurations and assignment of attributes, static security policies, pillar-level solutions with coarse dependencies on external systems, least-function established at provisioning, proprietary and inflexible pillars of policy enforcement, manual incident response and mitigation deployment.
- Advanced – some cross-pillar coordination, centralized visibility, centralized identity control, policy enforcement based on cross-pillar inputs and outputs, some incident response to predefined mitigations, increased detail in dependencies with external systems, some least-privilege changes based on posture assessments.
- Optimal – fully automated assigning of attributes to assets and resources, dynamic policies based on automated/observed triggers, assets have self-enumerating dependencies for dynamic least privilege access (within thresholds), alignment with open standards for cross-pillar interoperability, centralized visibility with historian functionality for point-in-time recollection of state.

Function	Traditional	Advanced	Optimal
Inventory Management	Agency manually categorizes data and has poor data inventorying, leading to inconsistent categorization.	Agency primarily inventories data manually with some automated tracking.	Agency continuously inventories data with robust tagging and tracking.
Access Determination	Agency governs access to data by using static access controls.	Agency governs access to data using least privilege controls that consider identity, device risk, and other attributes.	Agency's access to data is dynamic, supporting just-in-time and just-enough principles.
Encryption	Agency primarily stores data in on-premises data stores and where they are unencrypted at rest.	Agency stores data in cloud or remote environments where they are encrypted at rest.	Agency encrypts all data at rest.

Source: Adapted from Zero Trust Maturity Model, CICS.GOV

Maturity	Identity	Device	Environment (NW)	Application	Data
Traditional	Password or Multi-Factor (MFA)	Simple inventore	Macro segmentaion	Access based on local validation	Static control
Advanced	MFA or some Federation	Data access depends on device posture	Micro perimeters	Access based on central validation	Cloud data encrypted
Optimal	Continous realtime ML analysis	Data access depends on realtime analysis	ML threat protection	Access continously validated	All data is encrypted

Source: Adapted from CISA.org

These maturity stages, and the more specific details associated with each pillar below, can allow agencies to plan, assess, and maintain the investments needed to progress toward a ZTA. The following subsections provide high-level information to support agencies in transitioning to zero trust across the five different pillars: Identity, Device, Network, Application Workload, and Data. Each pillar also includes general details regarding Visibility and Analytics, Automation and Orchestration, and Governance for that pillar.

Pillar #5 Data

Agency data should be protected on devices, in applications, and networks. Agencies should include, categorize, and label data, protect data at rest and in transit, and deploy mechanisms for the detection data exfiltration. The table lists data functions pertaining to zero trust, as well as the considerations for Visibility and Analytics, Automation and Orchestration, and Governance within the context of data.

Zero Trust Maturity Model Stages and Descriptions

Maturity Stage	Initial (1)	Repeatable (2)	Defined (3)	Managed (4)	Optimized (5)
Description and Characteristics	The initiative is undocumented and performed on an ad hoc basis with processes undefined. Success depends on individual efforts	The process is documented and is predictably repeatable, using lessons learned in the initial phase	Processes for success have been defined and documented	Processes are monitored and controlled; efficacy is measurable	Focus is on continuous optimization

Source: Adapted from CISA.org

Maturity Stage	Initial (1)	Repeatable (2)	Defined (3)	Managed (4)	Optimized (5)
1. Define the Protect Surface	The DAAS element is unknown or discovered manually	The use of automated tools to discover and classify DAAS elements has begun but is not standardized	Data classification training and processes have been introduced and are maturing	New or updated DAAS elements are immediately discovered, classified as assigned to the correct protect surface in an automated manner	Discovery and classification processes are fully automated
2. Map the Transaction Flows	Flows are conceptualized-based interviews	Traditional scanning tools construct approximate flow maps	A flow mapping process is in place	Automated tools create precise flow maps	Transaction flows are automatically mapped in real time
3. Build a Zero Trust Architecture	With little visibility and an undefined protect surface	Protect surface is established based on current resources	The protect surface includes segmentation gateways	Additional controls added to evaluate multiple variables (e.g, SaaS and API controls)	Controls are enforced using hardware and software capabilities
4. Create a Zero Trust policy	Policy is written at Layer 3 (Network)	Additional "who" statements are being identified to address business needs	The team works with the business to determine who or what should have access	Custom user-specific elements are created and defined by policy, reducing number of users with access	Layer 7 (Application) policy is written for granular enforcement
5. Monitor and Maintain the Network	Visibility into what is happening on the network is low	Traditional security information and event management but the process is still mostly manual	Telemetry is gathered from all controls and is sent to a central data lake	Machine learning tools are applied to the data lake	Data is incorporated from multiple sources and used to refine steps 1–4

Source: Adapted from CISA.org

ZERO TRUST MATURITY MODEL SUMMARY

Maturity	1 Initial	2 Repeatable	3 Defined	4 Managed	5 Optimized
Description	Undocumented	Documented	Process defined	Process controlled	Optimized
1 Define the Surface	DAAS manual	No automation	Data classification starting	Automation starting	Discovery is automated
2 Map the Flows	Based on interviews	Scanning tools used	Flow mapping	Automation starting	Real time mapping
3 Build a Zero Trust Architecture	Undefined protect surface	Protect surface defined	Includes segmentation gateways	SaaS and API controls added	HW and SW controls added
4 Create a Zero Trust policy	Layer 3 policy	Address business needs	Identify who should have access	Reduce users with access	Layer 7 with granular enforcement
5 Monitor the Network	Network visibilty is low	Manual event management	Central data lake for events	Machine learning	Refine steps 1-4

Source: Adapted from CISA.org

ZERO TRUST MATURITY MODEL FOR DATA

Zero Trust Maturity
Examples of Functions

Function	Traditional	Advanced	Optimal
Inventory Management	Agency manually categorizes data and has poor data inventorying, leading to inconsistent categorization.	Agency primarily inventories data manually with some automated tracking.	Agency continuously inventories data with robust tagging and tracking.
Access Determination	Agency governs access to data by using static access controls.	Agency governs access to data using least privilege controls that consider identity, device risk, and other attributes.	Agency's access to data is dynamic, supporting just-in-time and just-enough principles
Encryption	Agency primarily stores data in on-premises data stores and where they are unencrypted at rest.	Agency stores data in cloud or remote environments where they are encrypted at rest.	Agency encrypts all data at rest.

Source: Adapted from Zero Trust Maturity Model, CICS.GOV

TECHNOLOGIES FOR DATA PRIVACY IN ZTA

Though numerous useful technologies are available for SRM leaders to consider, a lack of insight into the available markets with overlapping functions slows down operational readiness, according to Gartner. The required tooling must span the capabilities of discovery, mapping, classification, access controls, tokenization/encryption/pseudonymization or anonymization, and end-of-life controls. Integrated risk management (IRM) sets the outline of what is needed. The other markets of cloud access security broker (CASB), data security platforms (DSP), data-centric audit and protection (DCAP), data loss prevention (DLP), and file analysis (FA) bring the specific technologies to create cohesion between data security control and privacy. DSP and CSAB are discussed in separate chapters. This is an illustration of DSP that evolved from DCAP:

Technologies That Help Operationalize Privacy

Integrated Risk Management (IRM)	
Data Security Platforms (DSP) / Data-centric Audit and Protection (DCAP)	Cloud Access Security Broker (CASB)
Data Loss Prevention (DLP)	File Analysis (FA)

Source: Adapted from Gartner

MIGRATING TO PUBLIC CLOUD

DATA SECURITY FOR HYBRID CLOUD

Create data security policies and rules to protect data at rest and in transit. Use tokenization, anonymization, encryption, and other privacy models that are defined in the INTERNATIONAL DATA PRIVACY STANDARD ISO/IEC 20889. Centrally manage enterprise users and continuously monitors security behavior across a hybrid cloud.

Consistency across on-premises encryption and key management systems is often preferred to leverage the same tool and skills across multiple clouds. Issues with trust and cloud provider lock-in considerations are common concerns to enable easy migration to other cloud service providers.

EASIER SEGMENTATION THAT STARTS WITH A MAP

Host-based segmentation uses workload telemetry to create a real-time map of cloud and on-premises compute environments and applications. This map is used to visualize application connectivity, allowing teams to clearly see what they must protect. An advantage of using the host is seeing and enforcing segmentation down to the process level, which is more granular than just specific ports. Permitting only specific services between particular workloads is true micro-segmentation.

Another key difference is that micro-segmentation uses human-readable labels—not IP addresses or firewall rules—to create policy. Illumio assigns four-dimensional labels to workloads (bare-metal servers, VMs, containers, or processes running on hosts) to identify and provide context for each workload: role, application, environment, and location.

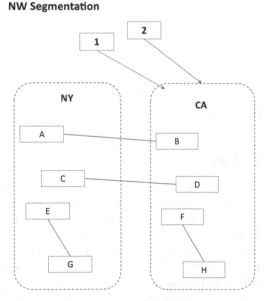

NW Segmentation

Source: Adapted from Illumio

VENDORS FOR ZERO TRUST NETWORK ACCESS

- Organizations cite VPN replacement as their primary motivation for evaluating ZTNA offerings but find that justification comes from risk reduction, not from any cost savings.
- Agent-based ZTNA is increasingly deployed as part of a larger SASE architecture or SSE offering for the extended workforce, while clientless ZTNA continues to grow in popularity to support third-party and BYOD use cases.

- Vendors continue to expand offerings into the data center with identity-based segmentation as separate products or combined with ZTNA offerings—blurring the lines between segmentation technologies.

MARKET DIRECTION

In the near midterm, stand-alone ZTNA vendors will find it increasingly difficult to compete with fully integrated SSE and SASE offerings. These vendors should expand their offerings to include SWG, DLP, and CASB offerings or partner with third-party providers.
Risks

- Some vendors have adopted the usage of dTLS to enable more effective transport for real-time communication applications. Clients should ensure that their providers support this protocol if they intend to leverage real-time applications over ZTNA.

Zero-knowledge proofs What is a zero-knowledge proof, and what does it do? A zero-knowledge proof (ZKP) refers to any protocol where a prover (usually an individual) is able to prove to another party (verifier) that they are in 29 possession of a secret (information they know but is unknown to the verifier). For example, a prover can prove their age without revealing what it actually is. The prover can use a ZKP to prove to the verifier that they know a value X (e.g., proof they are over 18), without conveying any information to the verifier apart from the fact that the statement is true. The verifier challenges the prover such that the responses from the prover will convince the verifier if the X is true (i.e., that the prover is over 18).

I know secret X

Prover needs to convince Verifier that he/she knows secret X

Prover   ⎯⎯⎯⎯⎯⎯⎯⎯⎯⎯⎯⎯⎯⎯⎯⎯⎯⎯⎯⎯⎯⎯⎯⎯→   **Verifier**

Source: Adapted from ICO ORG UK

PRIVATE SET INTERSECTION

(PSI) What is the private set intersection (PSI), and what does it do? PSI is a specific type of SMPC, which allows two parties, each with their own dataset, to find the "intersection" between them (i.e., the elements the two datasets have in common) without revealing or sharing those datasets. It can also be used to compute the size of the intersection or aggregate statistics on it. The client-server subtype is the most common type of PSI, where only the client learns the PSI result. Depending on the purposes, the client can be the user of a PSI service or the party who will learn the intersection or intersection size (the number of matching data points between the two parties). The server hosts the PSI service and holds data that the client can query to determine if it holds any matching data with the server. PSI can work in two ways:

- the data owners interact directly with each other and need to have a copy of their set at the time of the computation, known as traditional PSI; or
- the computation of PSI or the storage of sets can be delegated to a third-party server, known as delegated PSI. 21 The most efficient PSI protocols are highly scalable and use a variety of methods, including other privacy-enhancing techniques such as hashing or homomorphic encryption.

PSI result

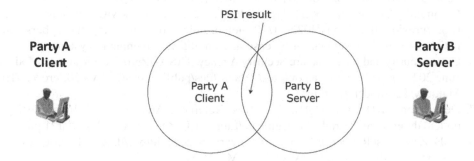

Source: Adapted from ICO ORG UK

SUMMARY

We discussed the need to change from "trust and verify" to "verify and then trust". We also discussed that another security aspect is Zero-knowledge proof, which means you actually possess knowledge without sharing the secret. Zero-knowledge can convince someone that you have a secret without disclosing the secret.

NOTES

1. Cybersecurity and Infrastructure Security Agency (CISA), Zero Trust Maturity Model (draft), June 2021,
2. Department of Defense (DoD), Zero Trust Reference Architecture, February 2021,
3. EO 14028: Improving the Nation's Cybersecurity, The White House, May 12, 2021, https://www.whitehouse.gov/briefingroom/presidential-actions/2021/05/12/executive-order-on-improving-the-nations-cybersecurity/
4. John Kindervag, No More Chewy Centers: Introducing the Zero Trust Model of Information Security, September 14, 2010, Updated September 17, 2010, https://media.paloaltonetworks.com/documents/Forrester-No-More-Chewy-Centers.pdf
5. National Security Memorandum 8 (NSM-8): Improving the Cybersecurity of National Security, Department of Defense, and Intelligence
6. NIST, SP 800-207: Zero Trust Architecture, August 2020, https://csrc.nist.gov/publications/detail/sp/800-207/final
7. OMB, M-22-09: Moving the U.S. Government Toward Zero Trust Cybersecurity Principles, The White House, January 26, 2022,
8. Sylvia Burns, Federal Deposit Insurance Corporation, "NSTAC ZT-IdM Subcommittee Briefing," Briefing to the NSTAC Zero Trust and
9. "Cloud Native Computing Foundation Announces Open Policy Agent Graduation". Announcements. Cloud Native Computing Foundation. 2021-02-04. Retrieved 2022-02-08.
10. "Open Policy Agent Accepted as CNCF Incubation Level Project". InfoQ. Retrieved 2020-01-21.
11. Alper Kerman, and Scott Rose, National Institute of Standards and Technology, "ZTA; Implementing a ZTA," Briefing to the NSTAC Zero Trust – Identity Management Subcommittee. Arlington, VA, September 22, 2021.
12. Building Consumer Confidence Through Transparency and Control, https://www.cisco.com/c/dam/en_us/about/doing_business/trust-center/docs/cisco-cybersecurity-series-2021-cps.pdf
13. CISA, Continuous Diagnostics and Mitigation, Accessed January 25, 2022, https://www.cisa.gov/cdm.

14. CISA, Zero Trust Maturity Model (draft), June 2021, https://www.cisa.gov/sites/default/files/publications/CISA%20Zero%20Trust%20Maturity%20Model_Draft.pdf
15. Community Systems, The White House, January 2022, https://www.whitehouse.gov/briefing-room/presidentialactions/2022/01/19/memorandum-on-improving-the-cybersecurity-of-national-security-department-of-defense-and-intelligencecommunity-systems
16. Cybersecurity and Infrastructure Security Agency (CISA), Zero Trust Maturity Model (draft), June 2021, https://www.cisa.gov/sites/default/files/publications/CISA%20Zero%20Trust%20Maturity%20Model_Draft.pdf
17. Department of Defense (DoD), Zero Trust Reference Architecture, February 2021, https://dodcio.defense.gov/Portals/0/Documents/Library/(U)ZT_RA_v1.1(U)_Mar21.pdf
18. DoD, Zero Trust Reference Architecture, February 2021, https://dodcio.defense.gov/Portals/0/Documents/Library/(U)ZT_RA_v1.1(U)_Mar21.pdf
19. EO 14028: Improving the Nation's Cybersecurity, The White House, May 12, 2021, https://www.whitehouse.gov/briefingroom/presidential-actions/2021/05/12/executive-order-on-improving-the-nations-cybersecurity/
20. https://dodcio.defense.gov/Portals/0/Documents/Library/(U)ZT_RA_v1.1(U)_Mar21.pdf
21. https://www.cisa.gov/sites/default/files/publications/CISA%20Zero%20Trust%20Maturity%20Model_Draft.pdf
22. https://www.cisa.gov/sites/default/files/publications/Final%20Draft%20NSTAC%20Report%20to%20the%20President%20on%20Zero%20Trust%20and%20Trusted%20Identity%20Management.pdf
23. https://www.cisa.gov/sites/default/files/publications/Final%20Draft%20NSTAC%20Report%20to%20the%20President%20on%20Zero%20Trust%20and%20Trusted%20Identity%20Management.pdf
24. https://www.cisco.com/c/dam/en_us/about/doing_business/trust-center/docs/cisco-privacy-benchmark-study-2022.pdf?CCID=cc000742&DTID=esootr000515
25. https://www.fedscoop.com/zero-trust-incomplete-experiment/
26. https://www.whitehouse.gov/wp-content/uploads/2022/01/M-22-09.pdf
27. ISO and IEC Joint Technical Committee (JTC 1) for Information Technology, ISO/IEC 27001: Information Security Management (landing page), https://www.iso.org/isoiec-27001-information-security.html
28. John Kindervag, ON2IT BV, "NSTAC ZT Briefing," Briefing to the NSTAC Zero Trust – Identity Management Subcommittee. Arlington, VA, September 8, 2021.
29. Lawrence Hale and Justin Morgan, General Services Administration (GSA), "How GSA Can Help Agencies with Their ZTA Journey," Briefing to the NSTAC Zero Trust – Identity Management Subcommittee. Arlington, VA, October 13, 2021.
30. National Institute of Standards and Technology (NIST), Special Publication (SP) 800-53 Rev. 5: Security and Privacy Controls for Information Systems and Organizations, September 2020, https://csrc.nist.gov/publications/detail/sp/800-53/rev-5/final
31. National Security Agency (NSA), Embracing a Zero Trust Security Model, February 2021, https://media.defense.gov/2021/Feb/25/2002588479/-1/-1/0/CSI_EMBRACING_ZT_SECURITY_MODEL_UOO115131-21.PDF
32. National Security Memorandum 8 (NSM-8): Improving the Cybersecurity of National Security, Department of Defense, and Intelligence Community Systems, The White House, January 2022, https://www.whitehouse.gov/briefing-room/presidentialactions/2022/01/19/memorandum-on-improving-the-cybersecurity-of-national-security-department-of-defense-and-intelligencecommunity-systems
33. NIST, Cybersecurity Framework, Accessed January 25, 2022, https://www.nist.gov/cyberframework
34. NIST, Cybersecurity Framework, https://www.nist.gov/cyberframework

35. NIST, SP 800-137: Information Security Continuous Monitoring (ISCM) for Federal Information Systems and Organizations, September 2011, https://nvlpubs.nist.gov/nistpubs/legacy/sp/nistspecialpublication800-137.pdf

36. NIST, SP 800-207: Zero Trust Architecture, August 2020, https://csrc.nist.gov/publications/detail/sp/800-207/final

37. NIST, SP 800-53 Rev. 5: Security and Privacy Controls for Information Systems and Organizations, September 2020, https://csrc.nist.gov/publications/detail/sp/800-53/rev-5/final

38. NIST, SP 800-53 Rev. 5: Security and Privacy Controls for Information Systems and Organizations, September 2020, https://csrc.nist.gov/publications/detail/sp/800-53/rev-5/final

39. NSA, Embracing a Zero Trust Security Model, February 2021, https://media.defense.gov/2021/Feb/25/2002588479/-1/-1/0/CSI_EMBRACING_ZT_SECURITY_MODEL_UOO115131-21.PDF

40. OMB, M-22-09: Moving the U.S. Government Toward Zero Trust Cybersecurity Principles, The White House, January 26, 2022, https://www.whitehouse.gov/wp-content/uploads/2022/01/M-22-09.pdf

41. Schalm, Deb (2019-10-08). "Fugue Adopts Open Policy Agent (OPA) for its Policy-as-Code Framework for Cloud Security". Security Boulevard. Retrieved 2020-01-21.

42. Sylvia Burns, Federal Deposit Insurance Corporation, "NSTAC ZT-IdM Subcommittee Briefing", Briefing to the NSTAC Zero Trust and Trusted Identity Management (ZT-IdM) Subcommittee. Arlington, VA, October 13, 2021.

43. Trusted Identity Management (ZT-IdM) Subcommittee. Arlington, VA, October 13, 2021.

44. U.S. Congress, Federal Information Security Management Act of 2002 (FISMA), March 2002, https://www.congress.gov/bill/107thcongress/house-bill/3844

45. U.S. Congress, Infrastructure Investment and Jobs Act, June 2021, https://www.congress.gov/bill/117th-congress/house-bill/3684

46. U.S. Congress, State and Local Cybersecurity Improvement Act, July 2021, https://www.congress.gov/bill/117th-congress/housebill/3138

6 Data Protection for Hybrid Cloud

INTRODUCTION

In this chapter, we will discuss Immutable Infrastructure, Container, and Kubernetes Security, Enterprise key management, Identity-based segmentation, Practical Guidance for Cloud Computing, and Critical Controls for SaaS.

USE CASES FOR DATA USE AND DATA SHARING

HEALTHCARE USE CASES

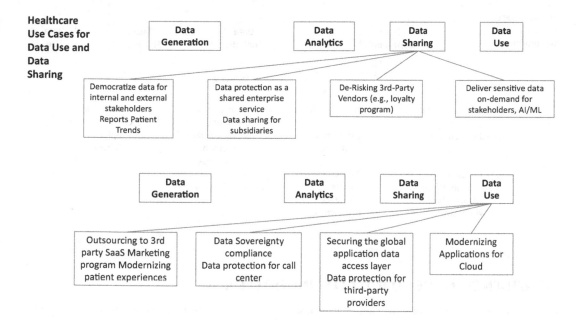

DOI: 10.1201/9781003254928-8

FINANCIAL SERVICES USE CASES FOR DATA USE

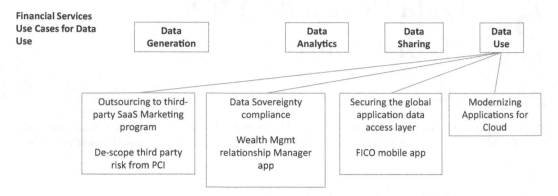

FINANCIAL SERVICES USE CASES DATA GENERATION

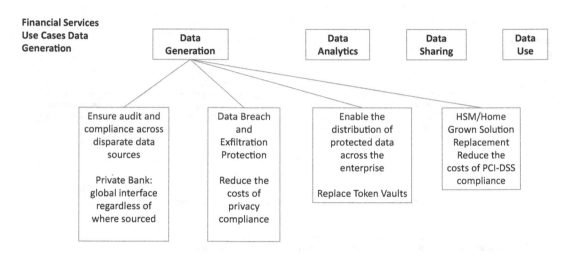

CONFIDENCE IN THE CLOUD CONTINUES TO GROW

Confidence in cloud infrastructure and platform services (CIPS) security continues to grow. "Cloud-first" strategies are now common, even among risk-averse organizations; however, execution remains impeded by a lack of necessary skills and tools to ensure secure deployment. In a recent Gartner survey, the most commonly cited challenge to cloud adoption was gaining security team approval and support for cloud migration strategies, suggesting that security teams are struggling to adapt to increasingly complex cloud technologies.

By 2023, 70% of all enterprise workloads will be deployed in cloud infrastructure and platform services, up from 40% in 2020, according to Gartner.

Through 2025, more than 99% of cloud breaches will have a root cause of preventable misconfigurations or mistakes by end users.

Obstacles
- Trust is slow to build and quick to evaporate, especially when experimental technology like confidential computing is paired with occasional hardware vulnerabilities.

- Because the technology is new and novel and touches sensitive data, potential clients have difficulty in identifying valid use cases for their business.
- Confidential computing can provide such protection now. Be mindful of the potential performance impacts and the extra cost. IaaS confidential computing instances (whether SGX-based or otherwise) will cost more to run.
- Confidential computing isn't usually plug-and-play and should be reserved for the highest-risk use cases. Depending on the vendor, it can require a high level of effort but offers diminishing marginal security improvement over more pedestrian controls like TLS, MFA, and customer-controlled key management services.

IMMUTABLE INFRASTRUCTURE

Immutable infrastructure is a process pattern (not a technology) in which the system and application infrastructure, once deployed into production, is never updated in place. Instead, the infrastructure and applications are simply replaced by the development pipeline when required changes.

Immutable infrastructure ensures that the system and application environment are accurately deployed and remain in a predictable, known-good-configuration state. It simplifies change management, supports faster and safer upgrades, reduces operational errors, improves security, and simplifies troubleshooting. It also enables rapid replication of environments for disaster recovery, geographic redundancy, or testing. This approach is easier to adopt and often applied with cloud-native applications.

CLOUD DATA PROTECTION GATEWAYS

Cloud data protection gateways (CDPGs) deploy a combination of forward/reverse proxy and API adapters to public Cloud SaaS providers. They can apply encryption or tokenization to structured or unstructured data, as it flows to the SaaS provider to mitigate inappropriate access to data that could lead to a breach. This helps meet data residency requirements for data protection and privacy. CDPG functionality is also provided by selected cloud access security broker (CASB) products. Why This Is Important Increasing volumes of sensitive data are stored across multiple public SaaS, which increases the risks of inappropriate access to data leading to security and privacy incidents. CDPG is increasingly important to help reduce these risks by restricting access to data to specific staff and potentially blocking access by the CSP.

DRIVERS

Organizations continue deploying an increasing number of SaaS and, to achieve consistent data security, they need CDPG deployed with multiple specific adapters, including Salesforce, ServiceNow, Box, Dropbox, G Suite, Office 365, and Workday.

- CDPG can provide encryption to protect stored files and also encryption or tokenization to protect fields within structured data stores.
- There is an increasing need to offer different key management options to either protect data independently of the SaaS with key management as a service (KMaaS), or integrate native SaaS protection through hold your own key (HYOK) or BYOK.
- A variety of international data residency and privacy requirements are increasing the needs to provide access privileges for staff and potentially to block or restrict access by the SaaS.
- The ability to integrate with SaaS native to bring your one key (BYOK) or maintain external control over key management are important choices to mitigate business risks.

CONTAINER AND KUBERNETES SECURITY

DRIVERS

Container and Kubernetes adoption is driven by developers and by a need for agility in service development and deployment.

- Multiple point solution vendors that have evolved (with some acquired) over the past several years can integrate transparently into the CI/CD pipeline and DevOps processes and are able to proactively scan containers for security and compliance issues.
- Traditional workload protection vendors such as McAfee, CrowdStrike, SentinelOne, and Trend Micro have now added support for containers and Kubernetes integration.
- DevOps-style development combined with containers and Kubernetes-based microservices applications deployed onto programmatic cloud infrastructure are a natural fit.

USER RECOMMENDATIONS

Use a hardened, patched OS for the container host OS. Scan containers in development for configuration and vulnerability issues of all code—custom, OS libraries, and third-party software—before production.

- Continuously assess the container orchestration environment's (typically Kubernetes) security posture for patch levels and correct and compliant configuration in development and in production using automated tools.
- Pressure existing workload protection vendors to provide complete solutions for container security that address end-to-end container security pipelines.
- Examine the processes expected to run in containers along with their behaviors, and use this information to replace signature-based deny-listing with allow-listing-based lockdown.
- Require container security solutions to explicitly support Kubernetes, including IaaSbased managed Kubernetes services.
- Design single-purpose containers and design clear tagging mechanisms to track data sensitivity.

CLOUD SECURITY POSTURE MANAGEMENT

Cloud Security Posture Management (CSPM) offerings continuously manage Cloud security posture through prevention, detection, response, and proactive identification of cloud infrastructure risk. The core of CSPM offerings apply common frameworks, regulatory requirements and enterprise policies to proactively and reactively discover and assess risk/trust of cloud services configuration and security settings. If an issue is identified, remediation options (automated or human driven) are provided. Why this is important assessing the secure and compliant configuration of a modern cloud hyperscale IaaS environment is extremely difficult. Even simple misconfiguration issues such as open storage objects represent significant and often unidentified risk.

ENTERPRISE KEY MANAGEMENT

Enterprise key management (EKM) provides a single, centralized software or hardware appliance for multiple symmetric encryption or tokenization-based cryptographic solutions. Critically, it enforces consistent data access policies across different structured and unstructured storage platforms, on-premises, and public cloud services. It facilitates key distribution and secure key storage.

DRIVERS

Cryptography is important for access control and EKM policies define the granularity of protection applied, typically linked to active directory.

OBSTACLES

EKM products typically comply with KMIP standards sponsored by OASIS. However, cryptography products typically do not comply with KMIP. This means that a different vendor's EKM cannot manage cryptography products.

MITIGATE DATA SECURITY AND PRIVACY RISKS

Data residency across cloud services creates complex choices in regard to balancing business needs against growing risks to provide adequate data security and compliance. This is due to the impacts of access by cloud service providers (CSPs), government authorities, and staff located around the world.

- There is a growing number of multicloud key management as a service (KMaaS) offerings provided by vendors and natively by each CSP that are independent or can integrate with bring your own key (BYOK) and hold your own key (HYOK) methods.
- Clients increasingly try to avoid data exposure and CSP trust issues by encrypting data on-premises. However, this may affect application performance and functionality.

IDENTITY-BASED SEGMENTATION

Identity-based segmentation (also called microsegmentation, zero-trust network segmentation, or logical segmentation) can create more granular and dynamic policies than traditional network segmentation, limited to IP/VLAN circuits. "Identitybased" refers to workload identity, not user identity.

DRIVERS

The shift to microservices container architectures increased the amount of east-west traffic and further complicated the ability of network-centric firewalls to provide this segmentation.

OBSTACLES

Legacy network firewalls: Some data centers have network firewalls for broader eastwest traffic segmentation, which is adequate for some organizations. Traditional firewalls can also present operational challenges to some identity-based segmentation solutions.

- Organizational dynamics: Cloud-centric organizations employing DevOps may value agility more than security, believing that any additional security controls will introduce operational friction.
- Expense: Full microsegmentation can come at a high price. Many organizations consider identity-based segmentation to be a net new budget item.

PRACTICAL GUIDANCE FOR CLOUD COMPUTING

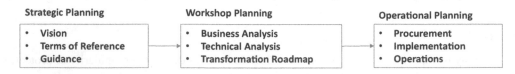

Source: Adapted from Object Management Group

NIST Cloud Computing Reference Architecture

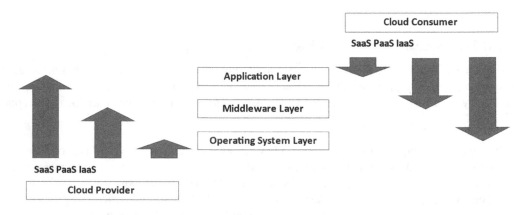

Source: Adapted from NIST

Assessing the Risks

Security, privacy, and data residency are risk management issues and should be treated using the same formal approaches: evaluate the probability and the impact of the potential threats, prioritize the risks accordingly, design and implement mitigation measures, test them, and keep monitoring the situation.

Adopting a cloud solution does not imply that the provider is solely responsible for security, privacy, and data residency issues. The customer and provider jointly share responsibilities. For example, in the case of an Infrastructureas-a-Service (IaaS), the provider is responsible for the compute, storage, and network, while the customer is responsible for hardening the operating system and middleware layers, implementing appropriate identity and access management, managing privileged access, encrypting data at rest and in motion, configuring the network and firewall to reduce the possibility of a breach, and so on.

The following considerations allow the risks to be discussed rationally:
Data residency is different, as this is clearly an issue that is exacerbated using cloud solutions.

- Inside threats are much higher than many would guess. Insiders were responsible for 39% of all data breaches in 2015. These breaches can be a result of malicious intent, accidental, or both. Insider breaches are often under reported and much harder to detect. Enterprises need to mitigate such risks with targeted programs to address deficiencies in training, communication, monitoring, policies, process, etc.

Five Sub-Steps for Data Residency Management

In the CSCC whitepaper, Data Residency Challenges, we offer five steps to assess and manage data residency risks:

1. Establish a governance structure—typically a team with representation from business lines, IT security, legal or compliance, and representatives from the organization's geographic areas.
2. Ensure proper metadata management by having a complete enterprise "data landscape" or information model in one place.
3. Define all the policies and rules on sensitive data elements—what can be located where, what needs to be anonymized or encrypted, etc.
4. Establish reports to monitor the application of policies; measure how much data resides in which country or jurisdiction; and identify deviations.
5. If possible, implement tools to track the provenance and pedigree of information—and how it moves across boundaries as it gets processed and transformed.

Security in the Cloud Service Agreements

Since a cloud service customer always transfers some responsibility to the provider, it is important to understand what the service agreements say about the relative roles and responsibilities of the parties.

The CSCC Practical Guide to Cloud Service Agreements calls out several issues with the current state of service agreements:

- Privacy and security considerations appear in different documents, with inconsistent titles and language.
- Most agreements impose stringent security obligations on the customer to protect the cloud provider—who decides unilaterally that a security violation occurred—but rarely any similar obligations or penalties regarding the harm that the provider might inflict on the customer.
- Privacy terms usually protect about the customer representatives' contact information, but not the customer's own users, who may be millions of end users.
- Escalation mechanisms are not specified or do not include response time commitments.

CRITICAL CONTROLS FOR SaaS

Salesforce implementations are usually composed of multiple environments that have diverse roles, such as sandbox, development, quality assurance, or production—to name a few.

The security of the overall environment is paramount to the security of the data that is hosted in the production system.

Likewise, organizations have fiduciary responsibilities to protect data wherever it exists.

In general terms, access to lower-risk environments such as development should not place sensitive data at risk. This means that, as much as possible, production and non-production environments should be separated (with different access controls) and that, unless sensitive information in non-production environments is appropriately secured (e.g., masked, scrambled, and/or redacted), these environments are secured with the same level and standards of protection.

Data Encryption

Business data stored and processed by Salesforce is its most crucial component. According to predefined rules and policies, sensitive data at rest should be encrypted and must be classified to avoid unauthorized access. Data encryption may impact functionality for search and sorting of data. Third-party product may help with these issues.

Salesforce Shield offers additional layers of data protection, including platform encryption, full event monitoring and field audit trail to track changes of the data. For companies handling sensitive data, such as financial service companies or healthcare companies, it should be evaluated if shield is necessary to fulfill compliance requirements.

HEALTHCARE STANDARDS

There are a variety of standards and best practices available which apply to specific aspects of healthcare IT and can be useful when considering the use of specific cloud services. Cloud services which support relevant standards should offer a better level of interoperability.

CLOUD DATABASES

Source: Adapted from Snowflake

MISTAKES IN MULTI-CLOUD ENVIRONMENTS

TOP THREE MISTAKES IN MULTI-CLOUD ENVIRONMENTS

1. Believing that Cloud is making you more secure
   Multi-cloud environments can have misconfigurations and basic multi-factor authentication (MFA) are often overlooked.
2. Trying to achieve visibility using multiple tools. You can't protect what you can't see, and your visibility is limited to that cloud provider.
3. Failure to incorporate an integrated approach, including people, process and tools. You need all three for a secure multi-cloud environment.

HYBRID CLOUD

Hybrid Cloud enables cloud service customers to leverage the wide-ranging capabilities of public CSPs while using private cloud deployment for more sensitive applications and data.

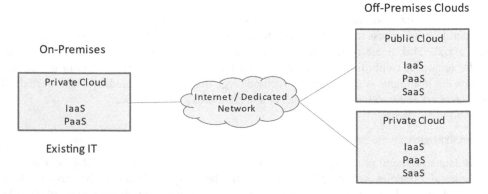

Source: Adapted from Object Management Group

Cloud Service Customer Points for Hybrid Cloud Computing:

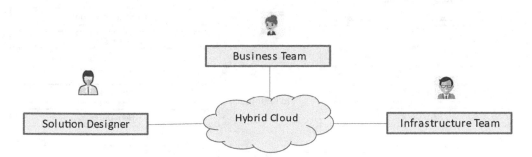

Source: Adapted from Object Management Group

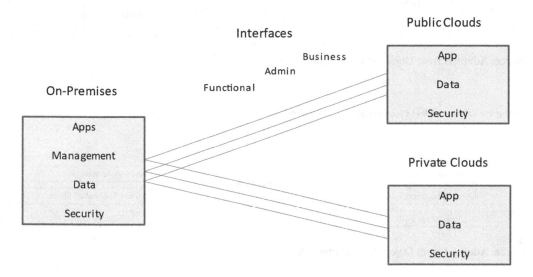

Source: Adapted from Object Management Group

DATABASE PROXY

JDBC driver-based to protect data in Cloud-managed databases that don't support external functions such as Google's Cloud SQL. (Snowflake and AWS Redshift have already added support for external functions and can integrate serverless protect() and unprotect() functions.)

Headcount Changes

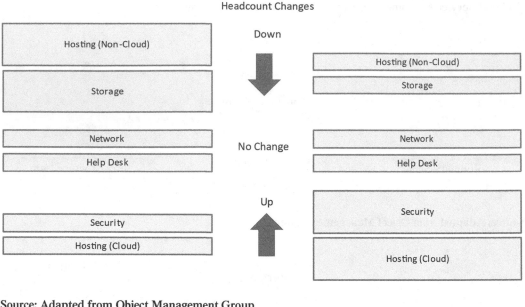

Source: Adapted from Object Management Group

Shifting the Values to Meet Changing Business Demands

Source: Adapted from Object Management Group

SUMMARY OF KEYS TO SUCCESS

Make learning a part of every job and project and ensure that it is part of the yearly objective of each staff member. Make mentoring within teams and sharing skills a yearly goal and requirement for advancement. Paired programming can be adapted for a "learn one, do one, teach one" training program. Leverage a variety of proven techniques (e.g., agile development practices, targeted online skills training, apprenticeships, lunch-and-learns, and mentoring) to include training more efficiently in day-to-day activities. Reward those who embrace and drive the change with recognition.

Keep track of where you are and where you want to be. To be successful, your program needs to be able to adapt to the ever-changing cloud technology and business landscape. Align your training program to your cloud adoption transformation so a twice-per-year assessment of current skills and gaps prevents surprises and gives a longer runway for the attainment of new business needs.

Don't reinvent the wheel. Leverage existing training capabilities and involve a range of IT staff members to build your specific education roadmap. Build an education program reflective of the mix of your new hires and skills growth for existing IT staff.

Enterprise Social Collaboration

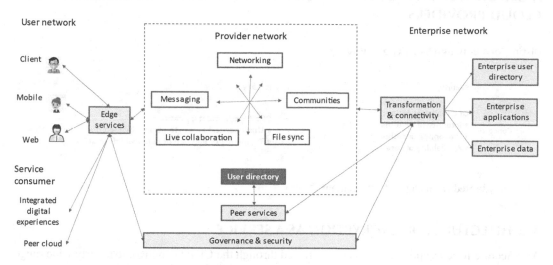

Source: Adapted from Object Management Group

SECURITY FOR CLOUD COMPUTING

Ten Steps to Ensure Success provides a practical reference to help enterprise information technology (IT) and business decision-makers analyze the security implications of cloud computing on their business.

Security for Cloud Services

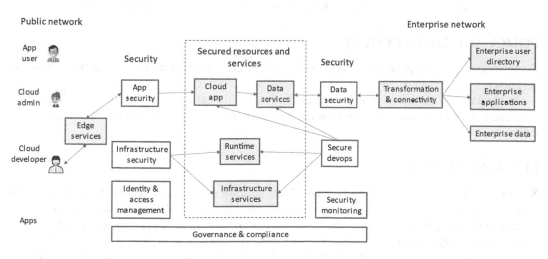

Source: Adapted from Cloud Standards Customer Council

Security and privacy challenges pertinent to cloud computing and considerations that organizations should weigh when migrating data, applications, and infrastructure.

Threats, technology risks and safeguards for cloud computing environments and the insight needed to make informed IT decisions on their treatment.

A CLOUD SECURITY ASSESSMENT TO ASSESS THE SECURITY CAPABILITIES OF CLOUD PROVIDERS

Distinctions between Security and Privacy

	Security	Privacy
Main Concerns	Of a technical nature: • Integrity of systems • Preventing unauthorized access to systems • Availability of service	Of a legal/regulatory nature: • Unauthorized access to personally identifiable information • Tampering or deletion of personal information

Source: Adapted from Object Management Group

ARCHITECTURE FOR ENCRYPTION AS A SERVICE

Architecture for encryption as a service delivered through the Cloud can involve a fairly wide range of applications. More specifically, the following are considered in scope:

- Key Management Systems (KMS);
- Control of Keys (Customer vs. Cloud Provider);
- Key Lifecycle.

DATA IN THE CLOUD

Data in the Cloud refers to data while it is being transmitted, stored or processed by a CSP. The organization should apply the same data classification used when the data is resident within the organization and therefore apply necessary cryptographic security requirements to data stored, transmitted, or processed by a CSP. CSP Service Level Agreements cannot replace cryptographic security controls.

POLICY AND ENFORCEMENT

Requirements for encryption to conform to established security policy do not stop at the on-premise perimeter.

As it relates to the use of cloud services, the issues of what is encrypted and when should be addressed in a similar way to on-premise methods through the establishment of file and data classification strategies.

KEY MANAGEMENT

Key management is the most complex part of any security system dealing with the encryption of data. An organization must define its cryptographic security and key lifecycle management policy. Access to these cryptographic keys should be granted to authorized users only and revoked when those users no longer need access.

Cryptographic keys for the encryption of data should be generated securely. This may include the use of an appropriately strong random number generator (RNG). Cryptographic keys should never be transmitted in the clear and should be stored inside a secure element, such as a smart card, or a service with the hardware security module (HSM).

However, based on the Segregation of Duties security principle, key management ideally should be separated from the cloud provider hosting the data. This provides the greatest protection against both an external breach of the service provider and an attack originating from a privileged user/employee of the provider.

Additionally, this segregation of duties prevents the cloud provider from unauthorized disclosure of customer data, such as compliance with a subpoena, without the customer's knowledge or approval. The customers should retain complete control over their data, and only they should be able to comply with disclosure requests.

Key management for Cloud can be complex and preferably, the customer maintains control of the encryption keys. Organizations need to match their risk tolerance and the compliance, government, audit and/or executive-mandated requirements they need to follow.

ENTERPRISEWIDE ENCRYPTION KEY MANAGEMENT (EKM)

A lack of encryption key management (EKM) strategy will increase the risk of data loss. According to Gartner, security and risk management leaders must develop an enterprisewide EKM strategy or lose the data.

EKM enforces consistent data access policies across different structured and unstructured storage solutions, on-premises, and public cloud services. It facilitates key distribution, secures key storage and maintains consistent key life cycle management.

Many security and risk management leaders struggle to understand the capabilities and limitations that EKM solutions provide, and how to properly configure them.

- Due to a diverse array of data silos and platforms located on-premises and in public clouds, investment in multiple data security products is required.
- SRM leaders cite that they struggle to support long-term access to encrypted data or established data encryption requirements to meet data residency, privacy, crypto-agility, compliance, and business needs.

According to Gartner, by 2023, 40% of organizations will have a multisilo, hybrid, and multi-cloud data encryption strategy, up from less than 5% in 2022. By 2024, 35% of organizations will leverage crypto and key orchestration platform to handle a variety of secrets and crypto-management, up from 0% in 2022.

Encryption Key Management mindshare by company size:

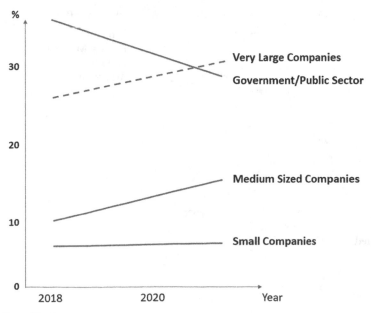

Encryption Key Management mindshare by company size:

Source: Adapted from Gartner

Encryption Key Management mindshare by Byer Role:

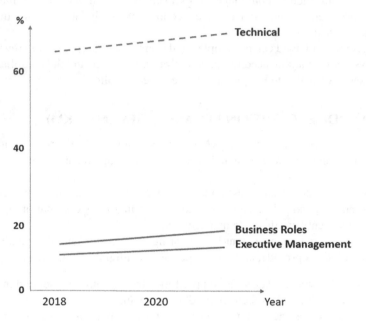

Source: Adapted from Gartner

Encryption Key Management mindshare by Region:

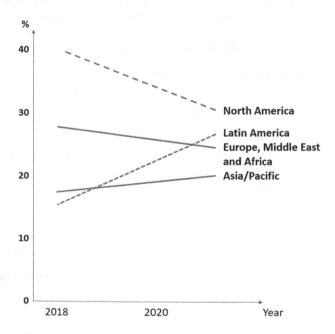

Source: Adapted from Gartner

Encryption Key Management mindshare by Industry:

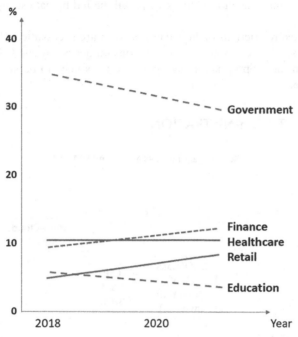

Source: Adapted from Gartner

SRM leaders are facing ever-increasing needs to protect and encrypt various critical and sensitive data stores, including public clouds, to protect themselves in the event of a data breach. A combination of privacy, data residency and compliance issues, internal security audits, and growing hacking threats are driving enterprises' requirements to develop a data security governance strategy to prioritize critical and sensitive data protection.

Regulations, such as the EU General Data Protection Regulation (GDPR) and the California Consumer Protection Act (CCPA), have dramatically increased pressure on SRM leaders to review and revamp their EKM strategy (see Hype Cycle for Privacy, 2020). COVID-19 has forced clients to leverage cloud services, thus revealing more data silos requiring data protection and management.

Areas for Enterprise Encryption Key Management

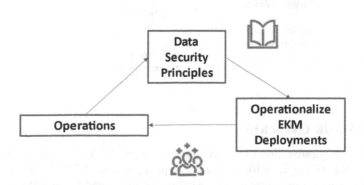

Source: Adapted from Gartner

CSP infrastructure security, basic storage encryption and cloud-native KMaaS services have strong track records. Malicious actors will try to exploit KM operations or, most likely, to compromise a client user account. The choices for KMaaS will be led by data security governance (DSG) policies.

These reflect desired restrictions on how data and keys are accessible, affecting risks associated with data residency, staff access issues and restrictions on access by the CSP. This will determine which KMaaS options are appropriate based on where keys need to be geographically stored and processed, see Figure:

KEY MANAGEMENT ADMINISTRATION

Key Management as a Service (KMaaS)

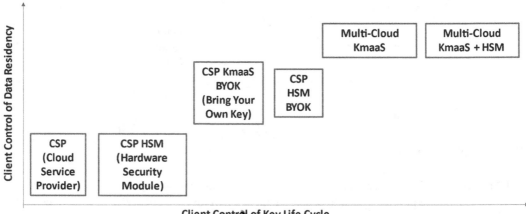

Source: Adapted from Garter

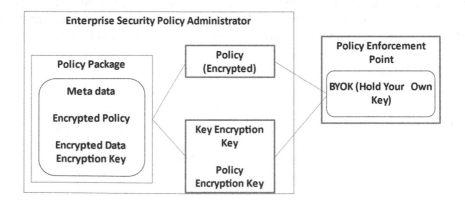

BRING YOUR OWN KEY

A number of popular cloud services currently support BYOK, which SRM leaders can leverage. However, BYOK carries with it a variety of pros and cons. BYOK allows SRM leaders to generate encryption keys on-premises (or via an external service) and to bring that key to their cloud service.

Thus, they gain the capability to generate their encryption keys (and full life cycles). However, SRM leaders will have to ensure that they include BYOK for all cloud applications in their comprehensive EKM strategy. Furthermore, differences in cloud services can also impact the approach of BYOK, which in turn causes key management issues for SRM leaders due to the management of different varieties. In addition, there are other methods, such as holding your own key, popularized by Microsoft. HYOK boasts some advantages over BYOK—specifically, minimizing the exposure time of key material.

DATA SECURITY GOVERNANCE

Data security governance refers to a subset of information governance that deals specifically with protecting corporate data (in both structured database and unstructured file-based forms) through defined data policies and processes and implemented via technologies that are drawn from products such as data-centric audit and protection (DCAP), cloud access security broker (CASB), and data loss prevention (DLP), among others.

CLOUD KEY MANAGEMENT

In Google Cloud, your data is encrypted at rest by default, and customers manage cryptographic keys in a central cloud service:

- A Cloud HSM to help ensure security
- Cloud KMS allows the import of your own cryptographic keys
- Cloud KMS can generate keys with other Google Cloud services
- Customer-managed encryption keys (CMEK) allow a customer to generate, use, rotate, and destroy encryption keys
- With Cloud External Key Manager (Cloud EKM)

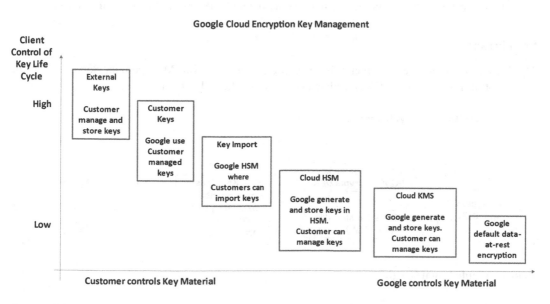

Source: Adapted from Google

KEYS, KEY VERSIONS, AND KEY RINGS

The Figure describes keys, key versions, and the grouping of keys into key rings:

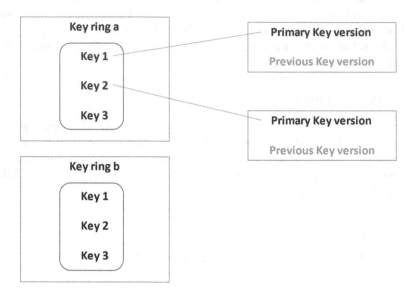

Source: Adapted from Google

- **Key:** A named object representing a cryptographic key
- **Key ring:** A cluster of keys for organizational purposes.
- **Key metadata:** Resource names, properties of KMS resources such as IAM policies, key type, key size, key state, and any data derived from the above.
- **Key version:** Represents the key material associated with a key at some point in time.

KEY HIERARCHY

The Figure illustrates the key hierarchy of Google's internal Key Management Service with the same root of trust as Google KMS. Related definitions follow the diagram.

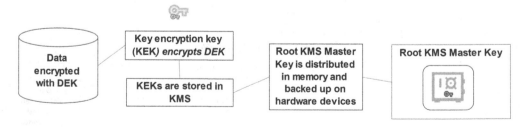

Source: Adapted from Google

- **Data encryption key (DEK):** A key used to encrypt data.
- **Key encryption key (KEK):** A key used to encrypt, or *wrap*, a data encryption key. All Cloud KMS platform options (software, hardware, and external backends) let you control the key encryption key.

- **KMS Master Key:** The key used to encrypt the key encryption keys (KEK). This key is distributed in memory. The KMS Master Key is backed up on hardware devices. This key is responsible for encrypting your keys.
- **Root KMS:** Google's internal key management service.

Cloud KMS Platform Overview

The Cloud KMS platform is integrated with Identity and Access Management (IAM) and Cloud Audit Logs.

Cloud KMS Platform for Key Management

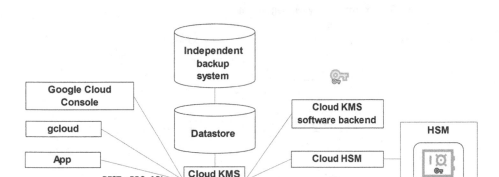

Source: Adapted from Google

Applications access key management services using a REST API or gRPC.

Cloud KMS Platform Architectural Details

Master Keys

Cloud KMS uses a Master Key to wrap all customer keys at rest. Each Cloud KMS server fetches a copy of the Master Key during startup as a hard dependency, and a new copy of the Master Key is retrieved every day. The Master Key is re-encrypted periodically.

Data Residency

The data underlying each Cloud KMS datastore remains exclusively within the Google Cloud region with which the data is associated. This applies to locations that are multi-regions as well, for example, the US multi-region. For more details on data residency.

Random Number Generation and Entropy

When generating encryption keys, Cloud KMS uses BoringSSL. FIPS 140-2 requires that its own PRNGs be used (also known as DRBGs). In BoringCrypto, Cloud KMS exclusively uses CTR-DRBG with AES-256. This provides output for RAND_bytes, the primary interface by which the rest of the system gets random data. This PRNG is seeded from the Linux kernel's RNG, which itself is seeded from multiple independent entropy sources.

Cloud KMS HSM Backend: HARDWARE Protection Level

Cloud HSM uses HSMs that are FIPS 140-2 Level 3–validated and are always running in FIPS mode. The FIPS standard specifies the cryptographic algorithms and random number generation used by the HSMs.

Cavium HSMs

The Cavium HSM PCIe card is validated by the vendor to be FIPS 140-2 Level 3–compliant. The current certificate is available on request.

HSM Key Hierarchy

In the following diagram, we see the Cloud KMS in the top half of the diagram. Cloud HSM wraps customer keys, and then, Cloud KMS wraps the HSM keys that are passed to Google's datastore.

Cloud KMS Platform for Key Management

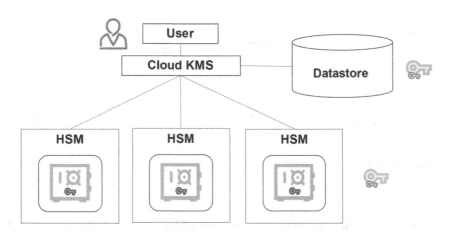

Source: Adapted from Google

The Cloud HSM has a key (not shown) that controls material migration inside the Cloud HSM administrative domain. A region might have multiple HSM administrative domains.

Datastore Protection

HSMs are not used as permanent storage for keys; they store keys only while they are being used. Because HSM storage is constrained, the HSM keys are encrypted and stored in the Cloud KMS key datastore.

Cloud KMS: Key Import

Cloud KMS allows the import of your own keys that you created on-premises or in an External Key Manager, including asymmetric keys, to extend your signing capabilities to the Cloud.

Lifecycle of a Request

This Figure describes the lifecycle of a Cloud KMS request.

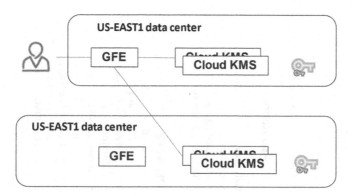

Source: Adapted from Google Cloud

These are the steps in this lifecycle:

1. A job running on behalf of a customer composes a request to the Cloud KMS service
2. The GFE provides public IP hosting of its public DNS name.
3. A request that arrives in us-east1 can be routed between us-east1 and us-west1 data centers.

Cloud EKM lets you protect data at rest in BigQuery and Compute Engine using encryption keys that are stored and managed in a third-party key management system that's deployed outside Google's infrastructure.

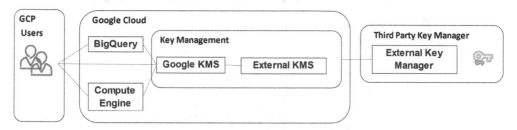

Source: Adapted from Google Cloud

Cloud Access Security Brokers (CASBs)

Cloud access security brokers (CASBs) can provide isolation of encryption keys and security policy enforcement for SaaS, IaaS, and PaaS. The majority of CASB deployments are cloud-based; on-premises deployments are rare. For example, a CASB can be implemented via a (JDBC) database driver:

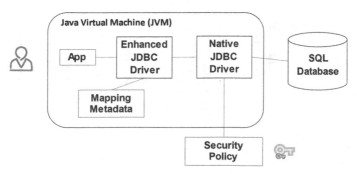

Source: Adapted from Google

PLATFORMS

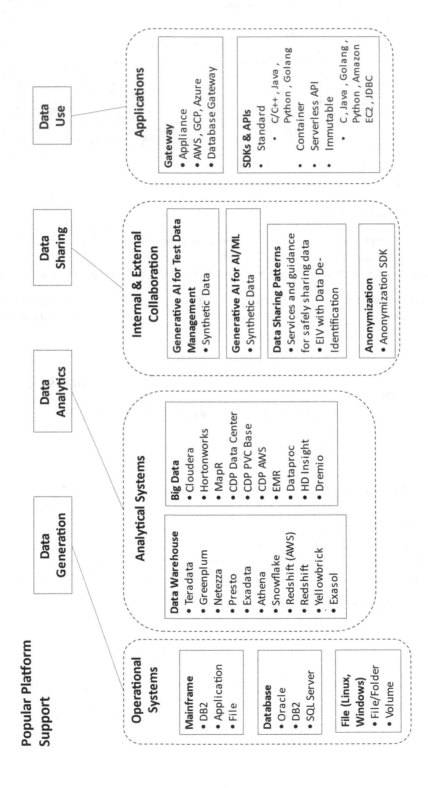

SUMMARY

We discussed Immutable Infrastructure, Container and Kubernetes Security, Enterprise key management, Identity-based segmentation, Practical Guidance for Cloud Computing, and Critical Controls for SaaS.

NOTES

1. ISO/IEC 19941 Information technology—Cloud computing—Interoperability and Portability. https://www.iso.org/standard/66639.html
2. RightScale 2017 State of the Cloud Report (2017). https://assets.rightscale.com/uploads/pdfs/RightScale-2017-State-of-the-Cloud-Report.pdf
3. https://a.sfdcstatic.com/content/dam/www/ocms/assets/pdf/platform/whitepaper-platform-shield.pdf
4. NIST Computer Security Resource Center | NIST Risk Management Framework SP 800-53 Revision 5.1: CM-6(1)
5. Center for Internet Security | The 18 CIS Controls, https://www.cisecurity.org/controls/cis-controls-list/
6. Ron Miller, "Palo Alto Networks intends to acquire Zingbox for $75M," TechCrunch, September 5, 2019 (https://techcrunch.com/2019/09/04/palo-alto-networks-intends-to-acquire-zingbox-for-75m/).
7. Blankenship, Joseph (2016). Hunting Insider Threats. Forrester Research report number 134865.
8. Cloud Standards Customer Council (2013). Convergence of Social, Mobile and Cloud: 7 Stepsto Ensure Success. http://www.cloud-council.org/deliverables/convergence-of-social mobile-and-cloud-7-steps-to-ensure-success.htm
9. Cloud Standards Customer Council (2013). Migrating Applications to Public Cloud Services: Roadmap to Success. http://www.cloud-council.org/deliverables/migrating-applications-to public-cloud-services-roadmap-for-success.htm
10. Cloud Standards Customer Council (2015). Practical Guide to Cloud Service Agreements. http://www.cloud-council.org/deliverables/practical-guide-to-cloud-serviceagreements.htm
11. Cloud Standards Customer Council (2015). Practical Guide to Platform as a Service. http://www.cloud-council.org/deliverables/practical-guide-to-platform-as-a-service.htm
12. Cloud Standards Customer Council (2015). Security for Cloud Computing: 10 Steps to Ensure Success. http://www.cloud-council.org/deliverables/security-for-cloud-computing10-steps-to-ensure-success.htm
13. Cloud Standards Customer Council (2016). Practical Guide to Hybrid Cloud Computing. http://www.cloud-council.org/deliverables/practical-guide-to-hybrid-cloud-computing.htm
14. Cloud Standards Customer Council (2016). Public Cloud Service Agreements: What to Expect & What to Negotiate. http://www.cloud-council.org/deliverables/public-cloud-service agreements-what-to-expect-and-what-to-negotiate.htm
15. Cloud Standards Customer Council (2017). Data Residency Challenges. http://www.cloud council.org/deliverables/data-residency-challenges.htm
16. http://cloud-council.org/resource-hub.htm#migrating-applications-to-public-cloud-services
17. http://csrc.nist.gov/publications/fips/fips140-2/fips1402.pdf
18. http://csrc.nist.gov/publications/nistpubs/800-57/SP800-57-Part2.pdf
19. http://docs.oasis-open.org/cmis/CMIS/v1.1/os/CMIS-v1.1-os.pdf
20. http://infrastructure-as-code.com/
21. http://media.amazonwebservices.com/CloudMigration-main.pdf
22. http://nvlpubs.nist.gov/nistpubs/Legacy/SP/nistspecialpublication800-64r2.pdf
23. http://searchcloudcomputing.techtarget.com/feature/When-to-adopt-the-lift-and-shift-cloud migration-model

24. http://standards.iso.org/ittf/PubliclyAvailableStandards/c060544_ISO_IEC_17788_2014.zip
25. http://standards.iso.org/ittf/PubliclyAvailableStandards/c060544_ISO_IEC_17788_2014.zip
26. http://www.cloud-council.org/deliverables/cloud-customer-architecture-for-api-management.htm
27. http://www.cloud-council.org/deliverables/migrating-applications-to-public-cloud-services-roadmapfor-success.htm
28. http://www.cloud-council.org/resource-hub.htm#practical-guide-to-cloud-service-agreements version-2
29. http://www.enisa.europa.eu/act/rm/files/deliverables/cloud-computing-risk-assessment
30. http://www.nist.gov/itl/cloud/upload/NIST_SP-500-291_Version-2_2013_June18_FINAL.pdf
31. http://www.oreilly.com/programming/free/migrating-cloud-native-application-architectures.csp
32. http://www.redbooks.ibm.com/redbooks/pdfs/sg248011.pdf
33. https://cloud.google.com/blog/products/identity-security/cloud-external-key-manager-now-in-beta
34. https://cloud.google.com/security/key-management-deep-dive
35. https://datatracker.ietf.org/doc/rfc6749/
36. https://gdpr.cloudsecurityalliance.org/wpcontent/uploads/sites/2/2017/11/EU_GDPR_Impact_for_BusinessesEstablished_Outside_the_EU_and_EEA.pdf
37. ISO/IEC 17788:2014 Information technology—Cloud computing—Overview and vocabulary.
38. ISO/IEC 19086-1:2016 Information technology—Cloud computing—Service level agreement (SLA) framework—Part 1: Overview and concepts. https://www.iso.org/standard/67545.html
39. ISO/IEC 20889. https://www.iso.org/standard/69373.html
40. Moore's Revenge' is upon us and will make the world weird, Mark Pesce, The Register. https://www.theregister.co.uk/2018/06/04/moores_revenge/ [2] 2017 State of Application Security: Balancing Speed and Risk, Jim Bird, SANS. Available at: https://www.sans.org/reading-room/whitepapers/analyst/2017-state-application-security-balancing-speed-risk-38100
41. National Institute for Standards and Technology (2011): NIST Cloud Computing Standards Roadmap. http://www.nist.gov/itl/cloud/upload/NIST_SP-500-291_Version-2_2013_June18_FINAL.pdf
42. National Institute for Standards and Technology (2014): NIST Cloud Computing Program. http://www.nist.gov/itl/cloud/
43. Open Container Initiative. https://www.opencontainers.org/

7 Web 3.0 and Data Security

INTRODUCTION

In this chapter, we will discuss Web3 Storage, Sharding and Pruning, Security Risks to Blockchain Ecosystems, Secure transaction ledgers, Blockchains in the Quantum Era, and Storing private keys.

ORACLE CONTRACTS

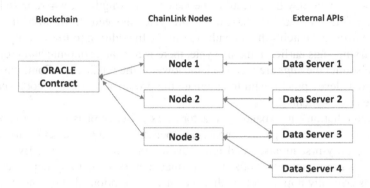

Source: Adapted from Drecom

Decentralized oracles –

Distributed RNGs or decentralized oracles can be used. Random numbers are generated based on random input from several participants. The input is then combined in some deterministic way to create the final random number.

- All participants can influence the outcome. No single participant can fully control it, so every endorsing peer of the RNG contract can use a high entropy function to generate a random number stored in private data.
- Endorsing peers of the lottery contract can then retrieve and combine the numbers to create the winning lottery number.

SECURITY TOOLS EMBEDDED IN THE SMART CONTRACT DEVELOPMENT LIFE CYCLE (DEVSECOPS)

Chaincode is a program that typically handles business logic agreed to by members of the network and is sometimes called a smart contract.

Chaincode in Hyperledger Fabric is similar to smart contracts.

Every chain code program must implement the Chaincode interface. In this recipe, we will explore chaincode implementation using Go.

https://developer.ibm.com/recipes/tutorials/writing-hyperledger-fabric-chaincode-using-go-programming-language/

DOI: 10.1201/9781003254928-9

SMART CONTRACT DEVELOPMENT LIFECYCLE

This paper does not attempt to prescribe or recommend a specific lifecycle, nor is it intended to replace any existing lifecycle that you or your enterprise employs. This section aims to provide useful guidance in a manner that is additive and augments your existing solution delivery lifecycle.

One of the keys to securing your lifecycle is by ensuring that it has the appropriate checkpoints, also known as milestones or security gates, in your processes so that a set of security function(s) can interrogate and attest to the security posture of the smart contract or software that is being built at a given point in time prior to deployment. There is much debate around when it is most useful or appropriate to apply a specific security control during a given lifecycle; however, we can rely on well-understood security and software engineering principles to guide us as to which controls should be applied and when.

A common phrase you may have heard is the idea of "shifting left", where introducing security controls into the leftmost or earliest phase of the lifecycle has been shown to be the most effective time to apply controls and catch software vulnerabilities. In addition to the security implications of identifying and fixing bugs earlier in the lifecycle, there is also an economic and project cost implication where the sooner the bugs are identified, the lower is the repair cost. Continuous delivery and quality enable your development team to automate the propagation of new code versions through multiple runtime environments.

The cost of remediation can expand by a factor of 5x for each phase. More importantly, fostering continuous quality can have greater impacts and benefits, such as greater customer satisfaction, promotion of a quality-first mindset, and fewer disruptions in the business. Everyone should be responsible for ensuring quality is built into the smart contracts and any dependent systems that rely on them. It is critically important to realize the false assumptions that the more bugs you find in smart contracts, the better the contract will be.

Secure Smart Contract Development Lifecycle (SSCDL)

To talk about DevSecOps, we must not lose focus that this is only the process of automating the tools used by the departments (QA, AppSec, CI) to automate a process.

Due to this, to cover the smart contract security process well, we must not only focus on the tools to carry out this process but also on the methodologies and techniques of these areas in the Smart Contracts process.

Risks Related to Quorum for Endorsement

If a channel peer does not upgrade to the newest version of the smart contract, that peer and any other peer that is not running the newest version will no longer be able to endorse transactions for the smart contract, which depending on the endorsement policy, creates a risk of not having enough endorsements to commit transactions. Note: It is possible for peers to catch up by installing the new smart contract version.

Private Data and Removal of Peers

When an upgrade removes an organization from private data collection, those removed peers continue to store data in the private data collection until the block that removes their membership is reached, at which point, the peers will no longer receive private data, and related clients will no longer be able to query the private data.

https://cloud.ibm.com/docs/blockchain?topic=blockchain-ibp-console-smart-contracts-v14

Fabric v2.0 uses a distributed process to manage the lifecycle of a smart contract and the allowed updates to a channel as part of the decentralization instead of a single organization's administrator making decisions for all organizations about when a smart contract is updated.

A DISTRIBUTED HASH TABLE (DHT)

DHT is a lookup service similar to a hash table: key-value pairs are stored in a DHT.

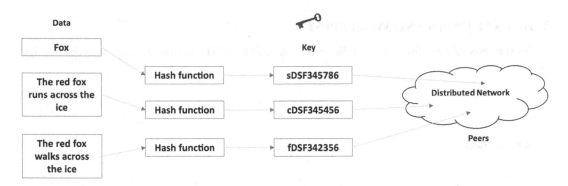

Source: Adapted from Drecom

WEB

History of the Web

While Web1 was a read-only web, and Web2 was a read-write web, Web3 instead promises to offer an unmediated read-write web, according to "The Ultimate Guide to Web3". Stages of the internet can be summarized like this:

1. Web1—Static
2. Web2—Dynamic
3. Web3—Decentralized

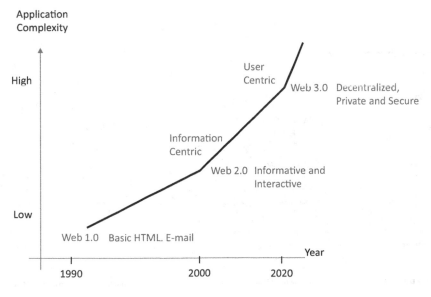

Source: Adapted from 101 Blockchains

Web1 was mainly about providing online content and information.

Web2 becomes dynamic, allowing users to consume or "read" information and create it themselves or "write" information.

WHAT ARE DAPPS AND WEB3 APPS?

Web3 supports dApps, distributed applications, according to "The Ultimate Guide to Web3 – What is Web3?"

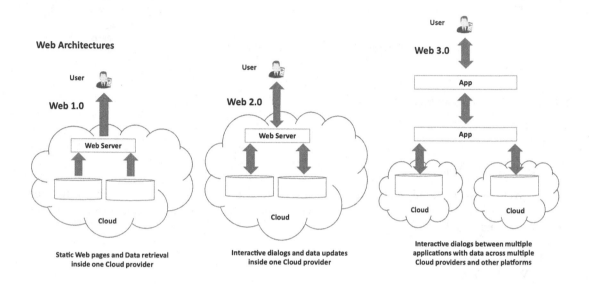

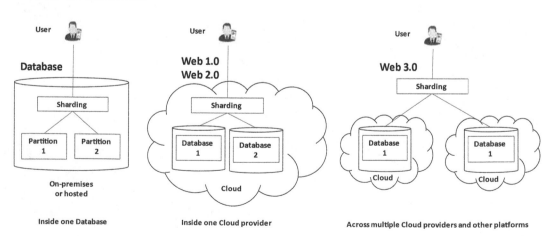

DISTRIBUTED TABLES

Kademlia Is a Distributed Hash Table

Kademlia is a distributed hash table for decentralized peer-to-peer computer networks designed by Petar Maymounkov and David Mazières in 2002.

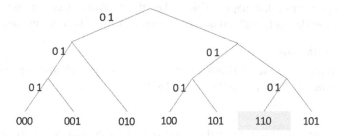

BLOCKCHAIN-BASED APPLICATIONS

So, what are Web3 apps? One integral part of many dApps or Web3 apps is so-called "smart contracts", according to "The Ultimate Guide to Web3 – What is Web3?"

SMART CONTRACTS OF WEB3 APPS

As such, you can largely regard Web3.js as your interface between JavaScript and the smart contracts of Web3 apps. Essentially, libraries like Web3.js allow you to interact with either a remote or local Ethereum node. This is commonly done through the use of an HTTP, IPC, or WebSocket connection, according to "The Ultimate Guide to Web3 – What is Web3?"

Ethereum JavaScript API

web3.js is a collection of libraries that allow you to interact with a local or remote Ethereum node, using an HTTP or IPC connection, according to "web3.js - Ethereum JavaScript API".

Dapp With Web3.js

According to "Build Your First Dapp With Web3.js", a decentralized application has three main components.

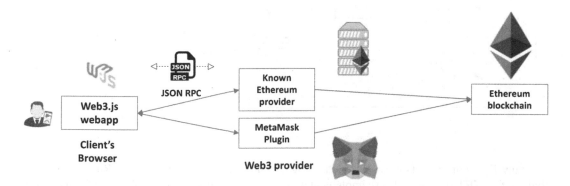

Source: Adapted from metter programming.pub

According to "Build Your First Dapp With Web3.js", you don't have to worry about the low-level details of JSON-RPC calls anymore since it provides an abstraction of the Ethereum json-rpc interface.

Clients

The Ethereum community maintains multiple open-source clients developed by different teams using different programming languages. This makes the network stronger and more diverse. The ideal goal is to achieve diversity without any client dominating to reduce any single point of failure.

Different Implementations

Each client has unique use cases and advantages, so you should choose one based on your own preferences, according to "NODES AND CLIENTS."

OpenEthereum

OpenEthereum is a fast, feature-rich, and advanced CLI-based Ethereum client. It's built to provide the essential infrastructure for speedy and reliable services, which require fast synchronization and maximum up-time. OpenEthereum's goal is to be the fastest, lightest, and most secure Ethereum client.

Overview of Strategies

Computers running software (known as nodes) can verify blocks and transaction data. According to "NODES AND CLIENTS", you need an application, known as a client, on your computer to "run" a node.

What Are Nodes and Clients?

"Node" refers to a running piece of client software.

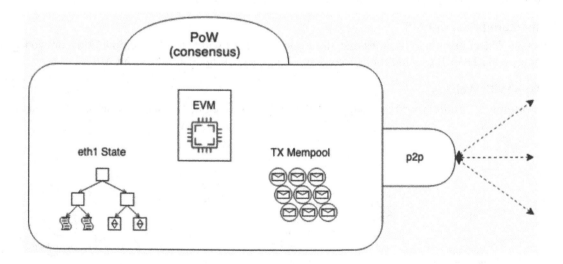

Many Ethereum clients exist in various programming languages such as Go, Rust, JavaScript, Python, C# .NET, and Java. These implementations have in common: they all follow a formal specification (originally the Ethereum Yellow Paper). This specification dictates how the Ethereum network and blockchain functions.

DECENTRALIZED APPLICATIONS (DAPPS)

DeFi revolves around decentralized applications, also known as DApps, that perform financial functions on distributed ledgers called blockchains, a technology that was first made famous by Bitcoin and has since been adopted more broadly. Rather than transactions being made through a centralized intermediary such as a cryptocurrency exchange or a traditional securities exchange on Wall Street, transactions are directly made between participants, mediated by smart contract programs.

SMART CONTRACTS AND DeFi

These smart contract programs, or DeFi protocols, typically run using open-source software that is built and maintained by a community of developers.

DAPPS AND WEB3

DApps are typically accessed through a Web3-enabled browser extension or application, such as MetaMask, according to "DeFi and Web3".

DECENTRALIZED FINANCE (DeFi)

Decentralized Finance (commonly referred to as DeFi) is a blockchain-based form of finance that does not rely on central financial intermediaries such as brokerages, exchanges, or banks to offer traditional financial instruments, according to "DeFi and Web3".

NAP—A TRUE CROSS-BLOCKCHAIN TOKEN

The token differs from atomic swaps in the sense that tokens are not exchanged between two different users on different blockchains, but rather the same token can be transferred to another blockchain with no other user involved, according to "NAP—A true cross-blockchain token".

WEB3 STORAGE

IPFS

IPFS allows users to host and receive content in a manner similar to BitTorrent. As opposed to a centrally located server, IPFS is built around a decentralized system, according to "IPFS".

STORJ

The individual file shards are sent to ordinary computers across Storj's network. But what if one of those computers gets turned off or stops running Storj and Kademlia is a distributed hash table for decentralized peer-to-peer computer networks, according to "Kademlia".

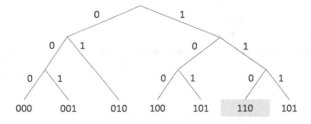

BLOCKCHAINS IN THE QUANTUM ERA

Transition from PreQuantum to Post-Quantum Blockchain Advances in quantum computing has triggered a growing sense of urgency within the DLT/ blockchain community to identify post-quantum algorithms that are both effective and practical to deploy. The transition from pre-quantum to post-quantum blockchain is necessary to ensure the security of blockchains in the quantum era. The extensive use of digital signatures in support of conducting blockchain transactions represents a prime vulnerability. Therefore, much attention is therefore being placed on developing and selecting suitable post-quantum digital signature algorithms, which are suitable for blockchain applications and can be phased over time.

First, some computationally intensive post-quantum cryptosystems may not be suitable for certain hardware currently used for implementing blockchain nodes. Therefore, post-quantum schemes should provide a trade-off between security and computational complexity in order to not restrict the potential hardware that may interact with the blockchain. One possibility is having gradations of key strength based on the hardware available.

Second, certain post-quantum cryptosystems generate large overheads that may impact the performance of a blockchain. To tackle this issue, future post-quantum developers will have to minimize ciphertext overhead and consider potential compression techniques.

Quantum Computing

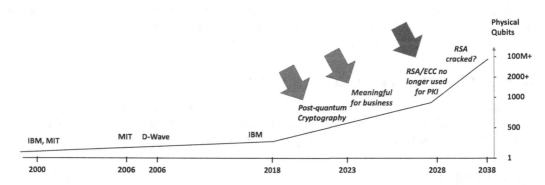

Source: Adapted from CBI Research and Gartner

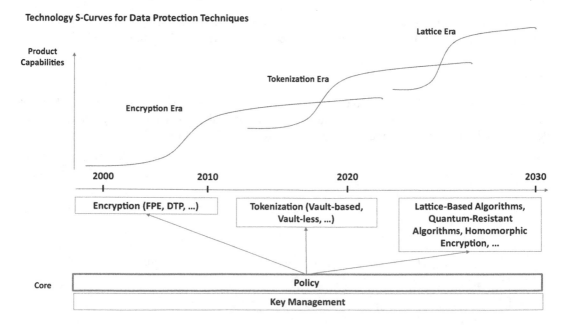

Storing Private Keys

Securely storing private keys.

These options tend to fall into hot, cold, or hardware-based storage.

- Hot Storage—copy-pasting of addresses, ever-changing whitelists, and constant 2FA rituals. Multi-sig is not protocol-agnostic (meaning it's not compatible with all blockchains) and lacks the operational flexibility to support growing teams.
- Cold Storage—Cold storage enables users to sign a transaction with their private keys in an offline environment. It takes 24–48 hours to make a transfer. not protect against credential theft.
- Hardware Wallet—if you lose the seed phrase, there is no other way of recovering your bitcoin.

Example:

The scam works like this:

The victim purchases cryptocurrency, likely for a "too good to be true" price.

The funds are sent to a multisig wallet the victim does not own but has access to. For example, the attacker may set up a 1–2 multisig wallet that lets the attacker move the funds without the victim's consent.

The attackers move the funds to a different wallet—one which the victim does not have access to. Our recommendations:

- If you are purchasing crypto, please make sure the wallet you are going to receive the funds in is a wallet that you own, a wallet that you have created that is not a multisig wallet and only you have access to it.
- If you are purchasing crypto, beware of "too good to be true" pricing or someone offering cryptocurrency at a much lower price than the current rate.

If someone tells you to create or join a multisig wallet to send you money, they are trying to scam you.

A secure messaging capability for Blockchain

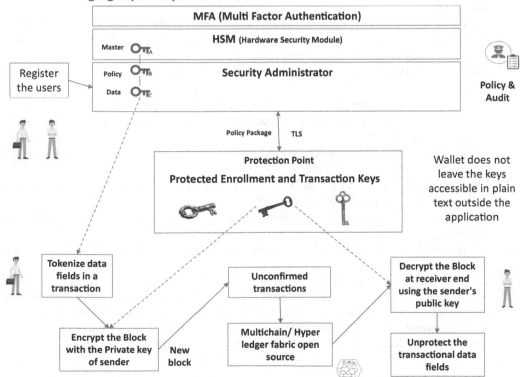

SUMMARY

We discussed Web3 Storage, Sharding and Pruning, Security Risks to Blockchain Ecosystems, Secure transaction ledgers, Blockchains in the Quantum Era, and Storing private keys.

NOTES

1. https://www.wto.org/english/res_e/booksp_e/blockchainanddlt_e.pdf
2. A Blockchain Platform for the Enterprise—Hyperledger-fabricdocs master documentation. (n.d.). Retrieved July 12, 2021, from https://hyperledger-fabric.readthedocs.io/en/release-2.2/
3. ALBREIKI, H., HABIB UR REHMAN, M., SALAH, K., & SVETINOVIC, D. (2020). Trustworth Blockchain Oracles: Review, Comparison, and Open Research Challenges. IEEE Access. 10.1109/ACCESS.2020.2992698
4. Allianz. (2021). Allianz Risk Barometer. https://www.agcs.allianz.com/news-and-insights/reports/
5. Allianz. (2021). Allianz Risk Barometer. https://www.agcs.allianz.com/news-and-insights/reports/allianz-risk-barometer.html
6. allianz-risk-barometer.html
7. Androulaki, E., Barger, A., Bortnikov, V., Christian Cachin, Christidis, K., De Caro, A., Enyeart, D.
8. Androulaki, E., Barger, A., Bortnikov, V., Christian Cachin, Christidis, K., De Caro, A., Enyeart, D., Ferris, C., Laventman, G., Manevich, Y., Muralidharan, S., Murthy, C., Nguyen, B., Sethi, M., SIngh, G., Smith, K., Sorniotti, A., Stathakopoulou, C., VukolićJuvoli, M., … Yellick, J. (2018).
9. Blockchain Oracles: Review, Comparison, and Open Research Challenges. IEEE Access. 10.1109/ACCESS.2020.2992698
10. Blockchain Provides an Alternative Trust Model, https://www.gartner.com/smarterwithgartner/cios-cant-ignore-these-5-realities-of-blockchain/
11. Blockchain Reseach Institute. https://evolutionq.com/quantum-safe-ublications/mosca_quantumproofing-the-blockchain_blockchain-research-institute.pdf
12. Blockchain with Hyperledger (ISBN: 9781788994521 ed.). Packt Publishing. https://www.packtpub.
13. Bundle of Rights, Retrieved July 15, 2021, https://en.wikipedia.org/wiki/Bundle_of_rights
14. C.-C. Yao. Protocols for secure computations (extended abstract). In 23rd FOCS, pages 160–164. IEEE Computer Society Press, Nov. 1982.
15. Carter, H. (2019). Journey to Blockchain: A Non-Technologist's Guide to the Internet of Value. BRI.
16. Chia, V., Hartel, P., Hum, Q., Ma, S., Piliouras, G., Reijsbergen, D., Staalduinen, M. v., & Szalachowski, P. (2019). Rethinking Blockchain Security: Position Paper. ArXiv:1806.04358. http://arxiv.org/abs/1806.04358
17. Cloud Security Alliance Hyperledger Fabric. http://maruyama-mitsuhiko.cocolog-nifty.com/security/2021/07/post-fdd305.html
18. Cloud Standards Customer Council 2017, Cloud Customer Architecture for API Management.
19. Conference, 1–15. 10.1145/3190508.3190538
20. Dabholkar, A., & Saraswat, V. (2019). Ripping the Fabric: Attacks and Mitigations on Hyperledger
21. Demystifying the blockchain, https://www.scrygroup.com/blog/2018-07-03/Demystifying-the-blockchain/
22. Dika, A., & Nowostawski, M. (2018). Security Vulnerabilities in Ethereum Smart Contracts.
23. Ethereum price prediction: ETH eyes $4,000 ahead of NFP data, https://www.bitcoininsider.org/article/129653/ethereum-price-prediction-eth-eyes-4000-ahead-nfp-data#:~:text=Ethereum%20and%20NFP%20data%20Ethereum%20is%20a%20blockchain,like%20Shiba%20Inu%20are%20built%20on%20Ethereum%E2%80%99s%20network

24. Ethereum Yellow Paper, https://ethereum.github.io/yellowpaper/paper.pdf
25. https://www.eublockchainforum.eu/sites/default/files/research-paper/wrks-main_1.pdf
26. European Commission. (2019). Legal and Regulatory Framework of Blockchains and Smart Contracts.
27. European Commission. (2020). 2018-2020 CONCLUSIONS AND REFLECTIONS. EU BLOCKCHAIN
28. Everything To Know About Utility Tokenization In Blockchain, https://bizzcoinhub.com/tokenization-in-blockchain/#:~:text=Tokenization%20is%20a%20method%20where%20some%20assets%20are,purchase%20or%20trade%20objects%20that%20aren%E2%80%99t%20easily%20available.
29. Fabric. Applications and Techniques in Information Security, 10th International Conference, ATIS 2019
30. Ferris, C., Laventman, G., Manevich, Y., Muralidharan, S., Murthy, C., Nguyen, B., Sethi, M., SIngh, G.
31. G. Rapier. From Yelp reviews to mango shipments: IBM's CEO on how blockchain will change the world. Business Insider, June 2017, https://www.businessinsider.com/ibm-ceo-ginni-rometty-blockchain-transactions-internet-communications-2017-6, 2017.
32. G. Zyskind, O. Nathan, and A. Pentland. Decentralizing privacy: Using blockchain to protect personal data. In IEEE Symposium on Security and Privacy Workshops, pages 180–184. IEEE Computer Society, 2015.
33. G. Zyskind, O. Nathan, and A. Pentland. Enigma: Decentralized computation platform with guaranteed privacy. CoRR, abs/1506.03471
34. Gartner. (2017). Blockchain Technology: How Security Relates to Use Cases. (ID:G00317396).
35. How blockchain will evolve until 2030 and today's hype versus reality, https://thepaypers.com/expert-opinion/how-blockchain-will-evolve-until-2030-and-todays-hype-versus-reality--1242127
36. http://arxiv.org/abs/1904.06898
37. http://ieeexplore.ieee.org/document/8666486/
38. http://www.cloud-council.org/deliverables/cloud-customer-architecture-for-api-management.htm
39. http://www.cloud-council.org/deliverables/data-residency-challenges.htm
40. https://arxiv.org/abs/2106.11210
41. https://blockchainlab.com/pdf/Hyperledger%20Whitepaper.pdf
42. Hyperledger – Open Source Blockchain Technologies. (n.d.). Hyperledger. Retrieved July 12, 2021, from https://www.hyperledger.org/
43. Hyperledger Architecture, Volume II
44. Hyperledger Fabric 2.0 Architecture Security Report, https://theblockchaintest.com/uploads/resources/CSA%20-%20Hyperledger%20Fabric%2020%20Architecture%20Security%20Report%20-%202021.pdf
45. Hyperledger fabric: a distributed operating system for permissioned blockchains. Proceedings of the Thirteenth EuroSys Conference, 1–15. 10.1145/3190508.3190538
46. Hyperledger. https://www.hyperledger.org/
47. IBM. (2020). Advancing global trade with blockchain. Institute for Business Value. https://www.ibm.com/downloads/cas/WVDE0MXG
48. Industry. https://query.prod.cms.rt.microsoft.com/cms/api/am/binary/RE1TH5G
49. International Conference on Blockchain (Blockchain), 313–320. https://doi.org/10.1109/Blockchain50366.2020.00046
50. Kademlia, https://en.wikipedia.org/wiki/Kademlia
51. Perez, D., & Livshits, B. (2020). Smart Contract Vulnerabilities:Vulnerable Does Not Imply Exploited. https://arxiv.org/pdf/1902.06710.pdf

52. Praitheeshan, P., Pan, L., Yu, J., Liu, J., & Doss, R. (2020). Security Analysis Methods on EthereumSmartContract Vulnerabilities — A Survey. https://arxiv.org/pdf/1908.08605.pdf
53. S. Nakamoto. Bitcoin: A peer-to-peer electronic cash system. https://bitcoin.org/bitcoin.pdf, 2008.
54. Security Controls for Blockchain Applications, Deloitte, https://www2.deloitte.com/ch/en/pages/risk/articles/security-controls-for-blockchain-applications.html

Section III

Data Quality

8 Metadata and The Provenance of Data

INTRODUCTION

In this chapter, we will discuss metadata as "data that provides information about other data", but not the content of the data, such as the text of a message or the image itself.

Types of Metadata

There are many distinct types of Metadata, including descriptive metadata, structural metadata, administrative metadata, reference metadata, statistical metadata, and legal metadata.

DATA CLASSIFICATION

Data classification is the process of organizing information assets using an agreed-upon categorization, taxonomy, or ontology. The result is typically a large repository of metadata useful for making further decisions or the application of a "tag" to an object to facilitate the use and governance of the data, including the application of controls during its life cycle.

Why This Is Important?

Data classification enables an effective and efficient prioritization for data governance, and business impact data classification can be used to support a wide range of use cases, for example:

- Applying data security controls, for example, DLP and EDRM
- Privacy compliance
- Risk mitigation
- Master data and application data management
- Data stewardship

Discover, Understand, and Leverage All Your Enterprise Data

Organizations rely on trusted data to make the best possible business decisions. But you're likely inundated with too much of a good thing. Data volumes are exploding. The number of data consumers is growing. Types of connected devices are proliferating. You have more data-driven business priorities. And your data is increasingly stored off-site in the cloud. How can your organization find all of this data, let alone harness it to support your business transformation? An enterprise-class catalog of catalogs helps you discover, understand, and leverage all your enterprise data. It goes to the heart of today's data-driven enterprises.

Why You Need a Catalog of Catalogs?

A data catalog that's limited to a specific tool, system, or use case can provide value, but you likely need to manage data across a wide range of enterprise data systems. These include

- On-premises databases and enterprise data warehouses
- Cloud data warehouses and cloud data lakes
- Business intelligence tools, such as Tableau, Microsoft Power BI, IBM Cognos, and others
- Extract, Transform, Load (ETL) tools for data integration
- Applications, such as Salesforce, Workday, SAP, and others

DOI: 10.1201/9781003254928-11

- Ecosystems including Microsoft Azure, AWS, and Google Cloud Platform. An enterprise-class catalog of catalogs complements your system-specific or use-case specific catalogs with universal metadata connectivity to all your data sources. Rather than requiring you to use a catalog of catalogs for some things and a specialized catalog for others, the catalog of catalogs can pull in metadata from all of your systems and catalogs. It thereby gives you a centralized, comprehensive view of all your data and end-to-end data lineage across your systems, cloud, and on-premises, and tools and ecosystems. You also benefit from standard cataloging functionality across your data, including artificial intelligence/machine learning-powered automated data curation, collaboration, social curation, lineage, and more.

DATA INTELLIGENCE

An Example of How Collibra Enables Data Intelligence:

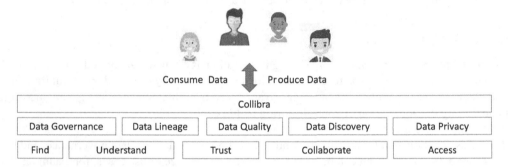

Source: Adapted from Collibra

A DATA MARKETPLACE

Source: Adapted from Collibra

DATA MONETIZATION

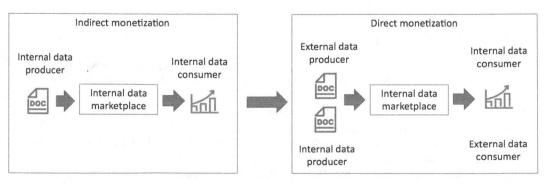

Source: Adapted from Collibra

BUILD A METADATA REPOSITORY

It's far easier to manage, categorize, segment, and secure your data if you can access and govern your metadata. For example, let's say you want to apply access controls to all of your customer data. Once you have your metadata in one place, you can segment data-bearing "customer" tags and apply specific protections to it.

You can even automate this process to avoid the time-consuming task of vetting each and every one of the data entities within the scope of your project.

As a result, scaling your project becomes a much simpler task. Once you've taught your security system what certain metadata tags mean, then it can protect new data entities automatically as and when they flow into your system.

Nurture collaboration Data governance isn't a one-person, or even a one-team job.

Although technology alone can't bring your people together, you'll need to provide stakeholders with a platform to share their knowledge of data lineage, business processes, and policies. Crucially, you need a system that can provide role-relevant experiences for both the business and IT. If a subject matter expert or line of business owner can't easily use your tool and understand how data governance relates to business processes, then they're unlikely to adopt it, or evangelize it to the rest of their team. At the same time, IT must be able to connect the dots between what the business wants and their role in implementing the systems and rules to automate and scale data governance policies and processes.

Email or spreadsheet-based systems simply can't support this type of teamwork.

Crucial data, documents, and files will end up stranded on individual computers or buried on disconnected applications.

A centralized data governance console, on the other hand, can help you get everyone on the same page. These tools connect data lineage to business processes, allow you to document policies, and align workflows across your business so that everyone is aware of their role in your strategy and how their use of data is aligned with the data governance standards and norms of the business importance. There's no getting around it, executing the first project in your data governance program is going to be big—you're breaking new ground, forming new relationships, and challenging what's gone before. You'll be transforming the way your business works, and transformation requires energy and perseverance.

But the outcome of your project will unquestionably be worth the effort.

Data governance has never been so important and valuable to your business.

And even on a small scale, it'll make your data more secure, trusted, and relevant so that everyone can leverage its full value.

Once you've demonstrated the value of data governance to the rest of your business, you can start rolling it out across the enterprise and laying the foundation for the data-driven digital transformation that will change the course of your business forever.

We hope that the advice and guidance we've shared in this eBook will help you along this journey.

You're about to start down the road to better quality data, more efficient processes, and data-driven digital transformation.

Data Asset Discovery and Lineage across different sources:

Source: Adapted from SAP

Examples of Metadata Connectivity with EDC:

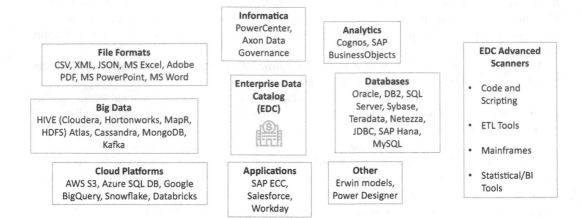

Source: Adapted from SAP

Enterprise Content Management: Find, Access, Discover, Ask

Source: Adapted from Wikipedia

SENSITIVE DATA MAPPING

Your organization needs to safeguard personally identifiable information (PII) and protected health information (PHI) data and comply with data privacy regulations such as the General Data Protection Regulation (GDPR) and the California Consumer Privacy Act (CCPA).

Intelligent data discovery leverages the power of advanced ML to identify sensitive data—it automatically evaluates and scores data that in combination can identify data subjects.

End-to-end data lineage and impact analysis capabilities then identify how sensitive data proliferates across repositories to support security and privacy compliance requirements. These capabilities can determine both upstream and downstream movement as well as related metadata, such as the specific type of data, process, protection status, and location of the data, to evaluate if violations have occurred.

For example, if personal data moves from a source to a target across geographic boundaries, you could be violating data sovereignty regulations. Or if data onboarded for billing processes is proliferated to other departments or locations for marketing processes, you could be violating privacy regulations. Intelligent data governance capabilities then notify policy or process stakeholders for remediation.

Domain Discovery

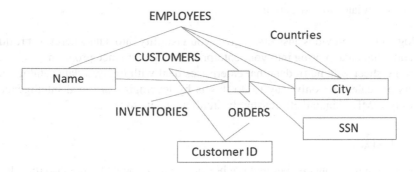

Source: Adapted from Informatica

Data Similarity and Clustering:

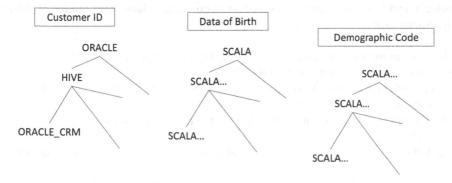

Source: Adapted from Informatica

DISCOVERING AND UNDERSTANDING RELEVANT DATA

A successful data governance program needs to include two very critical pieces: discovering and understanding relevant data. Your governance initiatives won't get far if they don't include these two essential processes.

However, the volume and variety of data that modern enterprises must govern pose a challenge. Relevant data may reside on-premises, in the cloud, or in multi-cloud environments.

And while data often exists in silos (walled off by boundaries such as business function, geography, or source), organizations must increasingly govern data holistically—whether to seize new opportunities or mitigate risk. For example, data-centric regulations such as the EU General Data Protection Regulation (GDPR) and California Consumer Privacy Act (CCPA) require an enterprise-wide view of customer personal data.

The degree to which you are successful at discovery and inventory, therefore, underpins the success of your data governance program. Let's look at these two processes more closely.

Discovering your data: Any data governance initiative needs to answer some simple questions:

- What data do I have?
- Where does it reside?
- What processes does it touch?
- What is its quality?

- Who's responsible for it?
- Where does it come from?
- What data is related to? And so on

A data catalog solution provides answers. It gives you visibility into data wherever it resides, so you can understand what data to bring into your enterprise data governance program.

But given the sheer volume of data that enterprises deal with today, a data catalog must deliver these answers at scale. The only way to do this is by leveraging artificial intelligence (AI) and machine learning (ML). Manual efforts simply aren't adequate to the task.

AI and Data Lineage

Data lineage is not a new concept, but modern business requirements far outstrip the siloed, limited features of the past. Organizations need enterprise scale, endto-end visibility, and AI-powered, intelligent capabilities for lineage that support any datadriven initiative. Before you can use data effectively, you need to understand it. Data lineage enables you to understand where data originates and how it changes over the entire data lifecycle. When you understand where your data comes from, who's using it, and how, you have the foundation to power any data-driven initiative. And you can answer questions like:

- What data in my enterprise needs to be brought into compliance with regulations like the General Data Protection Regulation (GDPR)?
- What data should we migrate to a cloud data warehouse—and which users will be impacted by the move?
- Where should our data scientists look for trusted data they can use in advanced analytics projects?
- Which data sources should we use for developing new customer experience initiatives?

The demand for data lineage comes from both technical and business users, including data architects, data engineers, data stewards, analysts and data scientists, as well as business managers, compliance professionals, and technical specialists. Data lineage empowers all of these users by providing them with a deeper understanding of their data and improving their confidence in the data. Lineage views at different levels—such as the business, logical, and detailed physical levels—provide the right level of detail for each type of user while allowing them to drill down. In addition, lineage helps improve collaboration by linking business views of data with underlying logical and detail information.

Data lineage gives you a visual representation of how data flows from its origin to its destination, showing the different processes the data undergoes and their dependencies as well as how data is transformed along the way. The problem is, today's data landscape is extremely complex. Data comes from many disparate sources across the enterprise, including on-premises and multi-cloud. An enterprise may have hundreds or thousands of data sources and millions of data objects.

Given the volume and scale of data today, it's virtually impossible for organizations to trace data's journey through their systems' infrastructure using manual processes. Many tools and technologies offer some limited lineage capabilities. But they provide a siloed view of data within an individual source. For instance, the lineage you may have for Hadoop provides visibility only as far as your Hadoop clusters. If you're relying on lineage at a datasource level, you have at best a patchwork view of your enterprise data.

For these reasons, enterprises are turning to the next evolution of data lineage: powered by AI and ML, with broad metadata connectivity to any data source, with the ability to drill down to a granular view or summarize at a high level for a business analyst, and the ability to automatically stitch together end-to-end lineage across cloud and on-premises.

For today's organizations, lineage is critical to address a wide range of data-driven business requirements. Let's examine the most important use cases in more detail. Regulatory compliance data lineage is critical for responding to regulators' increasingly frequent requests for granular transparency across a variety of financial regulations, such as the Basel Committee on Banking Supervision's standard number 239 (BCBS239), the Markets in Financial Instruments Directive (MiFID II), and the Comprehensive Capital Analysis and Review (CCAR). It also supports compliance with privacy and governance guidelines such as the GDPR, California Consumer Privacy Act (CCPA), and US Foundations for Federal Evidence-Based Policymaking Act. While individual regulations have many different provisions, compliance with all of these regulations requires you to provide reports and demonstrate their accuracy by showing how the key metrics in those reports were computed.

Lineage enables you to demonstrate where your data originated, trace its journey through your organization's systems, and show how it changed along the way. And the benefits of data lineage don't stop there. Because data lineage reveals any inconsistencies or inaccuracies in your analysis, it enables you to proactively identify and fix gaps in required data. You can also employ data lineage to harmonize data across multiple regulations by discovering different datasets that contain the same data, so you can reduce duplication.

Analytics data lineage improves understanding of your data and increases confidence in the data, leading to better business decisions. Data lineage helps both technologists and business analysts understand what data their organization holds, where it is located, and what it is used for. Because you can see where data from your most critical reports is coming from, data lineage helps you determine what data is most important for your business, so you can take appropriate measures to control its availability, quality, and security.

Cloud Modernization

As you migrate your on-premises data warehouses to the cloud to gain greater agility, flexibility, and scalability, you need to be strategic about how you migrate the data and manage the impact of migration.

Data lineage shows you where data originates and how it moves through your organization to its destination. You can view this data movement in high-level business terms or drill down to expand the lineage path to show columns and lineage diagram metrics. These capabilities enable your IT team to easily inspect source data warehouse schema structures to identify which structures need to be modified. Impact analysis tells you how data is used, what is dependent on it, how the migration will impact data assets, resources, and users, and the cost and benefits of moving certain data assets and workloads to the cloud. After the migration, end-to-end views into data lineage enable you to understand the data before and after it's moved to make sure that structure changes have been made correctly.

Customer Experience

Customers today are often more concerned with a business's experience than with the product's features or price. Delivering the experience customers expect requires your organization to have a 360-degree view of the customer and an end-to-end picture of each customer's journey and experience with the company each step. Master data management (MDM) is essential to delivering a single source of truth for all your business-critical customer data. An AI-powered data lineage solution helps identify the data that should be part of your master data.

Data lineage also provides insight into the quality of the data and how it's used, so that you can accomplish your customer experience goals faster.

Change Management and Impact Analysis

Reports and applications often include data from multiple sources. Changes to any of these sources can come in many forms: semantic changes, business logic changes, data model changes, process changes, and more. Data lineage is key to enabling effective change management in both business intelligence and application development contexts. By using the data lineage solution to perform "What If" analysis on potential changes on granular column-level data with business logic, you can understand how the change will potentially impact users, business processes, and reports.

Operational Efficiency

Data lineage can simplify your efforts to optimize your data footprint and reduce the costs and risks of data management. You can use lineage to identify and delete duplicate data, discover and deal with data silos, and locate and remove unused data and systems. Data lineage also supports and reduces the cost of data modernization and migration programs. By eliminating redundant data and providing a clear view of how data moves and changes within your organization, data lineage helps you reduce costs, improve operational efficiency, and provide the business with faster access to trusted data.

Data Security

Data breaches and disclosures of sensitive data come at a high cost. For example, the GDPR sets fines of up to 10 million euros or up to 2% of your global turnover for the fiscal year preceding a data breach, whichever is higher. Your organization must protect that data to meet regulatory requirements and reduce risk. Using data lineage, you can see exactly how your sensitive data flows throughout your organization so that you can ensure that you have proper controls in place every step of the way.

Data Governance

Data governance is the overall management of the ownership, quality, availability, and security of data used across your enterprise.

By clarifying where data is, who uses it, what they use it for, and how it is transformed, data lineage allows your organization to hand data ownership over to the relevant stakeholders who can ensure that your use of critical data complies with internal policies and external regulations. Data lineage enhances quality by tracking data elements, as they flow across the organization to ensure that business rules exist where expected, calculations and transformations are correct, and system inputs and outputs are compatible. By showing you what is your most critical data and where it flows, data lineage enables you to put in place solutions to maintain data availability and enhance security

Rabobank, a Dutch multinational banking and financial services company, moved from manual data lineage to an automated solution as part of an enterprise-wide digital transformation strategy. Rabobank uses an AI-powered data lineage solution through Informatica Enterprise Data Catalog to create business value in four essential areas:

- Regulatory requirements: Using end-to-end lineage to comply with BCBS 239 and other regulations
- Data quality management: Reducing time spent in root cause analysis of data quality issues
- Change management: Using lineage to view the impact of proposed changes to the data integration environment
- Data integration: Creating a better understanding of what the data means, where it comes from, where it's used, and how it's been transformed. Today, Rabobank is able to derive business lineage of its data assets through the Enterprise Data Catalog interface with an easy-to-use lineage view, enhancing confidence in data and promoting regulatory compliance.

AN AI-POWERED DATA CATALOG

Data governance should be designed to reduce the time-consuming manual processes that make it difficult or impossible to scale with the rise in the volume and variety of data. It should also accommodate the expansion in the number of end-users who expect easy, on-demand access to democratized data. By leveraging AI to automate and streamline processes like data discovery and cataloging, and adding rich business context to the data, data governance frees up talented personnel to focus on deeper analyses and higher-value processes.

An AI-powered data catalog provides a machine learning-based discovery engine to scan and catalog data assets across the enterprise, whether on-premises, in the cloud, or big data anywhere. Look for AI-powered auto discovery, enrichment, and curation capabilities that:

- Automatically identify and classify entities in structured and unstructured data
- Automatically detect similarity between datasets, and understand relationships and dependencies
- Automatically associate business terms and definitions to physical datasets.

While intelligent data catalogs have the ability to automatically scan and catalog assets across the enterprise, it's not enough to just provide visibility into all data. Your catalog should also guide users to the most relevant and trusted data for their business needs.

AI-Powered Data Catalog Components:

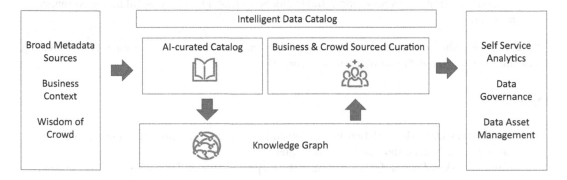

Source: Adapted from Informatica

Essential Capabilities

To support data governance programs that deliver trusted, governed, and protected data, make sure your data catalog solution provides these capabilities.

An enterprise data catalog not only supports data governance, but also provides a foundation for any initiative that depends upon trusted, governed, and protected data. Here's how an intelligent data catalog enables success.

1. Broad and deep metadata connectivity
   Successful data governance depends upon the ability to discover data by scanning and cataloging data assets across the enterprise.
2. Lineage and impact analysis
   To govern data effectively, you need to understand where data is located, who owns it, where it's coming from, and how it's being used. An effective data catalog will be able to provide a business-friendly view of the end-to-end lineage, so business users can understand the provenance of critical data. And by tying certain data.
3. Data quality monitoring
   At the end of the day, your data needs to be consistently trustworthy. Having visibility into the quality of your data is a must for any successful enterprise data governance program.

4. AI-powered scalability

Achieving enterprise scale is impractical without an AI-driven platform that can streamline processes, such as automated curation, tagging and classification, automatic detection of similar data, and automatic association of business terms to technical data assets. With thousands of datasets, each containing hundreds of columns and thousands of business terms, manual identification and tagging would be an impractical alternative. The results may have little or no value if it takes weeks or months to complete a data discovery process or generate a report.

To streamline the otherwise tedious process of associating technical metadata with business terms and policies, an AI-powered data catalog solution can automatically associate specific business terms and policies with the relevant datasets, a necessity for achieving and maintaining enterprise scale. Data stewards can focus on higher-value analyses of AI-curated datasets to deliver far more value.

5. Collaboration

In addition to harnessing the power of AI for scalability, a data catalog should harness the collective knowledge and subject matter expertise of all stakeholders in contact with the data. This includes IT architects, data owners, data stewards, and data consumers.

Collaboration across all of these stakeholders is critical to a successful data governance program.

The data catalog should enable IT to better support business requests and requirements by providing a holistic view of your data and rich business context.

Data Mesh

- The Gartner Data Mesh Network was coined in 2016 around building a metadata-driven data network built on data and use case patterns.
- Thoughtworks (Zhamak Dehghani) published a perspective on Data Mesh in 2019 around
- building decentralized, domain-driven data assets as products, leveraging a federatedcomputational governance model and shared data infrastructure.
- Based on the concept of placing the responsibility for the data with the people in closest proximity to the data.
- Delegates responsibility for specific data sets to members of a business domain that have the subject matter expertise to know what the data is supposed to represent and how it should be used.

Layers

- A data mesh consists of a connectivity layer to manage and support data access.
- A domain-driven analytical data architecture where data is treated as a product and owned by teams that most intimately know and consume the data.
- By decomposing the business into business domains, organizations narrow the impact of continuous change.
- Business data domains are tactical considerations for data governance while stewarding those business domains as cross-organizational assets becomes the most difficult aspect of governing data.

The following principles define Data Mesh:

- Domain-oriented, decentralized data ownership, and architecture.
- Data as a Product (DaaP)—Business domains defined by Service Level Agreements (SLA) and quality goals.

- Self-service data infrastructure as a platform.
- Focuses on federated-computational governance (overarching rules and regulation), including automation, classification, and learning from a perspective of curation (selecting, organizing, and looking-after).

CONSENT AND PREFERENCE MANAGEMENT PLATFORMS

Consent and preference management platforms consolidate end-user choices regarding how their personal data should be handled. Choices are synchronized across legacy, active and incoming repositories, both on-premises and in the cloud. The intent is to extend visibility and control to website visitors, allowing them to determine and change how much of their data to expose, to whom, and for what purpose. This also empowers marketers to respect customers' choices with a minimum of manual overhead.

WHY THIS IS IMPORTANT

A global wave of legislation and technology changes rapidly transforms norms and protections for personal data collected digitally. Organizations that fail to keep up with these changes now face substantial material risk. The result is an imperative for organizations to invest in consent and preference management platforms (CPMPs) to comply with new laws, preserve essential capabilities, and demonstrate to customers and stakeholders that they care about privacy.

METADATA

Organizations rely on trusted data to make the best possible business decisions. But you're likely inundated with too much of a good thing.

Data volumes are exploding. The number of data consumers is growing. Types of connected devices are proliferating. You have more datadriven business priorities. And your data is increasingly stored off-site in the cloud.

How can your organization find all of this data, let alone harness it to support your business transformation?

An enterprise-class catalog of catalogs helps you discover, understand, and leverage all your enterprise data. It goes to the heart of today's data-driven enterprises.

If your catalog is limited, you're essentially driving your business with blinders on. You see only a slice of the data you have—and your ability to leverage that data is correspondingly limited.

Many tools and solutions come with their own data catalog to inventory the data they store.

Other data catalogs have evolved to discover data in specific data domains or ecosystems, such as Amazon Web Services (AWS) or Microsoft Azure. You may already have a data catalog for your BI tool or cloud platform.

However, these data catalogs have a number of fundamental limitations. In particular, they're:

- System-Specific—If your catalog can't discover and trace data across all the various tools, applications, and processes in your organization, you're missing vast swathes of enterprise data. Can the data catalog for your cloud platform also give you visibility into the data in your Salesforce instance and your on-premises ERP system? For many data catalogs, visibility ends at the borders of a particular system.
- Use-Case Specific—Your organization may need your data catalog to support multiple use cases. These might include anything from analytics to data governance, Customer 360 initiatives, AI and machine learning projects for advanced analytics, compliance requirements, and more.

- Limited in Lineage Capabilities—Data lineage describes how data flows from its origin to its destination, indicating the different processes the data undergo, their dependencies, as well as how data is transformed along the way.

But many catalogs aren't able to trace lineage across systems or once data move from on-premises to the cloud.

- Limited in Metadata Capabilities—Many catalogs are able to scan certain types of metadata, but lack comprehensive capabilities. If your catalog isn't able to scan across a wide range of business, technical, operational, and usage metadata, it won't discover all your data.
- Not Scalable—Your catalog may be limited in the number of objects it can scan. You will be unable to view and manage all your enterprise data if your enterprise catalog cannot easily scan millions or tens of millions of objects.

The only way to overcome these limitations is with an enterprise-class catalog of catalogs.

A data catalog that's limited to a specific tool, system, or use case can provide value, but you likely need to manage data across a wide range of enterprise data systems. These include:

- On-premises databases and enterprise data warehouses
- Cloud data warehouses and cloud data lakes
- Business intelligence tools, such as Tableau

Microsoft Power BI, IBM Cognos, and others

- Extract, Transform, Load (ETL) tools for data integration
- Applications, such as Salesforce, Workday, SAP, and others
- Ecosystems including Microsoft Azure, AWS, and Google Cloud Platform

An enterprise-class catalog of catalogs complements your system-specific or usecase specific catalogs with universal metadata connectivity to all your data sources.

Rather than requiring you to use a catalog of catalogs for some things and a specialized catalog for others, the catalog of catalogs can pull in metadata from all of your systems and catalogs. It thereby gives you a centralized, comprehensive view of all your data, as well as end-to-end data lineage, across your systems, across cloud and on-premises, and across tools and ecosystems.

You also benefit from standard cataloging functionality across all of your data that includes artificial intelligence/machine learning-powered automated data curation, collaboration, social curation, lineage, and more.

Some Vendors

Big 5 CSP KMS Comparison
Presented below is an overview of four key public cloud service providers' KMS Offerings.

Alibaba Cloud

Alibaba has one managed service that is relevant to this document.

Alibaba Cloud KMS Alibaba Cloud Key Management Service (KMS) provides secure and compliant key management and cryptography services to help customers/users/organizations encrypt and protect sensitive data assets. KMS is integrated with a wide range of Alibaba Cloud services to allow customers/users/organizations to encrypt data across the cloud and to control its distributed environment.

AWS

KMS AWS Key Management Service (AWS KMS) is a managed service that makes it easy for customers to create and control the encryption keys used to encrypt the data. It uses hardware security modules (HSM) that have been validated under FIPS 140-2 or are in the process of being validated. AWS KMS allows users to manage customer master keys (CMK) and use them for various cryptographic operations. A CMK is a logical representation of a master key. CMKs are used for managing data encryption keys (DEK) that are used for encrypting data, including large amounts of data and other data encryption keys.

CloudHSM AWS CloudHSM is a cloud-based HSM that manages encryption keys on the AWS Cloud using FIPS 140-2 Level 3 validated HSMs. Customers receive dedicated, single-tenant access to each HSM instance in their cluster.

Each HSM instance appears as a network resource in their virtual cloud network. AWS provides HSM cluster management APIs.

Azure

Azure has two managed services that are relevant to this document.

Azure Dedicated HSM is an Azure service that provides cryptographic key storage in Azure using dedicated HSMs. It is the ideal solution for customers who require FIPS 140-2 Level 3-validated Thales Luna devices and complete and exclusive control of the HSM appliance. It is also suited for applications which need Common Criteria EAL 4+, NITES, or Brazil ITE and needs cryptography other than RSA and ECC. Azure Key Vault Azure Key Vault helps customers with secrets management, key management, and certificate management. Secrets and keys are safeguarded by Azure, using industry-standard algorithms, key lengths, and HSMs. The HSMs used are Federal Information Processing Standards (FIPS) 140-2 Level 2-validated.

Authentication is done via Azure Active Directory. Authorization may be done via role-based access control (RBAC) or key vault access policy.

RBAC is used when users deal with the management of the vaults, and key vault access policy is used when they are attempting to access data stored in a vault. This service has native integration with a large number of other Azure services.

Google Cloud

Google has two managed services that are relevant to this document.

GCP Cloud KMS GCP Cloud KMS is a scalable cloud-hosted key management service that lets customers manage cryptographic keys for their cloud services the same way they do on premises. It supports AES256, RSA 2048, RSA 3072, RSA 4096, EC P256, and EC P384 cryptographic keys. Cloud KMS is integrated with Cloud IAM and Cloud Audit Logging so that customers can manage permissions on individual keys and monitor how these are used. Cloud Key Management Service stores cryptographic keys in a hierarchical structure designed for useful and elegant access control management. Cloud KMS has a built-in 24-hour delay for key material destruction in order to prevent accidental or malicious data loss. Cloud KMS can also generate HSM-backed keys with GCP Cloud HSM.

GCP Cloud EKM GCP Cloud External Key Manager (EKM) is in early access and allows to encrypt data with encryption keys that are stored and managed in a third-party key management system.

IBM

IBM Cloud HSM IBM Cloud HSM Luna 7.0 from Thales protects the cryptographic infrastructure of some of the most securityconscious organizations in the world by securely managing, processing and storing cryptographic keys inside a tamper-resistant, tamperevident device.

IBM Key Protect IBM Key Protect is a cloud-based security service that provides life cycle management for encryption keys that are used in IBM Cloud services and non-IBM cloud applications.

Key Protect provides roots of trust, backed by a FIPS-140-2 Level 3 HSM. It supports importing the customer's root of trust encryption keys into the service. It can generate, store, and manage customer keys with a secure, application-friendly, cloud-based key management solution for encryption keys. When keys are deleted, they can never be recovered, and any data that is encrypted under those keys cannot be recovered. All programmatic interfaces are secured by TLS and mutual authentication.

THE PROVENANCE OF DATA

The provenance of data is a description of how the data came into being or was derived, according to "The provenance of data".

An Example of Tracking System-Level Provenance with SPADE:

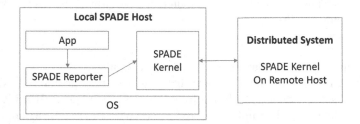

Source: Adapted from CSI

PROVENANCE SKETCHES

An Example of a Provenance Graph:

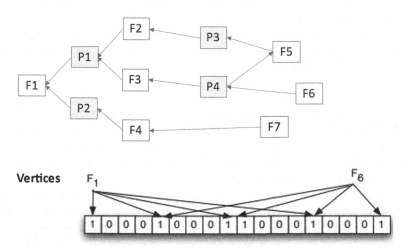

Source: Adapted from CSI

Matrix Filter

We introduce the matrix filter, a new data structure to probabilistically represent graph connectivity (or any other data that can be stored in a matrix). Whereas the original matrix may have a size of $\mu \times \mu$ for an arbitrary μ, the filter only uses $O(m \times m)$ space for a fixed m, thereby providing a compact representation of the matrix.

A matrix filter consists of (a) a row array of m bits, (b) a column array of m 2 bits, and (c) k independent hash functions $\{h1,\ldots,hk\}$, each of which has a range of $\{1,\ldots,m\}$. Further, the Ith bit bi of the row array defined in (a) is associated with the I th set of m bits in the column array defined in (b).

SPADE's Use of Matrix Filters

To collect the provenance of data created by a distributed application, SPADE is deployed on all the hosts where the application executes. Each instance operates independently, creating its own matrix filter to represent the provenance graph for the host on which it resides. Detailed provenance metadata in the form of process, file artifact, and network artifact vertices are collected in a local provenance store.

Intra-host provenance queries can be resolved using these provenance stores. What remains then is to determine the cross-host provenance relationships, which are captured by the set of network artifact vertices in a distributed provenance graph. Hence, the matrix filter on each host is used to store the set S of edges between the network artifact vertices and their ancestor vertices that are also network artifacts. Each network artifact is stored in the row array of the host's matrix filter. Its ancestor network artifact vertices are stored in the corresponding column array locations. This includes ancestors on the same host as well as on other hosts:

An Example of Distributed Data Provenance:

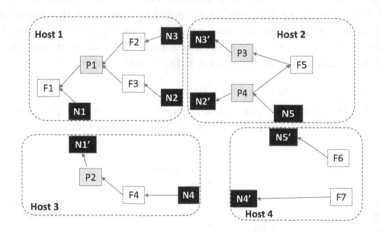

Source: Adapted from CSI

An Erosion of Anonymity

As digital resources become more and more critical to us, they're being linked together more tightly. Although we haven't hit yet a point where everything is integrated under a single account, we can see where things are headed based on what's already happened—specifically when it comes to using Facebook and Google accounts as a gateway to many different platforms.

DIFFERENTIALLY PRIVATE SYNTHETIC DATA

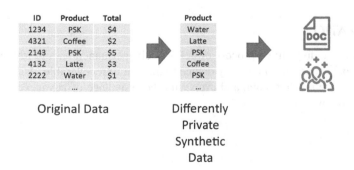

Source: Adapted from Collibra

Use Cases and Utility

Differentially private synthetic data has a huge advantage over other approaches for private data analysis: as shown in the figure, it allows analysts to use any tool or workflow to process the data.

Differently Private Synthetic Data

The primary challenge of differentially private synthetic data is accuracy. Constructing accurate differentially private synthetic data turns out to be extremely challenging in practice. As a rule of thumb, a purpose-built differentially private analysis, like the ones described in previous posts, will generally yield better accuracy than the same analysis on synthetic data.

On the other hand, a high degree of accuracy is not essential for every use case. Sometimes rough accuracy is enough to provide you with the insights and trends that you need to meet your objectives. Differentially private synthetic data can be an excellent solution in these scenarios.

Generating Synthetic Data

Conceptually, all techniques for generating synthetic data—privacy-preserving or not—start by building a probabilistic model of the underlying population from which the original data was sampled. Then, this model is used to generate new data. Suppose the model is an accurate representation of the population. In that case, the newly generated data will retain all the properties of that population, but each generated data point will represent a "fake" individual who doesn't actually exist.

Software Tools: Marginal Distributions

Imagine that we'd like to generate synthetic sales data for our pumpkin spice latte company. One way to accomplish this is using a differentially private marginal distribution:

Original Data				Histogram			Noisy Histogram	
ID	Product	Total		Product	Count		Product	Count
1234	PSK	4		PSK	54		PSK	55.3
4321	Coffee	2		Coffee	34		Coffee	34.7
2143	PSK	5		PSK	23		PSK	23.3
4132	Latte	3		Latte	12		Latte	12.9
2222	Water	1		Water	87		Water	87.2
	...			...			...	

Source: Adapted from Collibra

Now, we can use the one-way marginal to generate a "fake purchase" using weighted randomness. We pick a drink type at random, with the randomness weighted according to the one-way marginal we have generated. In the example, 60.8% of the generated purchases should be pumpkin spice lattes, 24.1% should be lattes, and 15.0% should be regular coffees.

DATA SANITIZATION

Data sanitization is the disciplined process of deliberately, permanently, and irreversibly removing or destroying the data stored on a memory device to make it unrecoverable. A device that has been sanitized has no usable residual data, and even with the assistance of advanced forensic tools, the data will never be recovered.

SUMMARY

We discussed different types of metadata as "data that provides information about other data".

NOTES

1. "A Guardian Guide to your Metadata". theguardian.com. Guardian News and Media Limited. 12 June 2013. Archived from the original on 6 March 2016.
2. "ADEO Imaging: TIFF Metadata". Archived from the original on 17 May 2013. Retrieved 20 May 2013.
3. "An Architecture for Information in Digital Libraries". Archived from the original on 27 March 2017. Retrieved 10 May 2017.
4. "Best Practices for Structural Metadata". University of Illinois. 15 December 2010. Archived from the original on 24 June 2016. Retrieved 17 June 2016.
5. "Data Catalog Vocabulary (DCAT) - Version 2". w3.org. 4 February 2020. Retrieved 23 November 2020.
6. "DCMI Specifications". Dublincore.org. 14 December 2009. Archived from the original on 17 August 2013. Retrieved 17 August 2013.
7. "Dublin Core Metadata Element Set, Version 1.1". Dublincore.org. Archived from the original on 16 August 2013. Retrieved 17 August 2013.
8. "Geospatial Metadata—Federal Geographic Data Committee". www.fgdc.gov. Retrieved 10 October 2019.
9. "How To Copyright Your Photos With Metadata". Guru Camera. gurucamera.com. 21 May 2016. Archived from the original on 30 June 2016.
10. "ISO 15836:2009 - Information and documentation - The Dublin Core metadata element set". Iso.org. 18 February 2009. Archived from the original on 27 March 2014. Retrieved 17 August 2013.
11. "ISO 25964-1:2011(en)". ISO.org. Archived from the original on 17 June 2016.
12. "ISO/IEC 11179-1:2004 Information technology - Metadata registries (MDR) - Part 1: Framework". Iso.org. 18 March 2009. Archived from the original on 17 January 2012. Retrieved 23 December 2011.
13. "ISO/IEC 11179-3:2013 Information technology-Metadata registries - Part 3: Registry metamodel and basic attributes". iso.org. 2014.
14. The provenance of dat,a http://www.csl.sri.com/users/gehani/papers/DPDM-2013.Sketch. pdf#:~:text=The%20provenance%20of%20data%20is%20a%20description%20of,can%20 audit%20events%2C%20read%20logs%2C%20and%20answerprovenance-related%20 questions
15. "Metadata = Surveillance". Archived from the original on 21 June 2016. Retrieved 6 June 2016.

9 Data Security and Quality

INTRODUCTION

In this chapter, we will discuss privacy-enhancing computation, differential privacy, the science of reidentifying data, attacks on privacy, deidentification technique choices, and secure multiparty computation (SMPC), and homomorphic encryption.

DATA QUALITY MODELS

Measuring data quality is a complex issue, and ARX supports multiple models that can be used as objective functions for optimizing the output data of an anonymization process. Cell-oriented and attribute-oriented models can be parameterized with different aggregate functions, which define how the individual measures will be compiled into a global measure for the overall dataset. The following aggregate functions are available:

- Rank
- Geometric mean
- Arithmetic mean
- Sum
- Maximum

Cell-Oriented General-Purpose Models

Granularity/loss: This measure summarizes the degree to which transformed attribute values cover the original domain of an attribute.

Attribute-Oriented General-Purpose Models

This model quantifies the loss of information based on mutual information that can be obtained about the original values of variables in the input dataset by observing the values of variables in the output dataset.

Record-Oriented General-Purpose Models

This model estimates data quality, but it does not take into account the actual attribute values in the output dataset.

Entropy-Based Model: This Model Has Been Proposed Here

Transformation Models
Supported Transformation Methods
    ARX supports a variety of common data transformation models, which can also be combined with each other.

1. Global and local transformation schemes
2. Value generalization

DOI: 10.1201/9781003254928-12

3. Random sampling
4. Record, attribute, and cell suppression
5. Microaggregation
6. Categorization
7. Graph databases

DATA QUALITY

DATA QUALITY SOLUTIONS

Data management solutions, augmented data quality, driven by metadata and AI, is a key dynamic driving the data quality solutions market. Leading vendors' augmented capabilities provide greater insights and automation, according to Gartner.

The data quality management practice has been maturing in recent years, and the vendor landscape is focused on addressing many of the market requirements. It covers much more than just technology. It includes workflow, roles, collaboration, and processes (such as those for monitoring, reporting, and remediating data quality issues). Gartner also sees end-user demand expanding toward broader capabilities that span data management and D&A governance.

STORING DATA

DISTRIBUTED FILE SYSTEMS AND OBJECT STORAGE

By 2025, 40% of infrastructure and operations (I&O) leaders will implement at least one hybrid cloud storage capability, up from 15% in 2021.

By 2025, 60% of the global unstructured data storage capacity will be deployed as software-defined storage (SDS), up from less than 25% in 2021.

Data Fabric

- Empowers data users to access data with improved efficiency and effectiveness.
- Eliminates many of the complexities that result from attempting to access data silos.
- The goal is to democratize and fully exploit and leverage the most important of data resources.
- The act of reducing complexity requires consistency and standardization that can only be addressed through adequate governance and formalized accountability for data management practices.
- Streamlines and incorporates next-gen enterprise data management (EDM).
- Democratizes data in a timely manner across hybrid, multi-cloud environments.
- Data Fabric is an architecture that relieves physical limitations, provides uniform access to data, and enables the acceleration of digital transformation.

Data Governance in Support of Data Mesh

- Data mesh design breaks giant, monolithic enterprise data architectures into subsystems or business domains, each managed by a dedicated team.
- With an architecture comprised of numerous domains, enterprises need to manage interdomain communication and shared services like environment creation and active metaorchestration.
- This management of inter-domain communications and active metadata orchestration is where data governance favorably supports data mesh architecture.

Governance in Support of Data Mesh and Data Fabric

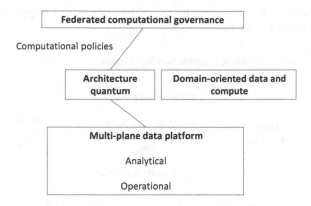

Source: Adapted from Informatica

Data Governance Areas Components of a Data Lake

Data Fabric Components

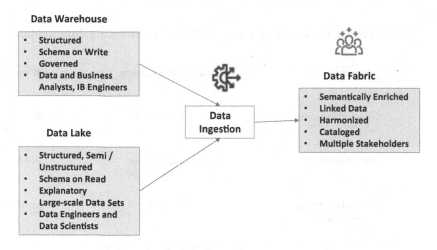

Source: Adapted from Gartner

PRIVACY-ENHANCING COMPUTATION

It supports use cases where data must remain confidential during processing and analytics and where the algorithms must remain confidential even if the data itself does not. It enables data monetization and privacy protection scenarios that were not possible with previous approaches.

- PEC is an overarching term for many techniques, each with different security and privacy guarantees. They can be used individually, but may also be combined for greater efficacy. The exact choice of techniques depends on the use case and implementation requirements.

- Techniques have matured to the point that commercial implementations are available. Trusted execution environments are available in computer processors and hyperscale cloud providers. Secure multiparty computation and homomorphic encryption products are available from increasing vendors.

Privacy-Enhancing Computation Techniques

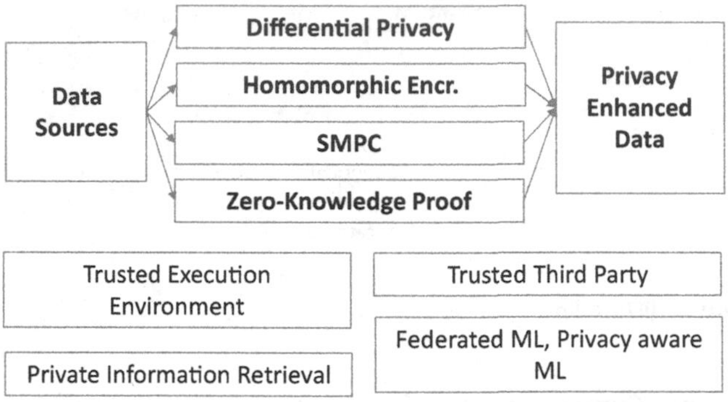

Source: Adapted from Gartner

PEC comprises three types of technologies that protect data while it's being used to enable secure data processing and data analytics: Each technology provides specific secrecy and privacy guarantees, and some can be combined for greater efficacy.

Top Strategic Technology Trends for Privacy-Enhancing Computation

People Centric	Location Independence	Delivery Resilient
Internet of Behaviors	Distributed Cloud	Intelligent Composable Business
Total Experience	Anywhere Operations	AI Engineering
Privacy-Enhancing Computation	Cyber Security Mesh	Hyperautomation
Combinatorial Innovation		

Source: Adapted from Gartner

ARX DATA ANONYMIZATION TOOL

ARX is a comprehensive open-source software for anonymizing sensitive personal data.

In this perspective, various metrics reflecting privacy risks are presented. Metrics implemented by ARX include re-identification risks for the prosecutor, journalist, and marketer attacks as well as estimates of population uniqueness, which can be calculated using different statistical models.

Example of input distribution:

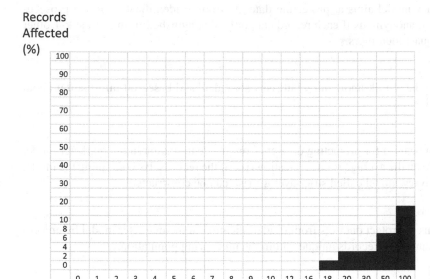

Distribution of Risk for Records with Maximal Risk

Source: Adapted from ARX

An Example of After-Distribution:

Distribution of Risk for Records with Maximal Risk

Source: Adapted from ARX

ARX supports (almost) arbitrary combinations of privacy models and different variants of most models.

k-Anonymity

This well-known privacy model aims at protecting datasets from re-identification in the prosecutor model. A dataset is k-anonymous if each record cannot be distinguished from at least k-1 other records regarding the quasi-identifiers.

k-Map

This privacy model is related to k-anonymity, but risks are calculated based on information about the underlying population.

Average Risk

This privacy model can be used for protecting datasets from re-identification in the marketer model by enforcing a threshold on the average re-identification risk of the records. By combining the model with k-anonymity, a privacy model called strict-average risk can be constructed.

Population Uniqueness

This privacy model aims to protect datasets from re-identification in the marketer model by enforcing thresholds on the number of records unique within the underlying population.

Sample Uniqueness

This privacy model can restrict the fraction of records that are unique regarding the quasi-identifiers.

ℓ-Diversity

This privacy model can be used to protect data against attribute disclosure by ensuring that each sensitive attribute has at least ℓ "well-represented" values in each equivalence class.

t-Closeness

This privacy model can also be used to protect data from attribute disclosure. It requires that the distributions of values of a sensitive attribute within each equivalence class must have a distance of not more than t to the distribution of the attribute values in the input dataset.

δ-Disclosure Privacy

This privacy model can also be used to protect data against attribute disclosure. It also enforces a restriction on the distances between the distributions of sensitive values but uses a multiplicative definition which is stricter than the definition used by t-closeness.

β-Likeness

This privacy model is related to t-closeness and δ-disclosure privacy and it can also be used to protect data against attribute disclosure. It aims to overcome limitations of prior models by restricting the relative maximal distance between distributions of sensitive attribute values, also considering positive and negative information gain.

δ-Presence

This model can be used to protect data from membership disclosure. A dataset is (δmin, δmax)-present if the probability that an individual from the population is contained in the dataset lies between δmin and δmax. In order to calculate these probabilities, users need to specify a population table.

Profitability

This model implements a game-theoretic approach for performing cost/benefit analyses of data publishing to create output datasets, which maximize data publisher's monetary benefit.

Differential Privacy

In this model, privacy protection is not considered a property of a dataset, but a property of a data processing method. Informally, it guarantees that the probability of any possible output of the anonymization process does not change "by much" if data of an individual is added to or removed from input data.

REGULATORY COMPLIANCE

First, for regulatory compliance, create policies based on any specifically defined requirements, such as the data deidentification rules that achieve HIPAA safe harbor and credit card number protection through tokenization in PCI DSS. Then, create policies that encompass more conceptual approaches, such as GDPR pseudonymization, according to Gartner.

Use static data masking (SDM) architecture to deidentify PII and PHI in nonproduction use cases where characteristics of the original data must be maintained. Still, data must be protected when at rest.

These use cases include data for development, testing, and training. SDM is also suitable for some analytics and data sharing.

USE TOKENIZATION AND FORMAT-PRESERVING ENCRYPTION

Use tokenization and format-preserving encryption architecture for production data where persistent protection of specific fields is critical. Apply dynamic data masking (DDM) when data needs protection only when accessed. These approaches may also apply to certain data analytics use cases.

Data can be protected from certain confidentiality or privacy violations by removing or changing specific data fields that contain personally identifiable information (PII)—aka nonpublic personal information (NPI)—or personal health information (PHI). PII and PHI are part of personal information defined in the General Data Protection Regulation (GDPR). For example, you can provide some protection against financial fraud by removing account numbers, or by replacing them with a unique substitute account number. And you can create some level of privacy protection by changing an individual's name and other identifying data fields. Depending on the approach and technology used, this type of field-level data transformation can be referred to as:

- Masking
- Tokenization
- Redaction
- Anonymization
- Pseudonymization
- Deidentification

These terms are often used interchangeably, even though they are not interchangeable. To achieve clarity in data security planning, it is important to define exactly what security or privacy goals must be met, or which specific technology implementation someone is referring to. For ease of reading, this research uses the terms "deidentification" and "data security" as goal and technology-independent terms.

Organizations should start by identifying which fields are present in the dataset, and how much protection must be applied to them. Applicability of Deidentification Architecture Options to PII and PHI Data Field Types Production use includes data in primary business applications and processes. The ability to deidentify data is greatly limited due to high utility requirements. In many cases, alternative controls must be used to reduce security risk.

- Nonproduction use covers data in development, test, and training environments. Data can often be significantly deidentified, and the subsequent risk is generally low enough that additional control requirements are few.
- Data warehousing and analytics include nontransactional use of data for a broad set of scenarios, such as fraud analytics and business analytics.

Applicability of Deidentification Architecture Options to PII and PHI Data Field Types:

Type of Data Field	Example Data Elements	Risk Level and Types	Business Value	Protection Approaches	Applicable Architectures
Fraud-sensitive PII	National identity number, credit card number, password	High—enables various fraud types	Low analytical value but critical for transactional applications	Omit, if possible, otherwise persistently substitute or randomize	Tokenization, FPE, DDM, and SDM
PII direct identifiers	Full name, email address, street address, phone number, username, social media identity	Moderate to high—enable phishing and trivial deidentification	Low analytical value but important for transactional applications	Omit, if possible, otherwise redact, substitute or randomize	Tokenization, FPE, DDM, and SDM
PII indirect identifiers	Postal code, city, state, date of birth	Low to moderate—may enable indirect deidentification	Moderate to high analytical value	Redact, generalize or randomize	SDM and DDM
PII/PHI attributes and behavioral data	Sex, gender, race, origin, health and medical data, genomic data, location data, search terms, activity, and so on	Up to high—may disclose very private information when deidentified	High analytical value	Varies—protection is challenging and requires in-depth risk analysis	SDM and DDM

Source: Adapted from Gartner

DATA FIELD SECRECY, PRIVACY, AND UTILITY

Data deidentification aims to balance data secrecy and privacy requirements with data utility requirements of specific business applications and processes. It takes advantage of the fact that not every process and application has to use the complete, original sensitive data and that sensitive data may be transformed to become less sensitive while still useful. For example, it may be sufficient to know a person's general location via part of their postal code in a business analytics scenario, rather than needing a complete street address. However, the complete data may be needed when testing a delivery routing system. The type of data field is a critical factor in determining this security-vs.-utility trade-off: Fraud-sensitive or "toxic" PII is a data field whose secrecy is a key concern for many organizations. These data fields cause a significant risk of harmful data breaches, but are critical for transactional applications. However, their nonproduction and analytical utility are low, so they should be omitted or persistently masked outside production. They are a strong candidate for DDM, tokenization, and/or FPE in production environments.

- PII direct identifiers are fields that allow trivial identification of a person or entity, and they are a key concern in privacy protection scenarios. Their utility is low outside of production systems and some data sharing scenarios, but they cause a significant compliance risk. Therefore, they are a strong candidate for irreversible deidentification in nonproduction environments and in PII and PHI attributes and behavioral data cover a large variety of data fields. They have strong utility in many scenarios, and protection is often challenging. Not only might these fields allow reidentification, but their contents themselves are often confidential. They are candidates for deidentification, but in-depth risk and utility analysis is required.

An Example of Degrees of Deidentification:

	Original data	Toxic data scrubbing	Psuedonymization	Anonymization	Advanced anonymization
Toxic Data	SSN 12345-6789	SSN A0677-8888	SSN A0677-8888	SSN A0677-8888	SSN A0677-8888
Direct Identifier	John Adams	John Adams	Neil Nelson	Neil Nelson	Neil Nelson
Direct Identifier	1 Center Street	1 Center Street	99 Tyson Street	99 Tyson Street	99 Tyson Street
Quasi-Identifier	New York, NY 10001	New York, NY 10001	New York, NY 10001	New York, NY 100xx	New York, NY 100xx
Quasi-Identifier	5-Dec68	5-Dec68	5-Dec68	1965-1970	1965-1970
Direct Identifier	212 111 1111	212 111 1111	555 555 5555	555 555 5555	555 555 5555
Direct Identifier	john@adams.us	john@adams.us	neil@domaimask.us	neil@domaimask.us	neil@domaimask.us

Source: Adapted from Gartner

DATA DEIDENTIFICATION ARCHITECTURE CHOICES

A major decision when implementing deidentification is picking the architecture options that implement the data transformation operations. Data use cases don't map directly to architecture choices, and it is easier to assess each architecture option to determine whether it can provide sufficient data security and data utility in a specific scenario.

SDM is used to create a deidentified copy of a dataset, and this copy is then used in one or more applications or processes. The deidentification does not happen in real time and is often initiated manually, as a scheduled batch task, or automatically, as part of a workflow. The SDM architecture can cross otherwise-separated application and data environments, such as production and training systems, without connecting them in real time. This figure shows an example of using SDM to create deidentified datasets for a nonproduction environment, where the relationships between records in the various datasets are maintained via unique mapping of key identifiers.

- Dynamic data masking architectures provide irreversible data field transforms applied in real time. They are designed mainly to transform the data when requested for extraction or use, but can also be used during data ingestion or load.
- Tokenization and format-preserving encryption architectures provide reversible data field transforms applied in real time. They are designed to protect data at rest and subsequent use by transforming it before it is stored in a repository and providing a real-time service to obtain the original data when needed.

STATIC DATA MASKING

SDM is used to create a deidentified copy of a dataset, and this copy is then used in one or more applications or processes. The deidentification does not happen in real time and is often initiated manually, as a scheduled batch task, or automatically, as part of a workflow. The SDM architecture can be used to cross otherwise-separated application and data environments, such as production and training systems, without connecting them in real time.

An Example of Static Data Masking:

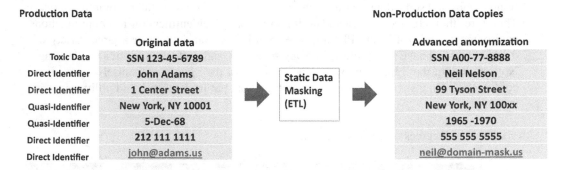

Source: Adapted from Gartner

Production Data

SDM is generally a weak fit for production data protection. Transforming data in batch does not fit most production data workflows, and the level of deidentification available in SDM goes beyond production data utility requirements. Rather than using SDM, organizations would generally consider DDM, tokenization, FPE, or alternative controls instead.

Some corner cases may still benefit from using SDM for production applications, but these tend to fall more into the data sharing and publishing categories. For example, when creating data for marketing communication purposes, SDM products can be put to good use. A major function of SDM in this case would be to scrub unnecessary data fields, but not to apply many field-level transforms.

Nonproduction Data

SDM is a strong fit for nonproduction development, test, and training environments. Data in these environments is often created through a batch process, and data utility requirements generally allow deidentification to an appropriate level. SDM is commonly deployed for this type of use case because it often satisfies data protection requirements without additional controls.

Data Warehousing and Analytics

SDM is a popular control in big data environments such as Hadoop. SDM does not negatively impact the response times when large datasets are queried. Clients who deploy Hadoop typically have the environment under their control, and the creation of additional columns and views is not perceived as invasive.

Data Sharing and Publishing

Dynamic Data Masking applies masking operations in real time when an application or person accesses data. The original data resides in the data repository; therefore, DDM protects data in use only.

The original data is accessible to a consuming entity when authorized by policy. Entities that are not authorized to access the sensitive information are provided with masked data instead. According to Gartner, the figure is an example of a DDM architecture, where applications and data repositories are combined with DDM policy enforcement points to provide data-in-use protection for specific data fields. It also provides downstream data-at-rest protection when loading data into another database.

An Example of Dynamic Data Masking:

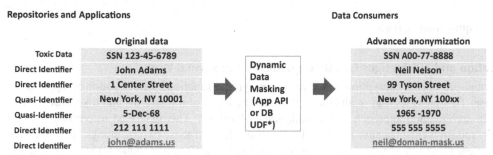

Source: Adapted from Gartner

DDM—excluding statistical databases, which are not as common as other masking solutions 4—is a relatively new market closely related to database security. Vendors include Dataguise, IBM, Informatica, Oracle, and Privitar. In addition, DDM can be a feature in other types of products, including databases such as Microsoft SQL Server and Oracle, access control products such as Axiomatics, and cloud access security brokers (CASBs).

Tokenization and Format-Preserving Encryption Tokenization and FPE architecture protect a data field by replacing its value with a substitute when loaded into an application or data store. This protects data at rest, as well as data in subsequent use. If an application or user needs the real data value, the substitute can be transformed back because the algorithms are designed to be reversible. The algorithms are designed to provide a unique and consistent mapping between the real value and token, making them applicable to directly identifying data fields.

The figure shows a tokenization architecture with tokenization on data entry, a tokenization service with a token mapping database, and two applications: one that uses only the stored, tokenized data and another that is connected to the tokenization service to provide the real data to some users:

An Example of Tokenization and FPE:

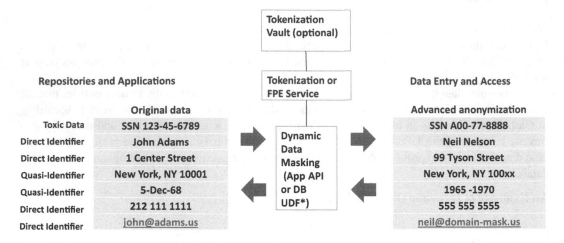

Source: Adapted from Gartner

Tokenization and FPE Designs Can Be Implemented in Several Ways

Local format-preserving encryption performs the encryption function entirely within an application or database. This provides high scalability, but limits the types of transforms, and tokenization may refer to an architectural approach and an individual algorithm. This may lead to confusion when discussing requirements, because it is not always clear which of these two meanings applies. Aside from Payment Card Industry Data Security Standard (PCI DSS), which makes a strict distinction between tokenization and encryption algorithms, organizations should focus on the tokenization service's architectural design and security. Production data can be tokenized when ingested or entered into a repository. The detokenization operation can then be applied in real time when an application accesses the data, or the application can be served as the substitute. Like DDM, the tokenization capability may be part of the repository, a mediator between the repository and the application, invoked by the platform or presentation infrastructure, or as part of the application. Because tokenization may need to store the mappings in a secure database and implement an algorithm for unique, consistent substitution, performance is critical in the architecture. Like DDM, tokenization works at the field level and is most applicable to fraud-sensitive and direct identifiers. Because tokenization aims to replace sensitive identifiers with surrogates in as many repositories and applications as possible, the substitute value itself may become a critically important data element. Ensuring its proper protection in the production environment is an important consideration even though certain confidentiality risks are reduced. Data warehousing and analytics tokenization is available for data stored in data warehouses and big data stores through the same architectural alternatives as production data stores.

Tokenization of sensitive identifiers during data ingest provides persistent protection—and reversibility—for data analytics use cases. As with production use cases, tokenization applies to a limited number of data fields. As a result, it cannot provide broader privacy protection.

DESIGN WITH DEIDENTIFICATION LIMITS IN MIND

When relying on data masking, customers should exercise caution to protect more complex privacy constructs, such as medical histories and personal behavioral information. In these scenarios, merely masking direct identifiers such as names, addresses, and phone numbers is often insufficient. Even masking well-known quasi-identifier combinations such as date of birth, ZIP Code, and sex may fall short if a person's attributes or activities are sufficiently unique. Especially because so much data about people is already out in public data sources, the risk of reidentification by combining data sources can be significantly higher than expected. Statistical analysis of reidentification risk is generally valid only in a specific dataset.

But even then, not all attribute and activity data types are easy to analyze—for example, location data. When keeping data in-house for development, testing, training, or even data analytics, it is exposed to a limited number of people. But sharing deidentified data with third parties increases the potential exposure and should always be done with caution; releasing it to the public means it cannot be taken back.

CHOOSE THE RIGHT FIELDS AND TECHNIQUES TO PROTECT THEM

The security team has to work with the application and data teams to find the best fit for each use case and match these with the masking technique options to create appropriate protection. Choosing techniques for higher-risk data fields and use cases involves experts and one should be aware that analyzing data for susceptibility to deidentification attack requires advanced statistical expertise.

PII direct identifiers should be deidentified in nonproduction environments and data publishing.

They should also be candidates for deidentification in data analytics and data sharing scenarios. Where possible, remove identifiers that are unnecessary to a specific use case.

- PII indirect identifiers should be deidentified in data sharing and be candidates for deidentification in nonproduction environments. They are usually necessary in data analytics environments due to their data utility.
- PII and PHI attributes and behavioral data should be candidates for masking in data sharing and nonproduction environments, but they are difficult to mask. They are almost always necessary in data analytics environments due to their data utility.

Relative Data Exposure Risk Potential by Use Case:

Risk Use	Lowest	Lower-medium	Medium	Medium-high
Production	In-house primary / transactional use	In-house secondary use		Third party
Analytics / Modeling		In-house		Third party
Non-production			In-house	Third party

Source: Adapted from Gartner

Three levels of utility:

Syntax: Ensure that specific data format requirements are maintained. For example, when a credit card number is masked, it may have to have a correct length, data type, and check digit.

- Semantics: Ensure that data maintains contextual correctness in the local and applied instances. The masked data appears to be logically consistent with unmasked data in the local instance. In the applied instance, the masked data behaves the same with respect to its intended use as does the unmasked data. For example, treatment and drug information may need to be changed when substituting one disease code with another.

- Statistics: Ensure that the masked dataset maintains the same frequencies and correlations as the original data. In other words, ensure that it maintains the intended meaning for a specific use case. For example, a masked dataset used for modeling must be realistic enough so as not to invalidate the analysis.

Utility Requirements by Use Case:

Use Case	Synthetic	Syntactically correct	Semantically correct	Statistically correct	Original
Production / transactional					
Production / secondary use					
Analytics / Sharing		Coarse-grained		Fine-grained	
Non-production Dev / test	Low context	Moderate context		Highly contextual	

Source: Adapted from Gartner

The Science of Reidentifying Data

Data deidentification is a complicated science because of the security-vs.-utility trade-offs that are required. Privacy protection, in particular, is an area that relies heavily on defending against attacks based on statistical analysis. Much like encryption, which requires the involvement of cryptographers, data deidentification, at some point, requires the involvement of statisticians. The difficulty of designing such systems is best understood by looking at the science of breaking them.

Attacks on secrecy may be attackable through context, and data deidentification often has to leave some context to maintain data utility. When redacting just a single word in a document with a fixed-pitch font, the surrounding text may provide sufficient context to determine the exact word, likely words, or the meaning of the sentence.

Attacks on Privacy

Privacy protection is more challenging than secrecy protection mainly because, in many use cases, the privacy-sensitive values cannot be masked or are difficult to mask. For example, masking a disease code makes the data unusable for analytics and such a change also requires ensuring consistency with any dependent data such as treatments, drugs, and even the patient's age and gender.

In addition, even nonsensitive data fields may aid an attacker in narrowing down the field of possible identities. And finally, more and more data is recorded in databases, accessible in various online services, and broadcast via social media. Given enough knowledge about the data and context, this could result in a privacy breach over time.

Deidentification Technique Choices

Masking techniques are the most important aspect of defining data deidentification policies because their choice and particular configuration ultimately determine what levels of security and utility can be achieved. The utility preservation attribute is a combined assessment of the masking technique's ability to satisfy several data utility requirements (syntax, semantics, statistics, internal and external referential integrity, uniqueness, repeatability, consistency, and reversibility). No single technique fits every situation because the fundamental tension between data utility and data security cannot be overcome.

Protection and Utility Preservation Attributes of Masking Techniques:

Secrecy	Best	Good	Good	Poor	Poor	Best
Privacy	Best	Fair	Fair	Fair	Fair	Best
Utility	Poor	Fair	Fair	Good	Fair	Poor

Source: Adapted from Gartner

Suppression, as shown in the Figure, omits specific fields or records. The greatest achievable privacy and secrecy control level is high because suppressed data is simply not visible in the resulting masked dataset. Suppression is used in production and nonproduction environments, but has low applicability in the more complex test environments and fine-grained analysis. Suppression in production environments is, in essence, access control. In nonproduction environments, suppression is often implemented as part of so-called "data subsetting" in data management solutions:

Original Data		
1	001-23-4567	Alice Johnson
2	000-01-4498	Bob Meyers
3	098-30-1588	Eve Mattson
4	045-75-9999	Mallory Hart

Data Suppression Technique	
1	Alice Johnson
2	Bob Meyers
4	Mallory Hart

Source: Adapted from Gartner

Redaction Redaction, as shown in the Figure, "blacks out" parts of data. It is mainly a secrecy control, although redaction can also provide some privacy control if the right sensitive data fields are included. It is an important technique for protecting unstructured data elements, such as sensitive parts of a document or photograph. Redaction is effective only if it consistently applies to the same parts of a data field; otherwise, data might be disclosed by combining different redacted versions.

Original Data		
1	001-23-4567	Alice Johnson
2	000-01-4498	Bob Meyers
3	098-30-1588	Eve Mattson
4	045-75-9999	Mallory Hart

Data Redaction Technique		
1	***-**-4567	Alice Johnson
2	***-**-4498	Bob Meyers
3	***-**-1588	Eve Mattson
4	***-**-9999	Mallory Hart

Source: Adapted from Gartner

As shown in the figure, substitution encompasses various methods to replace sensitive data with a surrogate or substitute value. The aim of substitution is to increase secrecy by replacing either all the data values with algorithmically related data (e.g., increasing the value by a set amount) or part of the data with a random value (e.g., replace the first five digits of a nine-digit social security number).

The secrecy of the substitution depends on the properties of the data as well as the complexity of the substitution algorithm. This method can provide strong secrecy control, but has varying efficacy for privacy control. For example, name substitution can provide good privacy control for direct deidentification attacks, but is still dependent on other identifiers, quasi-identifiers, and attributes and activities also being masked:

Original Data			Data Substitution Technique		
1	001-23-4567	Alice Johnson	1	465-82-4567	Alice Johnson
2	000-01-4498	Bob Meyers	2	762-98-4498	Bob Meyers
3	098-30-1588	Eve Mattson	3	567-45-1588	Eve Mattson
4	045-75-9999	Mallory Hart	4	567-45-9999	Mallory Hart

Source: Adapted from Gartner

As shown in the figure, generalization encompasses a variety of algorithms that modify data to become less specific but retains part of its meaning. Generalization can be implemented by replacing a value with a range or set, a set value from a generalized range or set, or a random value from a generalized range or set. Generalization aims to reduce privacy risk by making elements of quasi-identifiers nonspecific. In particular, the generalization is usually based on a statistical analysis of the data and designed to homogenize the data concerning the quasi-identifiers.

Although several generalization algorithms are known, many of them have known weaknesses for certain data distributions, and their efficacy for general datasets is hard to determine. Generalization also does not ensure secrecy because knowing a generalized value may well be as good as knowing the exact value. The security of generalization depends on the properties of the dataset. Small datasets are harder to generalize, and any outliers may remain recognizable when shuffling at the block level. Generalization thus offers low secrecy and moderate privacy control:

Original Data			Data Generalization Technique		
1	22	Alice Johnson	1	Alice Johnson	20 – 30
2	23	Bob Meyers	2	Bob Meyers	20 – 30
3	35	Eve Mattson	3	Eve Mattson	31 – 65
4	61	Mallory Hart	4	Mallory Hart	31 – 65

Source: Adapted from Gartner

Shuffling/swapping shuffling, as shown in the figure, moves around individual data items or groups of related data items. Shuffling aims to increase privacy control by disassociating sensitive values and other identifiers. Merely shuffling data does not keep data secret because the sensitive values are maintained, but privacy increases. Also, if data is sensitive only because of specific data field combinations, shuffling may be able to decouple—and thus desensitize—the combination. For example, you could shuffle Social Security numbers in a database to decouple them from a person's name. The security of shuffling depends on the properties of the dataset and whether individual values or related blocks of values are moved:

Original Data			Data Shuffling Technique		
1	Alice Johnson	Apples	1	Alice Johnson	Bread
		Oranges	2	Bob Meyers	Apples
2	Bob Meyers	Bread			Bananas
3	Eve Mattson	Apples			Grapes
		Bananas	3	Eve Mattson	Bananas
		Grapes			Oranges
4	Mallory Hart	Bananas	4	Mallory Hart	Apples
		Oranges			Oranges

Source: Adapted from Gartner

As shown in figure, randomization replaces a data value with a randomized value from an interval or set. Because there is no relationship between the original and masked data, secrecy of the original value is ensured. If identifiers and quasi-identifiers are randomized, privacy can be ensured because the subject is no longer distinguishable by those identifiers. For example, a randomized date of birth could thwart the "ZIP + DOB + gender attack" as described earlier in this section. However, these high protection levels come at the price of potentially low utility:

Original Data				Data Randomization Technique		
1	22	Alice Johnson		1	Alice Johnson	81
2	23	Bob Meyers		2	Bob Meyers	44
3	35	Eve Mattson		3	Eve Mattson	23
4	61	Mallory Hart		4	Mallory Hart	55

Source: Adapted from Gartner

SECURE MULTIPARTY COMPUTATION (SMPC)

Secure multiparty computation (SMPC) is a distributed computing and cryptography method that enables entities (applications, individuals, organizations, or devices) to work with data while keeping data or encryption keys in a protected state. Specifically, SMPC allows multiple entities to share insights while keeping data confidential from each other. Reason This Is Relevant Security and risk management (SECURITY) leaders struggle to balance data security and privacy when processing (personal) data. Regulations and overall operational objectives further complicate this.

The foundation for secure multiparty computation started in the late 1970s with the work on mental poker, cryptographic work that simulates game playing/computational tasks over distances without requiring a trusted third party. Note that traditionally, cryptography was about concealing content. This new type of computation and protocol is about hiding partial information about data while computing with the data from many sources and correctly producing outputs.

BARRIERS

SMPC algorithms can be latency-sensitive. As such, performance might sometimes not meet client requirements or expectations.

- Although considerable academic research has been conducted on SMPC, a relatively limited number of practical implementations have emerged.
- Compared to existing techniques (such as cryptography based on hardware generated and stored keys), clients could have potential issues with audits, especially if they have to adhere to standards like Federal Information Processing Standards (FIPS) certifications.

HOMOMORPHIC ENCRYPTION (HE)

Homomorphic encryption (HE) is a set of algorithms that enable computation on encrypted data. Fully homomorphic encryption (FHE) supports arbitrary mathematical operations, but has significant performance impact and is not practical. Partial homomorphic encryption (PHE) supports much more limited use cases with lower performance impact than FHE. Currently, commercial products are supported by some versions of PHE, but fast FHE over the Torus (TFHE) is beginning to appear in the market.

REASON THIS IS RELEVANT

When fully realized, homomorphic encryption will be an unparalleled advance in privacy and data processing. Benefits include

Performing data analytics on encrypted data such that the processor never sees the data in the clear, but delivers accurate results.

Sharing and pooling data among competitors allowing them to accomplish joint tasks (e.g., sharing AML data) without giving up secrets or privacy.

* Allowing data subjects to share all or part of their sensitive data without giving up privacy.

OPERATIONAL IMPACT

Even in its current restricted form (PHE), homomorphic encryption allows operationales to use data, send it to others for processing, and return accurate results without fear that the data will be lost, compromised, or stolen. Any data intercepted by a malicious actor will be encrypted and unreadable, even by the coming generation of quantum computers.

REQUIREMENTS

Enhanced enforcement of data residency restrictions globally forces organizations to protect data in use, rather than in transit and at rest only.

* Globally maturing privacy and data protection legislative frameworks demand more precise attention on sensitive data. As a result, data pooling, sharing, and cross-entity analysis use cases increasingly benefit from forward-looking and sustainable technologies like HE.
* Aside from conventional use cases like AML and cross-entity fraud analytics in the financial realm, the fight against COVID-19 has benefited from analysis of sensitive health-related data across various entities. At the same time, that data is protected in use.
* Application of HE has been observed in combination with secure multiparty computation (sMPC) to benefit from both internal and external data protection.

BARRIERS

The feasibility of application of (various forms of) HE in daily use cases leads to a certain complexity and reduced speed of operations, requiring highly specialized staff.

* The unfamiliarity of the market with this technology stands in the way of speedy adoption.
* FHE is not a Turing-complete framework, meaning an arbitrary set of instructions can't be executed. By its mathematical formalism, it's limited to operations based on addition and multiplication (and their inverses).
* While still highly useful, some scenarios will never be a good fit for THE, but could be addressed using an alternative technology: confidential computing.

GUIDANCE

Brainstorm with your technical and executive teams on opportunities. For example, come up with a list of 5–10 use cases for HE to improve adoption and remove barriers to adopting core solutions.

* Treat potential HE projects as experiments, keeping in mind both the early stage of the technology and the significant not-real-time nature of the products. Consider these experiments as proofs of concept until the technology matures.

- Continue existing security controls. PHE does not necessarily negate the need for other security controls (such as protecting decrypted text while in-memory), data residency requirements, and access control. Assess the core benefits of using homomorphic encryption combined with quantum-safe and privacy-preserving computation techniques.
- Integrate in-use protection through forms of HE into messaging and third-party analytics services.
- Consider piloting HE through the use of a vendor solution, which can offer functionality without the time investment of a custom solution.

SUMMARY

We discussed privacy-enhancing computation, differential privacy, the science of reidentifying data, attacks on privacy, deidentification technique choices, and secure multiparty computation (SMPC), and homomorphic encryption.

NOTES

1. Coop, Alex. "Sidewalk Labs decision to offload tough decisions on privacy to third party is wrong, says its former consultant". IT World Canada. Retrieved 27 June 2019.
2. de Montjoye, Y.-A. (2013). "Unique in the crowd: The privacy bounds of human mobility". Scientific Reports. 3: 1376. Bibcode:2013NatSR...3E1376D. doi:10.1038/srep01376. PMC 3607247. PMID 23524645.
3. de Montjoye, Y.-A.; Radaelli, L.; Singh, V. K.; Pentland, A. S. (29 January 2015). "Unique in the shopping mall: On the reidentifiability of credit card metadata". Science. 347 (6221): 536–539. Bibcode:2015Sci...347..536D. doi:10.1126/science.1256297. PMID 25635097.
4. El Emam, Khaled (2011). "A Systematic Review of Re-Identification Attacks on Health Data". PLOS ONE. 10 (4): e28071. Bibcode:2011PLoSO...628071E. doi:10.1371/journal. pone.0028071. PMC 3229505. PMID 22164229.
5. Fullerton, S. M.; Anderson, N. R.; Guzauskas, G.; Freeman, D.; Fryer-Edwards, K. (2010). "Meeting the Governance Challenges of Next-Generation Biorepository Research". Science Translational Medicine. 2 (15): 15cm3. doi:10.1126/scitranslmed.3000361. PMC 3038212. PMID 20371468.
6. Godard, B. A.; Schmidtke, J. R.; Cassiman, J. J.; Aymé, S. G. N. (2003). "Data storage and DNA banking for biomedical research: Informed consent, confidentiality, quality issues, ownership, return of benefits. A professional perspective". European Journal of Human Genetics. 11: S88–122. doi:10.1038/sj.ejhg.5201114. PMID 14718939.
7. Homer, N.; Szelinger, S.; Redman, M.; Duggan, D.; Tembe, W.; Muehling, J.; Pearson, J. V.; Stephan, D. A.; Nelson, S. F.; Craig, D. W. (2008). Visscher, Peter M. (ed.). "Resolving Individuals Contributing Trace Amounts of DNA to Highly Complex Mixtures Using High-Density SNP Genotyping Microarrays". PLOS Genetics. 4 (8): e1000167. doi:10.1371/journal. pgen.1000167. PMC 2516199. PMID 18769715.
8. Ito, Koichi; Kogure, Jun; Shimoyama, Takeshi; Tsuda, Hiroshi (2016). "De-identification and Encryption Technologies to Protect Personal Information" (PDF). Fujitsu Scientific and Technical Journal. 52 (3): 28–.
9. McGuire, A. L.; Gibbs, R. A. (2006). "GENETICS: No Longer De-Identified". Science. 312 (5772): 370–371. doi:10.1126/science.1125339. PMID 16627725.
10. McMurry, AJ; Gilbert, CA; Reis, BY; Chueh, HC; Kohane, IS; Mandl, KD (2007). "A self-scaling, distributed information architecture for public health, research, and clinical care". J Am Med Inform Assoc. 14 (4): 527–33. doi:10.1197/jamia.M2371. PMC 2244902. PMID 17460129.
11. Narayanan, A. (2006). "How to break anonymity of the netflix prize dataset". arXiv:cs/0610105.

12. PCAST. "Report to the President - Big Data and Privacy: A technological perspective" (PDF). Office of Science and Technology Policy. Retrieved 28 March 2016 – via National Archives.

13. Ribaric, Slobodan; Ariyaeeinia, Aladdin; Pavesic, Nikola (September 2016). "De-identification for privacy protection in multimedia content: A survey". Signal Processing: Image Communication. 47: 131–151. doi:10.1016/j.image.2016.05.020.

14. Simson, Garfinkel. De-identification of personal information: recommendation for transitioning the use of cryptographic algorithms and key lengths. OCLC 933741839.

15. Sweeney, L. (2000). "Simple Demographics Often Identify People Uniquely". Data Privacy Working Paper. 3.

16. Thorisson, G. A.; Muilu, J.; Brookes, A. J. (2009). "Genotype–phenotype databases: Challenges and solutions for the post-genomic era". Nature Reviews Genetics. 10 (1): 9–18. doi:10.1038/nrg2483. hdl:2381/4584. PMID 19065136. S2CID 5964522.

17. Abascal, Jackson; Faghihi Sereshgi, Mohammad Hossein; Hazay, Carmit; Ishai, Yuval; Venkitasubramaniam, Muthuramakrishnan (2020-10-30). "Is the Classical GMW Paradigm Practical? The Case of Non-Interactive Actively Secure 2PC". Proceedings of the 2020 ACM SIGSAC Conference on Computer and Communications Security. CCS '20. Virtual Event, USA: Association for Computing Machinery: 1591–1605. doi:10.1145/3372297.3423366. ISBN 978-1-4503-7089-9.

18. Andrew C. Yao, Protocols for secure computations (extended abstract)

19. Andrew Chi-Chih Yao:How to Generate and Exchange Secrets (Extended Abstract). FOCS 1986: 162–167.

20. B. Kreuter, a. shalet and C.-H. Shen, "Billion gate secure computation with malicious adversaries," USENIX Security Symposium 2012, pp. 285–300, 2012.

21. Bullock, William H.; Ignacio, Joselito S., eds. (2006). A Strategy for Assessing and Managing Occupational Exposures. AIHA. ISBN 978-1-931504-69-0.

22. David Chaum, Ivan Damgård, Jeroen van de Graaf: Multiparty Computations Ensuring Privacy of Each Party's Input and Correctness of the Result. 87–119.

23. Dons, E; Int Panis, L; Van Poppel, M; Theunis, J; Wets, G (2012). "Personal exposure to Black Carbon in transport microenvironments". Atmospheric Environment. 55: 392–398. Bibcode:2012AtmEn..55..392D. doi:10.1016/j.atmosenv.2012.03.020.

24. Dons, E; Int Panis, L; Van Poppel, M; Theunis, J; Willems, H; Torfs, R; Wets, G (2011). "Impact of time-activity patterns on personal exposure to black carbon". Atmospheric Environment. 45 (21): 3594–3602. Bibcode:2011AtmEn..45.3594D. doi:10.1016/j.atmosenv.2011.03.064.

25. Lioy, Paul (1990). "Assessing total human exposure to contaminants". Environmental Science & Technology. 24 (7): 938–945. Bibcode:1990EnST...24..938L. doi:10.1021/es00077a001.

26. Nieuwenhuijsen, Mark; Paustenbach, Dennis; Duarte-Davidson, Raquel (2006). "New developments in exposure assessment: The impact on the practice of health risk assessment and epidemiological studies". Environment International. 32 (8): 996–1009. doi:10.1016/j.envint.2006.06.015. PMID 16875734.

27. Oded Goldreich, Silvio Micali, Avi Wigderson: How to Play any Mental Game or A Completeness Theorem for Protocols with Honest Majority. STOC 1987: 218–229

28. Ott, Wayne R.; Steinemann, Anne C.; Wallace, Lance A. (2006). "1.4 Total Human Exposure Concept. 1.5 Receptor-Oriented Approach". Exposure Analysis. CRC Press. pp. 6–13. ISBN 978-1-4200-1263-7.

29. Ran Canetti, et al., "Adaptively Secure Multiparty", TOC/CIS groups, LCS, MIT (1996), p. 1.

30. Rights (OCR), Office for Civil (2012-09-07). "Methods for De-identification of PHI". HHS. gov. Retrieved 2020-11-08.

31. Shelat and C.-H. Shen, "Fast two-party secure computation with minimal assumptions," ACM CCS 2013, pp. 523–534, 2013.

32. T. Frederiksen and J. Nielsen, "Fast and maliciously secure two-party computation using the GPU", ACNS 2013, vol. Springer LNCS 7954, pp. 339–356, 2013.

33. US EPA, "Expocast" http://www.epa.gov/ncct/expocast/
34. Vallero, D.; Isukapalli, S.; Zartarian, V.; McCurdy, T.; McKone, T.; Georgopoulos, P.G.; Dary, C. (2010). "Ch. 44: Modeling and predicting pesticide exposures". In Krieger, Robert (ed.). Hayes' Handbook of Pesticide Toxicology. Vol. 1 (3rd ed.). Academic Press. pp. 995–1020. ISBN 978-0-08-092201-0.
35. Vallero, D.A. "Fundamentals of Air Pollution". Elsevier Academic Press.
36. Vallero, D.A. (2004). Environmental Contaminants: Assessment and Control. Academic Press. ISBN 0127100571.16.
37. Y. Huang, J. Katz and D. Evans, "Efficient secure two-party computation using symmetric cut-and-choose.," CRYPTO, vol. Springer LNCS 8043, pp. 18–35, 2013.
38. Y. Lindell and B. Pinkas, "An efficient protocol for secure two-party computation in the presence of malicious adversaries," Eurocrypt 2007, vol. Springer LNCS 4515, pp. 52–78, 2007.
39. Y. Lindell, "Fast cut-and-choose based protocols for malicious and covert adversaries," Crypto 2013, vol. Springer LNCS 8043, pp. 1–17, 2013.
40. Zvi Galil, Stuart Haber, Moti Yung: Cryptographic Computation: Secure Fault-Tolerant Protocols and the Public-Key Model. CRYPTO 1987: 135–155.

10 Analytics, Data Lakes, and Federated Learning

INTRODUCTION

In this chapter, we will discuss data quality, reliability, and trust. These are directly correlated to success in advanced analytics, the cornerstone of digital transformation. Investing now in cloud-native, AI-driven data management is key to modern data architecture. Essential business benefits include increased agility and reduced time to solution; democratization of data, empowering larger user populations; easy access to a large analytics ecosystem; and acceleration of innovation and time to value.

USE CASES FOR DATA ANALYTICS

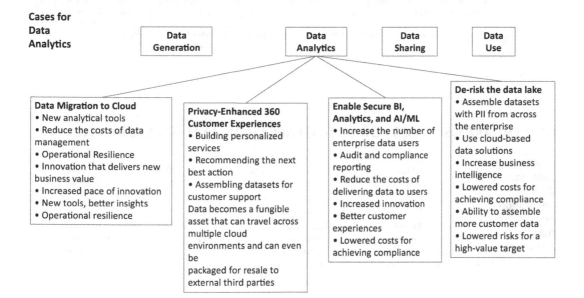

Cases for Data Analytics

Data Generation — Data Analytics — Data Sharing — Data Use

Data Migration to Cloud
- New analytical tools
- Reduce the costs of data management
- Operational Resilience
- Innovation that delivers new business value
- Increased pace of innovation
- New tools, better insights
- Operational resilience

Privacy-Enhanced 360 Customer Experiences
- Building personalized services
- Recommending the next best action
- Assembling datasets for customer support
Data becomes a fungible asset that can travel across multiple cloud environments and can even be packaged for resale to external third parties

Enable Secure BI, Analytics, and AI/ML
- Increase the number of enterprise data users
- Audit and compliance reporting
- Reduce the costs of delivering data to users
- Increased innovation
- Better customer experiences
- Lowered costs for achieving compliance

De-risk the data lake
- Assemble datasets with PII from across the enterprise
- Use cloud-based data solutions
- Increase business intelligence
- Lowered costs for achieving compliance
- Ability to assemble more customer data
- Lowered risks for a high-value target

DOI: 10.1201/9781003254928-13

FINANCIAL SERVICES USE CASES FOR DATA ANALYTICS AND DATA SHARING

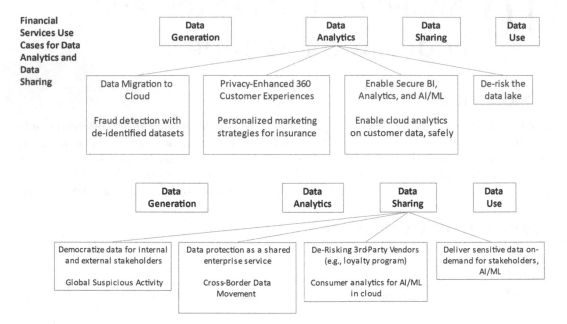

HEALTHCARE USE CASES FOR DATA GENERATION AND DATA ANALYTICS

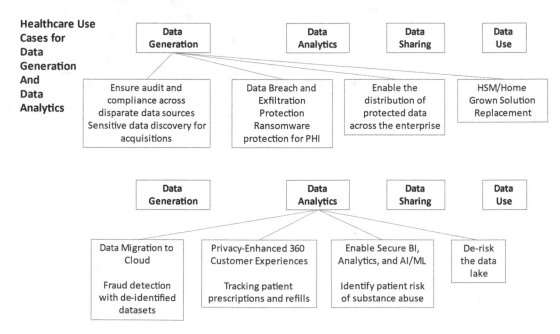

DATA AND ANALYTICS (D&A)

Gartner defines the market for data and analytics (D&A) services as consulting, system integration (SI), and managed services for the management of data for all uses (operational and analytical), and for the analysis of data to drive business processes and improve business outcomes through more effective decision-making:

- Data science and machine learning (aka AI)
- D&A governance
- Program management
- Enterprise metadata

Risks

Data and analytics leaders need to consider several risks when selecting and implementing a data science and machine learning platform.

Going too far in standardization: Many organizations seek to standardize as much as possible on a single DSML platform in order to reduce costs, enable collaboration, foster reuse, and allow staff rotation and easier exchange of models and insights between business units. However, this holds the risk of becoming too much like a one-size-fits-all approach, not recognizing significant differences in requirements between, for example, central DSML business teams or DSML teams in business units. Depending on those requirements, finding a single DSML platform that properly covers them all may be infeasible.

Going too far in taking different requirements and team preferences into account: This can result in the unnecessary investment in and use of multiple DSML platforms. This, in turn, hinders collaboration and creates bottlenecks for data and model governance as well as implementing standards and best practices across the organization. Different business and technical teams may have different requirements, which on a closer look may be covered by a single DSML platform. Also, different personas may have different preferences—which, of course, should be considered but should also be balanced with other buying criteria.

Underestimating the extent to which multipersona DSML platforms can support expert requirements or preferences: Often, due to a lack of information about capabilities, multipersona platforms may be dismissed prematurely as being not scalable, flexible, or sophisticated enough. Also, it may be unrightfully assumed that a multipersona platform does not support notebook-centric coding or the inclusion of open-source (frameworks). This may result in unnecessary investment in a separate DSML engineering platform, which in reality is only necessary after confirming that requirements or preferences are indeed not supported by a multipersona platform.

Not effectively addressing model validation when selecting multiple DSML platforms: This relates to the need to have proper validation by expert data scientists of DSML models that are produced by, for example, citizen data scientists. The use of different platforms for expert and citizen data scientists increases the risk of such validations not happening. Despite the growing ease of use of multipersona DSML platforms for nontechnical users, mistakes can still be made, and models should therefore be scrutinized before being deployed to production and used in decision-making.

Not effectively addressing cross-platform data and model operationalization and governance when selecting multiple DSML platforms: This includes the ethical use of data and AI, requiring privacy protection, explainability, bias mitigation, or fairness. Although such governance could be organized for each platform separately, a growing number of organizations seek a more enterprise-wide approach. This is often fueled by growing regulatory pressure and the growing business-critical role of DSML.

Recommendations

Data and analytics leaders responsible for data science and machine learning should:

- Determine which trends in DSML and neighboring technologies such as cloud services, business intelligence, or software engineering impact the scope and nature of DSML usage in your organization.

- Make an inventory of current and future DSML requirements by evaluating the scale and complexity of DSML applications and by identifying all relevant personas and their needs at the organizational unit level and common needs across the enterprise.
- Ascertain what DSML platform is best by matching requirements with one or multiple DSML multipersona or engineering platforms. This should be balanced with the importance of standardizing on one single platform to allow better collaboration, reuse, and governance across the enterprise.
- Determine strategic requirements for meeting organizational DSML goals by identifying patterns of DSML usage across the enterprise and the tools and infrastructure needed for present and future activity.

AUTO ANONYMIZATION

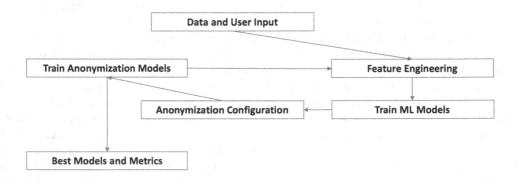

AUTO ANONYMIZATION BASED ON ML

Auto Machine Learning

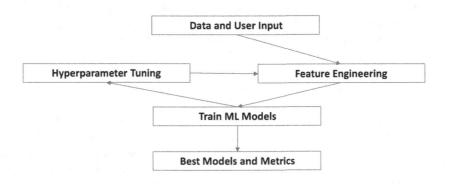

BIG DATA AND ANALYTICS

CLOUD CUSTOMER ARCHITECTURE FOR BIG DATA AND ANALYTICS

A hybrid cloud is a combination of on-premises and local cloud resources integrated with one or more dedicated cloud(s) and one or more public cloud(s), allowing for increased scalability and computational power for big data and analytics capabilities.

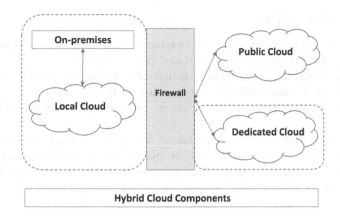

Hybrid Cloud Components

Source: Adapted from Gartner

Enterprise IT Domain Systems

Systems of Record

> Traditional enterprise systems that handles transactions

Systems of Automation

> Systems that measures multiple information points and trigger actions

Systems of Record

> Systems that bring together and analyze data from several sources

Systems of Engagement

> Systems that offer ways for users to engage with the company by combining front-end contextual information

Source: Adapted from Gartner

Self-service Data & Analytics

Public Cloud	Dedicated Cloud	On-premises
APIs	**APIs**	**Enterprise systems**
• Devices • IoT • Edge analytics • Social	• Advanced analytics • Big data • Sensors • Real-time analytics • Statistical modeling	• Local cloud • Analytics • Servers • Statistical modeling • Metadata catalog

Information Governance & Security

Source: Adapted from Gartner

DATA LAKE ARCHITECTURE

Data lakes can ingest and process volumes of data, but the real value of a data lake is realized only when the processed data is consumed to build data-driven applications.

Making the data available to downstream applications and consumers in the data lake lays the foundations for innovation and building data-driven applications. Easing the process of accessing the data lake allows business transformations to come from anyone in any line of business, not just your data scientists.

One of the main requirements from a data lake is to cater to a variety of consumers. Each consumer has different requirements regarding the attributes they want and in what format, according to Gartner. A high-level data lake architecture, along with key functional capabilities and major components needed to build a data lake, is shown in the Data Lake Reference Architecture:

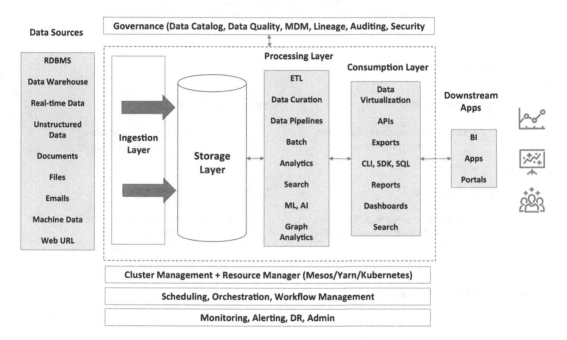

Source: Adapted from Gartner

A data lake is successful only when it allows rapid access and consumption with the right governance onboarding of users, irrespective of their location and which tools they use. Data lakes should support a wide variety of users, from data scientists, data engineers, data and business analysts, and product teams. These consumers should be able to point out their tools and access the data without development or operational skills. Consumers of data from a data lake consist of two types:

Data from a data lake can be accessed in two ways:

1. Processes and workloads within the data lake. For example: Extraction, transformation, and loading (ETL) workloads
2. Machine learning (ML) algorithms
3. Data-lake-based data marts
4. Search-based access
5. Data processing and analysis tools Data governance, data catalog, security, metadata, and MDM tools within the data lake
6. Processes and workloads outside the data lake. For example: Data pushed to data warehouses and/or data marts

7. Access to data visualization tools and business intelligence (BI) tools
8. Search-based access
9. Data analysis tools Data governance, data catalog, security, metadata, and MDM tools outside the data lake

Data from a data lake can be accessed in two ways:

BEST PRACTICES

Best practices that organizations, data lake architects, and data engineers should follow when building the consumption layer of the data lake:

Integrate the consumption layer with a data catalog/data governance and security tools to control access policies/authorization/authentication. Setting and enforcing security policies are essential for successful use of data within a data lake.

The data owners configure the security access requirements of the data, detailing who can access what data. The security details are stored as part of metadata, which data stewards use to enforce these policies.

- Support the most common ways of data access from the data lake, including SQL, APIs, search, exports, and bulk access.
- Ensure self-service capabilities, which are essential for a successful data lake. Different types of users consume the data, and they are looking for different things—but each wants to access the data in a self-service manner, without the help of IT.
- Track lineage, auditing, and logging of what data is consumed by whom, when, where, and how.

DATA GOVERNANCE

Data governance gives the data the right control and trust within the data lake. This gives confidence to the consumers of data in the data lake to make sound business decisions. Data governance is a set of formal processes that ensure that data within the enterprise meets expectations, such as:

1. Data is acquired from reliable sources.
2. Data meets quality standards.
3. Data conforms to well-defined business rules. Data is accessed and modified with the right policies, guidelines, and access controls.
4. Data follows a well-documented change control process.
5. Trustworthiness of the data remains intact as the data flows through the Data Governance Areas and Components of a Data Lake:

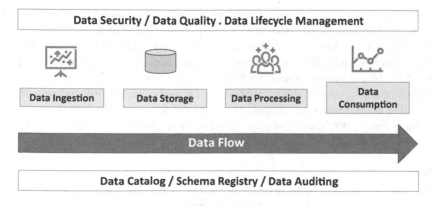

Source: Adapted from Gartner

At a high level, the best practices for data governance for a data lake should include Data governance has four major pillars: data quality, data catalog, data security, and data life cycle management. The following sections discuss details related to each of these pillars.

- Ensure that data access policies and governance solutions are not based on the storage system or analytics engine being used. Instead, the solution must be datacentric and enable consistent enforcement of policies using the tools you have deployed today and those you may deploy in the future.
- Ensure governance across all components of the data lake. Use data catalogs to ensure data quality at ingestion time, secure communication and every component within the data lake, and ensure the data life cycle is managed with the right kind of policies. Also, automate, configure, coordinate, and control the operationalization of data lakes.

Data Catalog

The single most important reason data lake implementations fail is because data lakes degenerate into data swamps due to a lack of proper metadata around them. Data lakes are reincarnated by making data catalogs an integral part of the ecosystem that is integrated across all layers and components.

Context is everything when it comes to data in the data lake. A data catalog helps companies build a map to organize and locate data stored in the data lake. It contains details on each dataset, both at a high level—in terms of its origin, date, and time of ingestion, and who ingested—and on a granular level regarding each piece of data, such as the data's profile and quality metrics, its data types, and their lineage. The catalog is the first tool anyone looking to work with the data lake should use to find data to build insights.

A data catalog solves multiple problems and data catalog vendors are innovating by building catalogs powered by AI, ML, and knowledge graphs:

1. Gives a comprehensive view of each piece of data across databases
2. Makes the data easy to find
3. Puts guardrails on the data and governs who can access it
4. Enables the data lake to support different use cases such as self-service analytics, self-service data preparation, data virtualization, and multicloud-based data architectures
5. Generate technical metadata
6. Enable semantic inference and recommendations
7. Catalog business context
8. Discover entities within unstructured data
9. Manage highly complex relationships, data quality, and data lineage

Metadata management tools and business glossaries are being integrated and are evolving as holistic data catalog tools. The data catalog becomes an indispensable guide to data, unlocking its potential and enabling organizations to be data-driven. The data catalog guides the producers and consumers of a data lake to find the right data for their interest. It provides clarity in the form of agreed definitions, supplied by subject matter experts, with a high-level view of the interconnectedness between data and the business processes that it supports. Data can be both a liability and an asset.

A data catalog is an important component to becoming a data-driven organization. It is not enough to simply have lots of data. The goal should be to maximize its findability and proper usage through ownership, understanding and trust.

A Data Fabric

A data fabric allows overlaying data applications access across data sources where data lakes and warehouses become network nodes. Data fabric combines the power of graph technology to capture and represent data complexity with rich semantics that allow end users to understand what the data means as it is ingested, stored, and delivered where and when needed. Data graphs enhanced with semantics have the power to capture and represent the complexity and heterogeneity of data available within an organization.

Data fabric aims to future-proof data architecture by providing a semantic buffer over data acquisition, storage, distribution, and underlying data sources. If data changes at sources, data fabric can mitigate the changes without breaking applications or requiring downtime. Data fabric can also elegantly query data across disparate data silos without data movement. The figure shows how the concept and capabilities of data fabric build on the concepts and capabilities of data warehouses and data lakes:

Data Fabric

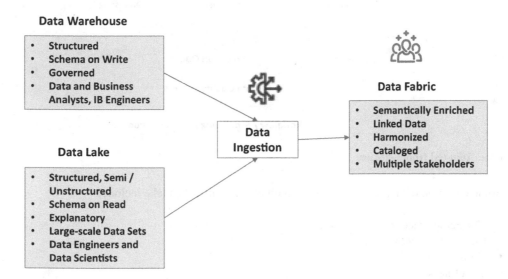

Source: Adapted from Gartner

Data and Governance

Understanding the data to be ingested in a data lake, whether it is external or internal, is extremely imperative. Determine the following before building a data lake:

1. Clearly identify the nature of the data in terms of volume, velocity, structure, source type, and location.
2. Define the data quality requirements, lineage, frequency of updates, and consistency and completeness.
3. Understand the security constraints of the data in terms of its usage and regulations. Identify data owners, data encryption requirements, access controls, and authorization and authentication policies.
4. Document the policies for data life cycle management.

Data Governance

Data governance comprises data quality, data catalog, data security and privacy, data lineage tracking, and data life cycle management components. These components cut across all the layers of the data lake. This section explores the data quality, catalog, and security aspects of data governance from an architectural lens.

Data Quality

For data democratization to be successful, organizations must ensure the data lake is filled with high-quality, well-governed data that is easy to find, easy to understand, and easy to determine for quality and fitness:

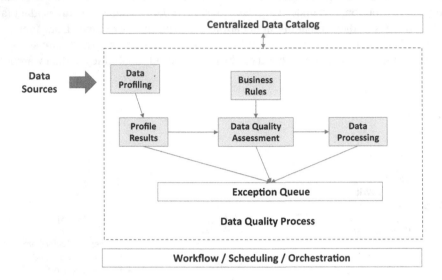

Source: Adapted from Gartner

Some common data quality issues that routinely arise in a data lake include:

- Correctness/accuracy
- Completeness/coverage
- Consistency
- Timeliness
- Data lineage embedded delimiters, where a value contains the delimiter that separates fields (e.g., commas)
- Corrupted records where an operational system may have inadvertently put control characters in values
- Data type mismatches, such as alphabetic characters in a numeric field
- Nonstandard representations of numbers and dates
- Multiple record types in a single file

A high-level architecture of how a data quality system should be architected is shown in the figure above.

Data Catalog

Data catalog tools should be able to extract entities from multistructured and unstructured data to build semantic metadata and to be able to identify relationships between entities. Data catalogs should also index the data to optimize and speed up data exploration and discovery. Data catalog tools should leverage semantic technologies to identify relationships and standardize methods expressing relationships to improve data visibility and reduce time to discover, integrate, and analyze the data.

Data catalog tools should identify latent topics from documents and then classify and annotate them based on the topics. After data ingestion, data catalog tools crawl the datasets in the Transient Zone and Raw Zone to build the metadata. Enterprise-wide data catalog tools that build a holistic enterprise catalog also crawl data sources outside a data lake and can also crawl to edge devices to gather technical and operational metadata. A high-level architecture of a data catalog is shown in the figure:

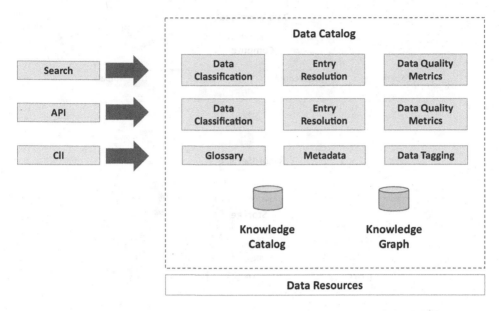

Source: Adapted from Gartner

Data Security

This section details some of the commonly used products and provides an overview of their architecture to implement security across the different layers of the data lake. Apache Knox is a reverse proxy that provides perimeter security to Hadoop clusters. It supports different policy enforcement like authentication, authorization, and host mapping by chaining these as specified in a topology deployment descriptor:

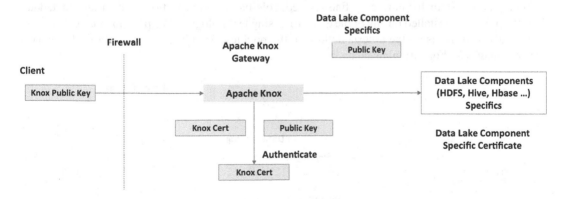

Source: Adapted from Gartner

As the data lake ecosystem grows, different products have different security implementations. Duplicate policies are often needed to provide the same user with seamless access to different tools in the ecosystem. Cloudera's RecordService is a new security layer that sits between the storage managers and compute frameworks to provide a unified data access path, fine-grained data permissions, and uniform enforcement across the stack to minimize duplication of policies. The figure below shows how RecordService fits into the architecture:

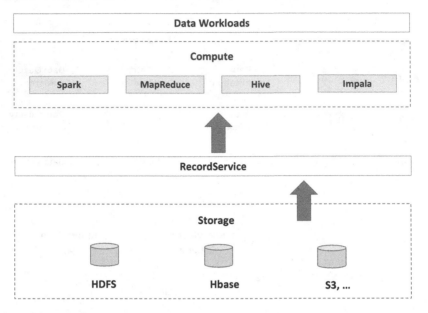

Source: Adapted from Gartner

Apache Ranger's concept of a RecordService is a framework to enable, monitor, and manage security across a Hadoop ecosystem. It provides authorization for a range of technologies in the ecosystem. It is based on attribute-based access control (ABAC). The Ranger plug-in is installed with the product—for that, authorization needs to be enforced. It synchronizes user data with the enterprise directory (where user credentials are stored) and uses that to set up appropriate security policies. When a user tries to access data for products for which the Ranger plug-in is installed, it retrieves the stored policies and does appropriate checks before users gain access to the required data. Another example of a record service is Apache Sentry.

Sentry is a system for enforcing fine-grained, role-based authorization to data and metadata. Sentry's plug-in is installed on any of the data processing technologies. The plug-in intercepts access to data, and if it meets all the criteria defined in the policies, metadata access is allowed. Sentry's server manages authorization metadata.

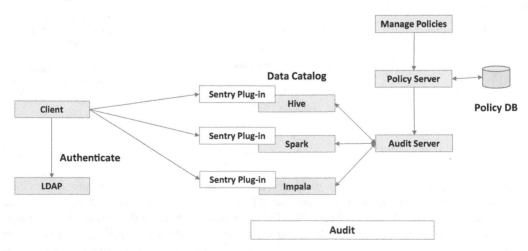

Source: Adapted from Gartner

Most components in the Hadoop ecosystem now include a built-in key management service (KMS) to secure the transport protocol over HTTP. It provides both client and server REST APIs for securing the communication channel.

It is a Java application that includes support for the Java key store to hold multiple keys and an API to access and manage key metadata. It also includes an access control list (ACL)-based support for multiple authentication and authorization protocols like Kerberos, Microsoft Azure Active Directory, and Lightweight Directory Access Protocol (LDAP) with Secure Sockets Layer (SSL).

The Hadoop Key Management Server (KMS) includes end-to-end encryptions covering data at rest and in motion. Data written into Hadoop Distributed File System (HDFS) is immediately encrypted using a specific algorithm and assigned a security zone.

Data lakes contain a large number of files, and setting permissions for each manually is not possible. Instead of defining ACLs at a file level, these tools allow you to set up policies using tags by simply tagging files and folders instead of manually creating ACLs. Catalog tools allow you to set these tags, and they can get automatically applied by the policy-based access control tools.

This approach provides a powerful way to manage and organize the data without trying to shoehorn the organizational, hierarchy-based access rules into the file management structure. Tagging can be applied to data at the ingest layer and policies can be applied to restrict access to files.

Automation is the ideal solution for handling sensitive data and the access control management around it. Tools from vendors like Informatica and Waterline Data automatically scan ingested files and detect sensitive data with advanced ML algorithms and tag them. These tags are then used by the data catalog tools to enforce tag-based policies.

DATA SHARING

Data sharing creates opportunities for data providers and consumers. For providers, sharing data can provide new sources of revenue and opportunities to get feedback from users. For consumers, data sharing enables enrichment of existing data to better inform business decisions and expand analysis capabilities. Data application builders should look for data platforms that provide the ability to share data easily and avoid creating copies of data.

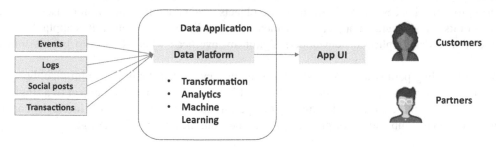

Source: Adapted from Snowflake

Creating copies of data to share entails paying to store duplicate data, increasing costs, and once data is copied out of the data producer's system it is no longer fresh, requiring systems to repeatedly copy and handle new versions of the data to stay up to date. Sharing through data copy also carries the overhead of building and maintaining systems to incorporate copied data into the consumer's system.

DESIGN PATTERNS FOR SECURITY

With security breaches frequently in the news, you should expect customers to have concerns about their data security. Security features in a multitenant data platform should include guarantees for regulatory and contractual security requirements and managing access to data and computing resources. Access control within a multitenant system is important to have some way of granting and restricting access for different users.

Access control broadly refers to the mechanisms systems put in place to achieve this goal. In this section, we will talk about two types of access control: role-based (RBAC) and discretionary (DAC). It is useful to think of access management in terms of relationships between users and objects in the system. In a data application, objects include databases, tables, configuration controls, and compute resources. Relationships between users and objects are set by privileges generally falling into the categories of create, view, modify, and delete. As it is typical for a user to have more than one of these privileges, grouping multiple privileges into a role used to control access is common. This is the RBAC model, shown in the figure:

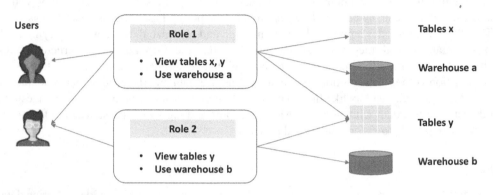

Source: Adapted from Snowflake

As depicted in the figure above, Role 1 and Role 2 each encapsulate multiple privileges for interacting with the available assets, and each individual user may be assigned one or both roles. In addition to typical access controls for database objects, Snowflake includes warehouses and other entities in its set of securable objects, or elements that can have access constraints applied to them. This can save data application developers significant overhead when setting up permissions for tenants.

When handling permissions, one aspect to keep in mind is that it's best to minimize the spread of privileges to a given object across several roles. Limiting access to a given object to a single role reduces overhead if there is a need to modify that permission in the future. A role hierarchy can then be used to create combinations of privileges, as in the example depicted in the figure:

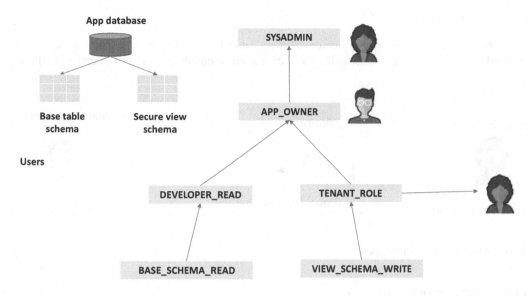

Source: Adapted from Snowflake

AUDITING

The ability to audit changes in access controls is critical for assessing system vulnerabilities, tracking down the source of corrupt data, and complying with regulations such as the European Union's General Data Protection Regulation (GDPR).

ACCESS AND AUTHORIZATION CONTROLS

Another important area of security is ensuring the connections between the application tier and the underlying data platform are secure. Considerations in this space include authentication, encryption management, and secure network design. To guarantee a secure connection between the application and the Snowflake Data Cloud, you can use AWS5 or Azure PrivateLink.

These services allow you to create direct, secure connections between Snowflake and your application tier without exposure to the public internet. Snowflake allows connections from any device or IP by default, but you can limit access using allow and block lists.

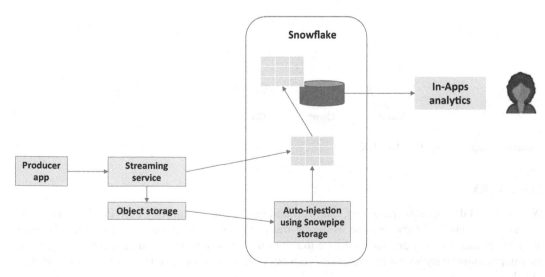

Source: Adapted from Snowflake

SHARING BY REFERENCE

A modern approach to data sharing replaces copying data with referencing data. Without the cost and overhead of copying data, the velocity increases dramatically, enabling data to be shared immediately.

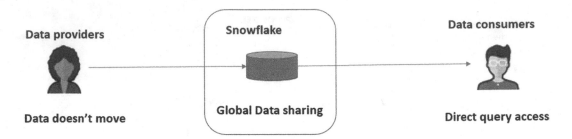

Source: Adapted from Snowflake

FEDERATED LEARNING

What is federated learning and what does it do? For example, the processing involves multiple entities. However, FL is not necessarily a type of SMPC. There are two approaches to federated learning: centralized design and decentralized design. In centralized FL, a co-ordination server creates a model or algorithm, and duplicate versions of that model are sent out to each distributed data source.

The duplicate model trains itself on each local data source and sends back the analysis it generates. That analysis is synthesized with the analysis from other data sources and integrated into the centralized model by the coordination server. This process repeats itself to constantly refine and improve the model.

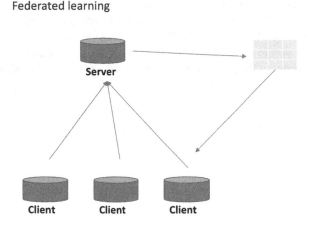

Source: Adapted from ICO Org UK

SUMMARY

We discussed data quality, reliability, and trust and how these are directly correlated to success in advanced analytics, the cornerstone of digital transformation, and the essential business benefits include increased agility and reduced time to solution; democratization of data, empowering larger user populations; easy access to a large analytics ecosystem; and acceleration of innovation and time to value.

NOTES

1. D. J. Power (10 March 2007). "A Brief History of Decision Support Systems, version 4.0". DSSResources.COM. Retrieved 10 July 2008.
2. https://ico.org.uk/
3. Dedić N. & Stanier C. (2016). "Measuring the Success of Changes to Existing Business Intelligence Solutions to Improve Business Intelligence Reporting" (PDF). Measuring the Success of Changes to Existing Business Intelligence Solutions to Improve Business Intelligence Reporting. Lecture Notes in Business Information Processing. Lecture Notes in Business Information Processing. Vol. 268. Springer International Publishing. pp. 225–236. doi:10.1007/978-3-319-49944-4_17. ISBN 978-3-319-49943-7.
4. Evelson, Boris (21 November 2008). "Topic Overview: Business Intelligence".
5. Evelson, Boris (29 April 2010). "Want to know what Forrester's lead data analysts are thinking about BI and the data domain?". Archived from the original on 6 August 2016. Retrieved 4 November 2010.
6. H P Luhn (1958). "A Business Intelligence System" (PDF). IBM Journal of Research and Development. 2 (4): 314–319. doi:10.1147/rd.24.0314. Archived from the original (PDF) on 13 September 2008.
7. Henschen, Doug (4 January 2010). "Analytics at Work: Q&A with Tom Davenport" (Interview). Archived from the original on 3 April 2012. Retrieved 26 September 2011.
8. Jump up to:a b c Rao, R. (2003). "From unstructured data to actionable intelligence" (PDF). IT Professional. 5 (6): 29–35. doi:10.1109/MITP.2003.1254966.
9. Kobielus, James (30 April 2010). "What's Not BI? Oh, Don't Get Me Started….Oops Too Late…Here Goes…" Archived from the original on 7 May 2010. Retrieved 4 November 2010. "Business" intelligence is a non-domain-specific catchall for all the types of analytic data that can be delivered to users in reports, dashboards, and the like. When you specify the subject domain for this intelligence, then you can refer to "competitive intelligence", "market intelligence", "social intelligence", "financial intelligence", "HR intelligence", "supply chain intelligence", and the like.
10. Miller Devens, Richard (1865). Cyclopaedia of Commercial and Business Anecdotes; Comprising Interesting Reminiscences and Facts, Remarkable Traits and Humors of Merchants, Traders, Bankers Etc. in All Ages and Countries. D. Appleton and company. p. 210. Retrieved 15 February 2014. business intelligence.
11. Power, D. J. "A Brief History of Decision Support Systems". Retrieved 1 November 2010.
12. Springer-Verlag Berlin Heidelberg, Springer-Verlag Berlin Heidelberg (21 November 2008). Topic Overview: Business Intelligence. doi:10.1007/978-3-540-48716-6. ISBN 978-3-540-48715-9.
13. "Decoding big data buzzwords". cio.com. 2015. BI refers to the approaches, tools, mechanisms that organizations can use to keep a finger on the pulse of their businesses. Also referred by unsexy versions—"dashboarding", "MIS" or "reporting".
14. "Experimental Characteristics Study of Data Storage Formats for Data Marts Development within Data Lakes". Retrieved 18 September 2021.
15. [94th Congress of the United States of America, 1975] 94th Congress of the United States of
16. [Abowd et al., 2019a] Abowd, J., Ashmead, R., Simson, G., Kifer, D., Leclerc, P., Machanavajjhala, A., and Sexton, W. (2019a). Census topdown: Differentially private data, incremental schemas, and consistency with public knowledge. US Census Bureau.
17. A smarter way to jump into data lakes. McKinsey. 1 August 2017.
18. [Abowd et al., 2019b] Abowd, J., Kifer, D., Moran, B., Ashmead, R., and Sexton, W. (2019b).
19. Abowd, 2018a] Abowd, J. M. (2018a). Staring-down the database reconstruction theorem. In Joint Statistical Meetings, Vancouver, BC.

20. Abowd, 2018b] Abowd, J. M. (2018b). The U.S. Census Bureau Adopts Differential Privacy. In Proceedings of the 24th ACM SIGKDD International Conference on Knowledge Discovery & Data Mining, pages 2867–2867.

21. AI in cybersecurity, https://swisscognitive.ch/2021/12/10/the-artificial-intelligence-trajectory-an-outlook-of-2022/

22. America (1975). PL 94-171: Redistricting Data.

23. "Are Data Lakes Fake News?" Sonra. 8 August 2017. Retrieved 10 August 2017.

24. [Ashmead et al., 2019] Ashmead, R., Kifer, D., Leclerc, P., Machanavajjhala, A., and Sexton, W. (2019). Effective Privacy After Adjusting for Invariants with Applications to the 2020 Census.

25. [Asi and Duchi, 2020] Asi, H. and Duchi, J. C. (2020). Instance-optimality in differential privacy via approximate inverse sensitivity mechanisms. In Larochelle, H., Ranzato, M., Hadsell, R., Balcan, M. F., and Lin, H., editors, Advances in Neural Information Processing Systems, volume 33, pages 14106–14117. Curran Associates, Inc.

26. "Business Analytics vs Business Intelligence?". timoelliott.com. 9 March 2011. Retrieved 15 June 2014.

27. Census TopDown Algorithm: Differentially Private Data, Incremental Schemas, and Consistency with Public Knowledge.

28. Cloud Standards Customer Council 2017, Cloud Customer Architecture for Big Data & Analytics.

29. Cloud Standards Customer Council 2017, Data Residency Challenges.

30. Data, machine learning and chaos. https://swisscognitive.ch/2021/12/08/faster-smarter-approach/

31. David Jensen (2004). "6. Using Scripts". Proximity 4.3 Tutorial.

32. G. Zyskind, O. Nathan, and A. Pentland. Enigma: Decentralized computation platform with guaranteed privacy. CoRR, abs/1506.03471

33. http://standards.iso.org/ittf/PubliclyAvailableStandards/c060544_ISO_IEC_17788_2014.zip

34. http://www.cloud-council.org/deliverables/cloud-customer-architecture-for-big-data-and-analytics.htm

35. http://www.cloud-council.org/deliverables/data-residency-challenges.htm

36. https://www.frontiersin.org/articles/10.3389/fpubh.2022.814163/full

37. https://www.r-bloggers.com/2019/01/generating-synthetic-data-sets-with-synthpop-in-r/

38. https://www.tetrate.io/

39. ISO 17788 Cloud Computing Overview and Vocabulary.

40. Jump up to: a b c Blumberg, R. & S. Atre (2003). "The Problem with Unstructured Data" (PDF). DM Review: 42–46. Archived from the original (PDF) on 25 January 2011.

41. L-diversity: privacy beyond k-anonymity, https://ieeexplore.ieee.org/document/1617392

42. What Is Blockchain Sharding?, https://changelly.com/blog/what-is-sharding/#:~:text=%E2%80%9CSharding%20is%20a%20database%20partitioning%20technique%20that%20will,is%20not%20the%20prerogative%20of%20the%20Ethereum%20network

11 Summary

One of the most gratifying outcomes of writing this book is the dialog with people about their view of data Privacy and security. I reconnected with people I worked with in the past, and they also introduced me to new people.

We discussed Web 3.0, zero trust, and data integrity aspects:

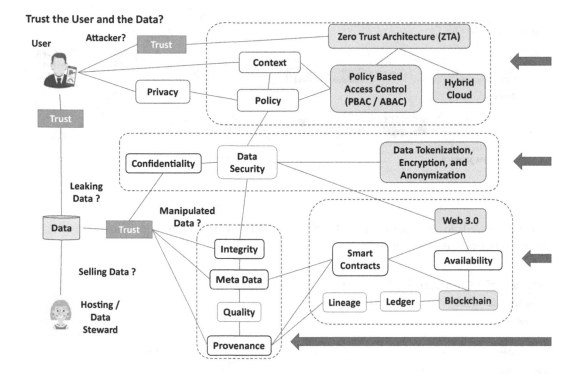

DOI: 10.1201/9781003254928-14

We discussed how ZTA and Web 3.0 can address different issues:

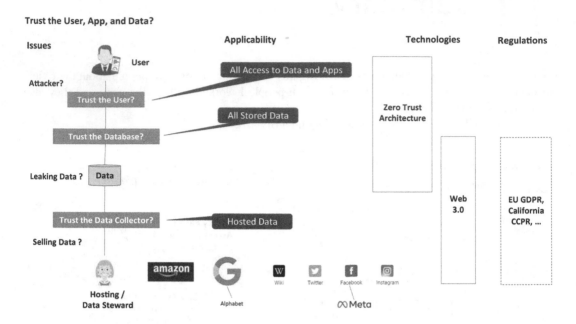

We discussed an example of a roadmap that is implementing zero trust and addressing the discussed issues that we discussed:

Example of a Data Security Roadmap

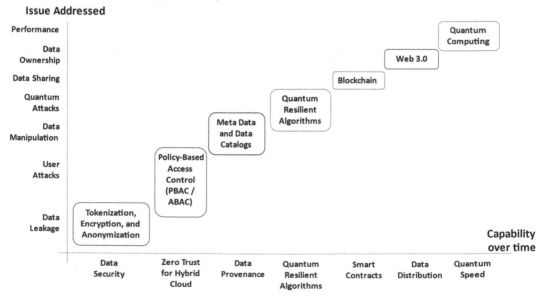

Volume I discussed different forms of access control, including "dynamic authorization to resources", including ABAC (attribute-based access control) or PBAC (policy-based access control). This book discussed the jouney into zero trust that can address several of the issues. We also discussed the small steps that can be taken by implementing multifactor authentication and policy-based and dynamic authorization to resources.

We discussed zero trust:

Zero Trust Maturity Model

Areas

Identity	Device	Environment (NW)	Application	Data
Analytics				
Automation				
Governance				

Maturity Levels

Maturity	Identity	Device	Environment (NW)	Application	Data
Traditional	Password or Mult Factor (MFA)	Simple inventore	Macro segmentaion	Access based on local validation	Static control
Advanced	MFA or some Federation	Data access depends on device posture	Micro perimeters	Access based on central validation	Cloud data encrypted
Optimal	Continous realtime ML analysis	Data access depends on realtime analysis	ML threat protection	Access continously validated	All data is encrypted

Source: Adapted from CISA.org

Glossary

Access Control: The process of granting or denying specific requests to 1) obtain and use the information and related information processing services and 2) enter specific physical facilities (e.g., federal buildings, military establishments, border crossing entrances).

Actuarial Pricing: Actuarial pricing is the discipline that applies mathematical and statistical methods to assess risk and price policies in insurance, finance, and other industries and professions.

Advanced Encryption Standard (AES): AES is a block cipher encryption algorithm.

Advanced Persistent Threat: An adversary with sophisticated skills and resources provides opportunities to achieve its goals using multiple attack vectors (cyber, deception, physical, malware).

Advanced Threat Prevention (ATP): Advanced Threat Prevention is a cybersecurity tool that identifies malware, quarantines it, and allows it to be analyzed and identified in and between organizations.

Alert: A notification that can detect an incident, vulnerability, or finding.

Annual Revenue: Annual Revenue is the amount of yearly income of an organization before taxes.

Antivirus Software: A program that monitors the network to detect malicious code and to prevent malware insertion.

API: Application programming interface.

Architecture: A highly structured specification of an acceptable approach within a framework for solving a specific problem according to "Glossary of Terms, Acronyms, and Notations".

Assumption of Breach: Assumption of a breach is a model that dictates that you have been breached and will be breached again. Robert Mueller defined it at the RSA Security Conference in 2013.

Attack: An attack is an assault perpetrated by a threat source that attempts to exfiltrate data, interruption processes, or alter data or system operations.

Audit: Independent review and examination of records and activities to assess the adequacy of system controls and ensure compliance with established policies and operational procedures.

Authentication: Verifying the identity of a user, process, or device.

Authorization: The ability to determine if a user has the right to create, read, update, or delete specific data.

Availability: Availability is the ability to ensure the data is available to users.

Backdoor: An undocumented way of gaining access to a computer system. A backdoor is a potential security risk.

Backup: A copy of files and programs made to facilitate recovery if necessary.

Board of Directors: In a public company, a board of directors (BoD) is a group of individuals elected to represent the shareholders. A board's mandate is to establish corporate management and oversight policies and make decisions on major company issues, including cybersecurity. Every public company must have a board of directors.

Botnet: A collection of computers compromised by malicious code and controlled across a network.

Breach: A data breach is an incident where information is stolen or taken from a system without the knowledge or authorization of the system's owner. A security breach is an incident that results in unauthorized access to networks, devices, or data without knowledge or authorization of the system's owner.

Bug: An unexpected detect in a system or device.

Business Continuity Management (BCM): Business Continuity Management is the process of creating systems of prevention and recovery to deal with potential threats to a company.

Business Interruption: Business interruption is when business as usual is interrupted and when the authorized users cannot access an application. In cyber, it is typically a result of a denial of service attack.

Business Process: Business process is a set of digital rules utilized by one or more systems to take inputs, transform them, and produce outputs reported or utilized by other systems.

Capability Maturity Model Integration (CMMI): Impact and likelihood information can be obtained by using CMMI as the basis for the answer ratings developed at Carnegie Mellon University (CMU). CMMI is used in terms of process level improvement training and appraisal programs. CMMI defines the following maturity levels for processes: Initial, Managed, Defined, Quantitatively Managed, and Optimizing.

Category Domains: In risk modeling, category domains are subsets of data that can be allocated into further categorization.

Chief Information Security Officer (CISO): Chief Information Security Officer (CISO) is a senior-level executive within an organization responsible for establishing and maintaining the enterprise vision, strategy, and cybersecurity program to ensure digital assets are adequately protected.

Clickjacking: Clickjacking is an attack that unwittingly has a user click a web page element disguised as another element. Typically, this results in malware being deployed unknowingly.

Cloud: Technology services and software that run on the Internet instead of on-premises computers.

Cloud Computing: Cloud computing provides on-demand work access to a shared pool of computing capabilities or resources that can be provisioned rapidly with minimal management effort.

Common Vulnerability Exposure (CVE): Common Vulnerability Exposure (CVE) is a database of vulnerabilities published by NIST. The CVE system provides a reference method for publicly known information-security vulnerabilities and exposures.

Compliance Manager or Officer: A compliance manager or officer is an employee whose responsibilities include ensuring the company complies with its outside regulatory requirements and internal policies. A compliance officer may craft and update internal policies to mitigate the risk of the company breaking laws and regulations and lead internal audits of procedures. In cyber, there are many regulations based on type of data processed, geography, and industry that a compliance manager must be familiar with.

Confidentiality: Confidentiality is the ability to ensure that only authorized and approved users have access to the data.

Consensus: This refers to a majority of participants of a network agreeing on the validity of a transaction. In the context of Hyperledger Fabric Consensus, a network of nodes provides a guaranteed ordering of transactions and validates the block of transactions.

Consensus Security: An application of security protocols, such as encryption and hashing, to protect data integrity and safeguard Consensus Algorithm against proof of work, proof of stake, etc.

Container Image: Package of software that can run within a container.

Control Assessment: Control assessment is a security assessment that uses policies, and controls tests to ascertain the effectiveness of a cybersecurity control both organizationally and technically.

Cookie: A cookie is a small text file that is placed on your computer by some websites you visit. Cookies can then be used to track you through the site, or when you revisit. Some cookies will allow you to save information about yourself, to prevent you re-entering it. When used correctly, cookies can be very useful; however, some websites use them to track you without your consent.

Critical Infrastructure: Critical Infrastructure represents the digital assets that are instrumental for society to function without a debilitating impact on the security, economy, health, safety, or environment.

CVE: Common Vulnerabilities and Exposures (CVE) is a list of publicly disclosed computer security flaws.

Cyber Budget: Cyber budgets are a combination of fixed and variable costs and delineated by capital and operational expenses. The cyber budget should be aligned with the fixed operational costs (the security team personnel), the capital fixed costs (the tools and their licensing costs), and the variable costs.

Cyber Insurance: Cyber Insurance is a risk transference mechanism to reduce business interruption, data exfiltration, and regulatory losses due to cyber-attacks.

Cyber Legal Team: Cyber legal team is the legal team that will be involved in cyber when a breach occurs. All communications will likely be run by legal before they are released to the media or a regulator. The communications team usually crafts any breach notifications with the CISO and legal collaborating.

Cyber Resilience: Cyber resilience measures an entity's ability to continuously deliver the intended outcome despite adverse cyber events. It can be used to benchmark and define organizations goals in terms of cybersecurity.

Cyber Risk: Cyber risk is the risk at the digital asset level; system, process, technology, and data can have reputational, organizational, legal, and/or financial impacts. It is the cornerstone of measuring cyber resiliency.

Cyber Simulation (SIM): Cyber simulation (SIM) is an automated approach to train Cybersecurity Operations (SOC) teams to adequately respond to evolving threats.

Cyber Threat: Cyber threat is a malicious attempt to damage or disrupt a computer network or system.

Cyber Threat Intelligence (CTI): Cyber threat intelligence (CTI) is a cybersecurity tool that works in the deep and dark web to identify hackers and track their malicious activities. CTI provides detailed information about potential or current attacks that threaten an organization.

Cybergeddon: A term defined by the author to indicate the worst-case scenario of inherent risks analysis in terms of zero percent effectiveness of controls of an organization.

Cybersecurity: Cybersecurity is a program of activities that utilize people, process, and tools to protect an organization's information systems.

Cybersecurity: Cybersecurity is the body of technologies, processes, and practices designed to protect networks, computers, programs and data from attack, damage or unauthorized access.

Cybersecurity Posture: Cybersecurity posture refers to the maturity and effectiveness of the various cybersecurity control measures.

Data: Data is the information that is processed and stored. Data can be classified into different types including privacy, credit card, intellectual property, customer data, supply chain data, etc.

Data Breach: Data breach is the unauthorized movement or disclosure of information.

Data Exfiltration: Data exfiltration is when cyber criminals steal data. This can be due to many causes including and not limited to misconfigured systems, poor access controls, from insiders or external actors. Specifically, it is the unauthorized copying, transfer, or retrieval of data from a computer or server. Data exfiltration is a malicious activity performed through various techniques, typically by cybercriminals over the Internet or other networks.

Data Loss: Data loss can happen due to theft, deletion, or misplacement of data.

Data Loss Prevention (DLP): Data loss prevention (DLP) is a cybersecurity tool that provides rules to identify when data is accessed by authorized users and sent outside the organization and add additional rules to prevent unauthorized data leakage. It is found mostly in large organizations and in those with privacy issues.

Data Privacy Officer (DPO): Data privacy officer (DPO) is a senior-level executive within an organization responsible for data privacy. The DPO must ensure that the organization complies with GDPR if it processes EU citizen privacy data regardless of where it is located.

Data Type: Data type is the classification of data processed. This can be one or more types, including but not limited to privacy, personally identifiable (PII), patent, formula, healthcare, federal, business, credit card, etc.

Deepfake: Deepfake is a video of a person in which their face or body has been digitally altered so that they appear to be someone else, typically used maliciously or to spread false information.

Detect: Detect is the third of the five NIST functions. The detect function defines the appropriate activities to identify the occurrence of a cybersecurity event. The detect function enables timely discovery of cybersecurity events.

Digital Asset: Digital asset refers to the systems, business processes, technologies, and data type used to automate work using computer technology.

Disaster Recovery (DR): DR is a discipline to recover from a disaster using a redefined plan tested and ready to execute.

Distributed Denial of Service (DDOS): Distributed denial of service (DDOS) happens when a cyber-offender takes action that prevents legitimate users from accessing targeted computer systems, devices, or other network resources.

DLT: Distributed Ledger Technology (DLT) is technological infrastructure and protocols that operate a decentralized network allowing simultaneous secure access, validation, and record updating using cryptographic signatures and with no central authority.

Domain: In cyber risk modeling, domain is a specific set of data. In this invention, it is related to the cyber risk engine. However, other domains can be created.

Encryption: Encryption is a process used in cybersecurity that provides data scrambling so that only authorized parties can access it.

Enterprise Risk Management: Enterprise risk management is a business program that combines risk management disciplines across several operational, credit, cyber, etc.

Event: An event is a suspicious occurrence that may be an indication that an incident is occurring.

Exploit: This term is used generally to represent any method deployed by unauthorized users to gain access to computers or networks.

Exposure: Exposure is a condition where the system is unprotected, and an attacker can obtain access to the system or network.

FERPA: The Family Educational Rights and Privacy Act (FERPA) is a federal law that protects the privacy of student education records by the U.S. Department of Education.

FI: Financial Institutions.

Financial Cyber Impacts: Financial cyber impacts are defined in three categories; data exfiltration, business interruption, and regulatory loss and are aligned to what cyber insurance companies will pay out claims against.

Finding: A finding is a result of a control assessment.

FIPS: US Federal Information Processing Standards.

FIPS 199: The loss of confidentiality, integrity, or availability could be expected to have: (i) a limited adverse effect (FIPS Publication 199 low); (ii) a serious adverse effect (FIPS Publication 199 moderate); or (iii) a severe or catastrophic adverse effect (FIPS Publication 199 high) on organizational operations, organizational assets, or individuals.

Firewalls: Firewalls are a cybersecurity tool that prevents unauthorized access to or from a private network. This a basic cybersecurity tool and most SMEs will also have firewalls.

Fully Homomorphic Encryption (FHE): FHE has numerous applications. For example, it enables private queries to a search engine—the user submits an encrypted query and the search engine computes a succinct encrypted answer without ever looking at the query in the clear.

GDPR: GDPR is the General Data Protection Regulation that came into effect May 25, 2018, protecting the EU citizen privacy data.

GWAS: A genome-wide association study (GWAS) is used in genetics research to associate specific genetic variations with particular diseases.

Hacker: A Hacker is someone who makes things. In this context, it's someone who makes things by programming computers. This is the original, and purest definition of the term, that is, you have an idea and you "hack" something together to make it work. It also applies to people who modify things to significantly change their functionality, but less so.

HIPAA: The Health Insurance Portability and Accountability Act of 1996 (HIPAA) is a U.S. federal law that required national standards to protect sensitive patient health data.

Homomorphic Encryption (HE): HE allows operations on encrypted data.

Hyperledger: This umbrella project of open source blockchains and community focused on developing a suite of stable frameworks, tools, and libraries for enterprise-grade blockchain (DLT) deployments.

Hyperledger Fabric: Distributed ledger software that can be used as a foundation for developing blockchain-based solutions or applications.

Hypervisor: Virtual machine monitor software that virtualizes physical resources and allows for running virtual machines.

IAPP: International Association of Privacy Professionals, https://iapp.org, is the largest and most comprehensive global information privacy community and resource. Founded in 2000, the IAPP is a not-for-profit organization that helps define, promote, and improve the privacy profession globally.

Identify: Identify is the first of the five NIST functions. The identify function assists in developing an organizational understanding to managing cybersecurity risk to systems, people, assets, data, and capabilities.

Identity Access Management (IAM): Identity access management (IAM) is a cybersecurity tool that provides authorization and authentication of users to systems.

Impact: Impact is the degree to which a cyber-issue may have an adverse outcome on the organization. Several factors can influence impact in cybersecurity.

Incident: An incident is an occurrence that may result in a loss or adverse consequence to the digital asset.

Incident Response: Refers to cybersecurity remediation work where an incident is confirmed, and resources respond to mitigate and repair the damage to the digital assets.

Inherent Cyber Risk: Inherent cyber risk is the cyber risk without controls in place or as if there was zero percent effectiveness of cybersecurity controls. It is the worst-case scenario and is also called "cybergeddon" risk.

Innovation: Innovation is the act or process of introducing new ideas, devices, or methods.

Insured: Insured is a first- or third-party organization that has purchased cybersecurity insurance to transfer risk and increase cyber resiliency.

Integrity: Integrity ensures that the data is unaltered and is consistent, accurate, and trustworthy over its entire life cycle.

Inter-cloud computing: Paradigm for enabling the interworking between two or more cloud service providers.

Interconnectivity: The term defines the electronic connections between businesses, systems, processes, vendors, suppliers, governments, and the like.

International Standards Organization (ISO): ISO is the International Standards Organization. It publishes the ISO/IEC 27001, an information security standard, part of the ISO/IEC 27000 family of standards. ISO/IEC 27001 specifies a management system intended to bring information security under management control and gives specific requirements. Organizations that meet the requirements may be certified by an accredited certification body after completing an audit.

Intrusion Detection System (IDS): Intrusion Detection System (IDS) is a cybersecurity tool that monitors systems for malicious activity or policy violations.

IP Address: An Internet protocol is a numerical label connected to a computer network used for communications.

IT Auditors: IT auditors are responsible for developing, planning, and executing IT audit programs based on risk assessments in a highly integrated audit environment. This includes documenting and communicating risks, providing counsel on control issues and recommended process changes, and monitoring corrective actions to improve the organization's existing practices reducing cyber risk.

Lattice-based cryptosystems (LBE): LBE can build systems that securely and privately handle computation on encrypted data. Some homomorphic encryption schemes use it. LBE can be quantum-resistant. Lattice-based cryptography is based on cryptographic systems such as Learning With Errors, LWE. Lattice-based cryptography has been published and analyzed increasingly during 2011 to 2020.

Likelihood: Likelihood is a probability that a cyber-attack will cause damage.

Malware: Malware is software that is intended to damage or disable computers and computer systems.

Mergers and Acquisitions (M&A): Mergers and Acquisitions (M&A) is the area of corporate finance, management, and strategy that deals with purchasing and/or joining with other companies. Two organizations join forces to become a new business in a merger, usually with a new name. In terms of digital assets, not all digital assets will be acquired or utilized in the merger or acquisition.

Microsharding: Microsharding splits a file up into multiple pieces, but the pieces are extremely small. Theoretically, as small as a single byte, each microshard tends to be just a few bytes in practice. Each of these microshards are stored in different locations.

Mitigation: Mitigation uses measures to reduce the likelihood of risk or implement risk reduction controls based on the impacts.

MLOps: MLOps (machine learning operations) is a discipline that enables data scientists and IT professionals to collaborate and communicate while automating machine learning algorithms.

National Institute of Standards and Technology (NIST): NIST is the National Institute of Standards and Technology, a unit of the U.S. Commerce Department. The NIST Cybersecurity Framework (CSF) is a set of 98 control tests. The CSF provides a policy framework of computer security guidance for how private sector organizations in the United States can assess and improve their ability to prevent, detect, and respond to cyber-attacks.

New York State (NYS) Part 500 regulation: New York State (NYS) Part 500 regulation establishes cybersecurity requirements for financial services companies.

Nonpersonal data: Class of data objects that does not contain PII Personal data objects that were originally made anonymous are nonpersonal data.

OPD: Organizational data whose protection is required based on the policies established by governance of data process. Organizations have policies that govern the data under their control. ISO/IEC 38505-1 identifies and examines higher level governance concerns regarding the use of data, which is relevant from the perspective of governance of data.

Operational Risk: Operational risk is the prospect of loss resulting from inadequate or failed procedures, systems, or policies.

Opt-in/Opt-out: An important distinction in the privacy debate concerns the terms under which e-mail marketers (legitimate ones, not spammers that ignore ethical and legal concerns) can contact users. Opt-in is the consumer-friendly position, where companies can send e-mail only to people who have directly given their consent for such communications, typically by signing up at a website.

Partially Homomorphic Encryption (PHE): PHE allows only one operation on the encrypted data (i.e., either addition or multiplication but not both). PHE are in general more efficient than SHE/SWHE and FHE, mainly because they are homomorphic with respect to only one type of operation: addition or multiplication.

Payment Industry Data Security Standard (PCI-DSS): PCI-DSS is the Payment Industry Data Security Standard. It applies to banks, merchants, and data processors who process credit card data.

Penetration Testing: Penetration testing is a method that searches for vulnerabilities and attempts to circumvent the system's security features.

PHI: Protected Health Information.

Phishing: Phishing is the fraudulent practice of sending emails from reputable companies to induce users to reveal personal information, such as passwords and credit card numbers.

Physical Security: Physical security are controls for physical access to the organization. These controls are locks, cameras, doors, fire suppression systems, personnel identification (badges), visitor security, etc. All organizations usually have some level of physical security. More mature have electronic means.

Privacy: Privacy is related to the confidentiality and integrity of data.

Privacy Policy: Privacy policy is a disclaimer placed on a website informing users about how the website deals with a user's personal information and is a disclaimer placed on a website informing users about how the website deals with a user's personal information. This is a disclaimer placed on a website informing users about how the website deals with a user's personal information.

Process Revenue: Process revenue is the amount of revenue based on the use of a particular process.

Programmer: A programmer is someone who can solve problems by manipulating computer code. They can have a wide range of skill levels—from just being "ok" with basic scripting to being an absolute sorcerer with any language.

Protect: Protect is the second of the five NIST functions. The protect function outlines appropriate safeguards to ensure delivery of critical infrastructure services. The protect function supports the ability to limit or contain the impact of a potential cybersecurity event.

Pseudonymity: This concept originated in the field of cryptography. Pseudonymity can prove a consistent identity without revealing one's actual name, instead of using an alias or pseudonym. Pseudonymity combines many of the advantages of both a known identity and anonymity.

Public domain data: It is a class of data objects over which nobody holds or can hold copyright or other intellectual property rights. Data can be in the public domain in some jurisdictions, while not in others.

Qualitative: Qualitative data is information about qualities; information that can't actually be measured from a subjective viewpoint.

Quantitative: Quantitative research is used to quantify the problem by generating numerical data or data that can be transformed into usable statistics. It is objective.

Ransomware: Ransomware is a type of malicious software intended to block access to network systems until the target pays some form of ransom to the deployer.

Recover: Recover is the fifth of the five NIST functions. The recover function identifies appropriate activities to maintain plans for resilience and to restore any capabilities or services that were impaired due to a cybersecurity incident. The recover function supports timely recovery to normal operations to reduce the impact from a cybersecurity incident.

Regulatory Loss: Regulatory loss happens when a regulator fines an organization for a cyber-breach. The costs of the fines are defined by the regulator(s).

Regulatory Risk: Regulatory risk is defined as having privileges withdrawn by a regulator or having conditions applied by a regulator that adversely impact the economic value.

Reputational Risk: In cyber, reputational risk is a matter of corporate trust. The loss can be demonstrated in lost revenue; increased operating, capital or regulatory costs, or destruction of shareholder value.

Residual Cyber Risk: Residual cyber risk is the cyber risk with controls in place. It is the best-case scenario.

Resources: Resources are an operational or capital item. Operational resources are personnel and capital resources are equipment.

Respond: Respond is the fourth of the five NIST functions. The respond function includes appropriate activities to act regarding a detected cybersecurity incident. The respond function supports the ability to contain the impact of a potential cybersecurity incident.

Risk: A risk, in plain language, is a chance of something bad happening combined with how bad it would be if it did happen.

Risk Accumulation: Risk accumulation or amplification is the aggregation of losses from a single event due to the concentration of cyber risk exposed to that single event. In cyber risk, this based on the digital assets. Some examples are cloud compromise and data exfiltration.

Risk Amplification: Risk amplification is the aggregation of financial losses from a cyber event due to reputational, operational, or legal impacts.

Risk Calculation: In risk modeling, risk calculation is a mathematical determination of the risk exposures.

Risk Names: In risk modeling, risk names are measurable exposures that use algorithms to express their value.

Risk Parameters: In risk modeling, risk parameters are specific numerical or other measurable factors forming one of a set that defines a digital asset risk or sets the conditions of its operation.

Risk Qualifications: In risk modeling, risk qualifications are calculations that use subjective data from the business.

Risk Quantifications: In risk modeling, risk quantifications are calculations that use objective financial metrics derived from the business and cyber-related metrics derived from metric-based organizations.

Risk Questionnaire: In risk modeling, risk questionnaire is a set of questions that are used in the risk qualification metrics.

Rootkit: A rootkit is a set of software tools that enable an unauthorized user to gain control of a computer system without being detected.

Secure multitenancy: Type of multitenancy that employs security controls to explicitly guard against data breaches and provides validation of these controls for proper governance.

Security and Exchange Commission (SEC): The Securities and Exchange Commission is a U.S. governmental agency that oversees securities transactions, the activities of financial professionals, and mutual fund trading to prevent fraud.

Security Control Measures: Security control measures refers to the means taken by organizations to identify, protect, detect, recover, or respond to cybersecurity. This includes people, process, and tools.

SIEM: Security incident event management (SIEM) is a cybersecurity tool that provides real-time analysis of security alerts generated by applications and network hardware to identify brute force, viruses, and firewall attacks.

SMPC: Secure Multi Party Computing.

Somewhat Homomorphic Encryption (SWHE): SWHE allows a limited number of either addition or multiplication operations of the data, but not both. SHE (Somewhat Homomorphic Encryption also called SWHE) is more general than PHE because it supports homomorphic operations with additions and multiplications.

Spam: Spam is any unsolicited electronic message. Often spam messages will be commercial in nature. "Spammers" usually harvest email addresses from websites or buy them from other companies.

Spyware: Any technology that aids in gathering information about persons or organizations without their knowledge. On the Internet, spyware is programming that's secretly installed in a computer to gather information about the user and relay it to advertisers or other interested parties. Spyware can infiltrate a computer as a virus or as a surprise result of installing a new program.

System: System is a consolidated set of technologies that provides the basis for collecting, creating, storing, processing, and distributing information.

Tabletop Exercise: A discussion-based exercise where resources meet and work through a scenario to validate plans, procedures, policies regarding an incident.

Technology: Technology is computer-related components that typically consist of hardware and software, databases, messaging, and devices.

Threat: A negative event can lead to an undesired outcome, such as damage to or loss of an asset. Threats can use—or become more dangerous because of—a vulnerability in a system.

Threat Actor: Threat Actor is an entity that is partially or wholly responsible for an incident that impacts—or has the potential to impact—an organization's cybersecurity. In threat intelligence, actors are generally categorized as external, internal, or partners.

Unicode: The Unicode Standard provides a unique number for every character, no matter what platform, device, application, or language. It has been adopted by all modern software providers and now allows data to be transported through many different platforms, devices, and applications without corruption. Support of Unicode forms the foundation for the representation of languages and symbols in all major operating systems, search engines, browsers, laptops, and smart phones—plus the Internet and World Wide Web (URLs, HTML, XML, CSS, JSON, etc.).

Vendors: Vendors are third parties that provide goods or services to an organization.

Vendor Cyber Risk: The measurement of cyber risk that a third party possesses in relationship to digital assets of the first party.

Vendor Cyber Risk Management: Vendor cyber risk management (VCRM) is the measurement and management of cyber risk that focuses on third-party products (such as cloud service providers) and services (system integrators, management consultants, and the big 4), and the digital assets they provide or work with.

Verizon Data Breach Report (VRR): The VRR is annual security report from Verizon that provides vast statistics on data breach information.

Virtual Machine (VM): Isolated execution environment for running software that uses virtualized physical resources.

Virus: A piece of code capable of negatively affecting computer systems and networks by corrupting or destroying data.

VPN: A virtual private network is an encrypted connection over the Internet to protect it from unauthorized access. It allows for the safe transmittal of data from one location to another.

Vulnerability: Vulnerabilities are weaknesses in a system. They make threats possible and/or more significant.

Vulnerability Management System (VMS): A VMS is a cybersecurity tool that cyclically uses software to identify and classify vulnerabilities. VMS vendors include Qualys, Rapid7, Tripwire, Saint, Tenable, Core Security, Critical Watch, Beyond Security, and many others.

Web Bug/Beacons: A web beacon is a clear image (you cannot usually see it). They are often placed in email messages. When you open the message, the bug will notify the sender. Web bugs are often used by services such as MSGTag.

Weights: Cyber risk refers to probability weighting used for percent complete metrics and maturity weighting to define which parameters are more critical than others.

White Hat/Black Hat: White hat hackers (also known as ethical hackers) are the polar opposite of their black hat counterparts. They use their technical skills to protect the world from bad hackers according to "Different Types of Hackers: The 6 Hats Explained".

Willful Neglect: Cybersecurity means conscious, intentional failure or reckless indifference to the obligation to comply with cybersecurity measures.

ZTA: Zero Trust Architecture.

NOTES

1. Glossary of Terms, Acronyms, and Notations. https://pages.nist.gov/FIPS201/glossary/
2. Privacy Glossary. https://www.privacytrust.com/guidance/privacy_glossary.html
3. Different Types of Hackers: The 6 Hats Explained - InfoSec .... https://sectigostore.com/blog/different-types-of-hackers-hats-explained/

Appendix A: The 2030 Environment

INTRODUCTION

We will discuss quantum cryptography, threat solution, deployment of quantum systems in different countries, and trends in Data Security.

SOME ERAS IN DATA SECURITY

We will discuss cryptography, tokenization, and lattice-based encryption. These techniques provide different application transparency levels and resistance to quantum computing attacks.

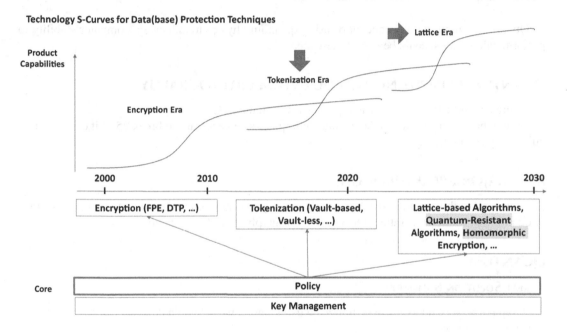

Quantum Attacks?

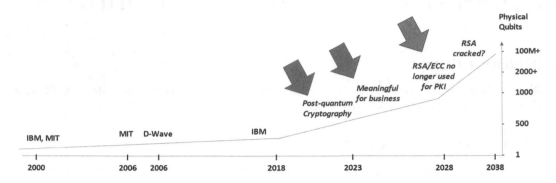

Source: Adapted from CBI Research and Gartner

Quantum computing, the concept of using quantum physics to enhance a computer's ability to perform calculations, could be one of these areas.

QUANTUM COMPUTING AND QUANTUM CRYPTOGRAPHY

Breaking 256-bit Elliptic Curve Encryption with a Quantum Computer
Researchers have calculated the quantum computer size necessary to break 256-bit elliptic curve public-key cryptography:

ANY MAJOR BREAKTHROUGHS

Of course, all of this assumes that there aren't any major breakthroughs like quantum in silicon chips or quantum at room temperature. On a desktop or graphics card form factor.

QUANTUM

THREAT SOLUTION SUMMARY

Each type of quantum threat can be mitigated using one or more known defenses. Depending on the threat, they include:

- Physical isolation
- Increasing symmetric key sizes
- Using Quantum Key Distribution (QKD)
- Replacing quantum-susceptible cryptography with quantum-resistant cryptography
- Using hybrid solutions
- Using quantum random number generators (QRNG)
- Using quantum-enabled defenses

Major Project Steps Estimated Timeline

- Education and Awareness 1 month
- Get Senior Management Support 1 month
- Form a Project Team, Plan, and Estimated Timeline 1 month
- Perform a Data Protection Inventory 3–12 months
- Analyze Collected Data and Make Mitigation Decisions 3–6 months

- Testing, Experimentation, R&D 1–2 years
- Implement Post-Quantum Mitigations 1–5 years

Re-Assess Project End

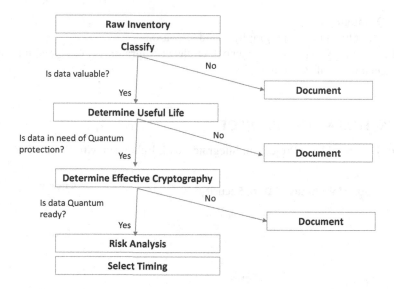

Taking a Data Protection Inventory

Source: Adapted from Amazon AWS

DATA PROTECTION INVENTORY FIELDS

A data protection inventory should include at least the following components:

- Description of devices and/or data, including any version information
- Location of all sensitive data and devices
- Identification of owners, stakeholders, and vendors (if any)
- Criticality of the data to the organization
- Determination of how long the data or devices need to be protected from unauthorized eavesdropping (e.g., useful life)
- Identification of data protection systems currently involved
- Effective cryptography they use, particularly cryptographic algorithms, algorithm type (e.g., symmetric, asymmetric, hash, etc.), existing key sizes, and maximum configurable key size
- Cryptography name/description
- Cryptographic type (e.g., symmetric, asymmetric, key exchange, hash, digital signature, etc.)
- Current key size
- Maximum key size
- Vendor support timeline for data protections
- Other post-quantum mitigations already involved (e.g., physical, QKD, PQC, etc.)
- Post-quantum protected already (Y/N?)

TESTING

Organizations with the appropriate resources are encouraged to begin testing potential PQC solutions in their own environments and applications. PQC solutions can impact performance and usability. By testing PQC solutions, an organization may learn about particular challenges in their own environment and be better prepared for the post-quantum migration project overall. There are many resources available to help developers and testers with PQC implementations, including

- Open Quantum Safe
- NIST Post-Quantum Cryptography Standardization
- NIST National Cybersecurity Center of Excellence Migration to Post-Quantum Cryptography
- ETSI Quantum-Safe Cryptography

QUANTUM THREAT AND PROJECT

Evolution of Enhanced Data Protection integrated with Enhanced with Policy Control:

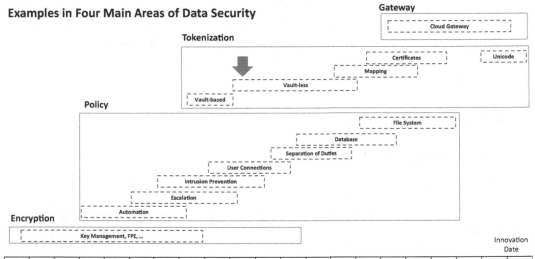

SUMMARY

We use cryptography, tokenization, and lattice-based encryption. These techniques provide different levels of application transparency and resistance to quantum computing attacks.

NOTES

1. https://techxplore.com/news/2022-03-homomorphic-encryption.html
2. https://phys.org/news/2022-01-quantum-silicon-accuracy.html
3. https://www.sciencedaily.com/releases/2021/06/210617082723.htm
4. https://newatlas.com/quantum-computing/quantum-computing-desktop-room-temperature/
5. https://www.schneier.com/blog/archives/2022/02/breaking-245-bit-elliptic-curve-encryption-with-a-quantum-computer.html

6. https://openquantumsafe.org/
7. https://csrc.nist.gov/projects/post-quantum-cryptography/post-quantum-cryptography-standardization
8. https://www.nccoe.nist.gov/projects/building-blocks/post-quantum-cryptography
9. https://www.etsi.org/technologies/quantum-safe-cryptography
10. https://nvlpubs.nist.gov/nistpubs/CSWP/NIST.CSWP.04282021.pdf
11. https://nvlpubs.nist.gov/nistpubs/ir/2016/NIST.IR.8105.pdf

Appendix B: Synthetic Data and Differential Privacy

INTRODUCTION

We will discuss synthetic data, generating microdata artificially, synthetic data in A.I., and synthesising data.

SYNTHETIC DATA

Synthetic data is a class of data that is artificially generated, that is, not obtained from direct observations of the real world. Data can be generated using different methods such as statistically rigorous sampling from real data, semantic approaches, generative adversarial networks, or by creating simulation scenarios where models and processes interact to create completely new datasets of events.

Why this is important one of the major problems with A.I. development today is the burden of obtaining real-world data and labeling it, so A.I. models can be trained effectively. Synthetic data can rectify this. Furthermore, synthetic data is critical in removing personally identifiable information (PII). Business impact adoption is increasing across various industries and is used in natural language processing (NLP) applications. We predict a massive increase in the adoption of synthetic data:

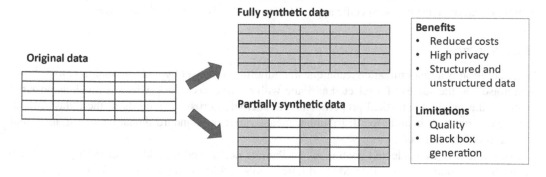

Source: Adapted from Statice and Gartner

- Avoids using PII when training machine learning (ML) models via synthetic variations of original data or synthetic replacement of parts of data.

GENERATING MICRODATA ARTIFICIALLY

Synthetic data is an approach to generating microdata artificially to represent a predefined statistical data model. By definition, a synthetic dataset does not contain any data collected from or about existing data principals, but looks realistic for the intended purposes. Synthetic data fitting the original data too closely can reveal information about genuine data principals, such as their personal data.

There are various ways to create synthetic data. Theoretically, data can be randomly generated based on a number of selected statistical properties. Key characteristics of such a model are the distributions of each attribute (overall and in subpopulations) and the internal relationships among the attributes.

In practice, the generation of synthetic data can involve multiple or continuous transformations on real datasets using randomization techniques and sampling, as described in this document.

Typically, synthetic data is used for testing tools and applications.

Synthetic data can be used for developing queries. In some applications, synthetic data can be used as a surrogate for real data: in these cases, the data curator should reproduce queries performed on synthetic data on actual data, to ensure that inferences drawn on the synthetic data are correct when drawn on real data.

The privacy guarantees of synthetic data can be evaluated using the differential privacy model.

RANDOMIZATION TECHNIQUES

General

The term "randomization" refers to a category of de-identification techniques in which values of an attribute are modified so that their new values differ from their true values in a random way. Such a process reduces the ability of an attacker to deduce the value of an attribute from the values of other attributes in the same data record, thereby reducing the effectiveness of inference attempts.

NOTE Another term sometimes used to describe "randomization" is "perturbation".

Randomization techniques do not preserve data truthfulness at the record level. To achieve the chosen objectives, an effective randomization process resulting in useful data needs to be tailored on a case-by-case basis. Such tailoring involves both a detailed understanding of the nature of the data and the choice of appropriate parameters for the selected randomization techniques (and typically involves performing a statistical evaluation).

The output of randomization is microdata.

Certain randomization techniques, such as permutation, are applicable to both numerical and nonnumerical data attributes. Specific approaches to randomization are described below.

NOISE ADDITION

Noise addition is a randomization technique that modifies a dataset by adding random values, "random noise", to the values of a selected attribute with continuous values, while as much as possible retaining the original statistical properties of the attribute across all records in the dataset. Such statistical properties include the distribution, mean, variance, standard deviation, covariance, and correlation of the attribute.

Noise addition to a selected continuous attribute is performed by adding, or multiplying by, a stochastic or randomized number. Many different noise addition algorithms have been developed with the goal of preserving the statistical properties of the de-identified data and its usefulness for different use cases.

A general review of these techniques is outside the scope of this document.

PERMUTATION

Permutation is a technique for reordering the values of a selected attribute across the records in a dataset without modification of values. As a result, permutation retains the exact statistical distribution of the selected attribute across all records in the dataset.

NOTE: Other terms used to describe the process of permutation are "data confusion", "shuffling", and "attribute substitution".

Permutation techniques are applicable to both numeric and non-numeric values. Special considerations need to be taken to ensure that the resulting dataset appears to be consistent and realistic, because observable inconsistencies can help to reconstruct the permutation algorithm. For example, it is to be expected that men are taller than women on average; it is also to be expected that first or given names typically correspond to the listed gender.

Permutation approaches or algorithms differ both in their approach and their complexity. Some algorithms are based on repeatedly swapping values between records until all values are replaced for the selected attribute; other algorithms follow logic designed for the specific application needs. In order to preserve the correlation among the distributions of selected attributes (i.e., selected columns in a table), the same perturbation algorithm needs to be applied to all these attributes.

Knowledge of a deterministic permutation algorithm typically allows the data to be restored to its original state by back-tracking the algorithm, which makes a controlled re-identification possible. On the other hand, using a non-deterministic permutation algorithm (i.e., an algorithm that employs a degree of randomness as part of its logic) makes the process of re-identification less trivial and more resilient to re-identification attacks.

Because of this, specific organizational objectives for controlled re-identification as well as appropriate technical and organizational measures to safeguard the knowledge of the algorithms from unwarranted access need to be taken into consideration while choosing or designing the algorithm.

MICROAGGREGATION

The term "microaggregation" refers to a category of de-identification techniques that replace all values of continuous attributes with their averages computed in a certain algorithmic way. For each continuous attribute (or for a selected set of continuous attributes), all records in the dataset are grouped such that the records with closest values of the attribute (or attributes) belong to the same group and there are at least k records in each group, for a sufficiently large value of k. The new value of each attribute is then computed to be the average of the attribute's values in the group. The closer the values in each group are, the more data usefulness is preserved.

The output of microaggregation is microdata. Microaggregation does not preserve data truthfulness.

Sampling

Data sampling is a statistical analysis technique that selects a representative subset of a larger dataset in order to analyze and recognize patterns in the original dataset. To reduce the risk of re-identification, sampling is performed on data principals.

Performing a random sampling adds uncertainty about the dataset. For example, an attacker, by merely matching attributes of a certain record from the sample with external information, cannot be sure that the record corresponds to the specific data principal since there is no certainty that the data principal is present in the sample dataset. More generally, applying generalization or randomization techniques on a sample, rather than on a whole population, can increase the effectiveness of these de-identification techniques.

The methods for drawing samples from data vary broadly and their selection depends on the dataset and the anticipated use cases. An example of a common algorithm is a simple probability sampling where random numbers are used to select the records in a dataset ensuring that there is no correlation among the records in the resultant sample.

The output of sampling used in this way is microdata.

Disruptions using Technology Innovation

According to Gartner, to best sense and respond to disruptions using technology innovation, enterprise architecture and technology innovation leaders should:

Summary Translation: Innovation Insight for Synthetic Data

- Poor data quality, lack of adequate data, siloed data and bias in training data are among the top data-related challenges with A.I. initiatives.
- Artificial data generated using A.I. techniques (synthetic Data) can improve A.I. model accuracy, time to value, aid with regulatory compliance, and lower the cost of data acquisition.

- Synthetic data can be both structured and unstructured data, with tabular data and images being the most commonly used forms today.
- There is a growing ecosystem of startups in this space, with levers of competition being the impact on model performance, types of data they can generate, privacy filters they offer, and the industry use case focus.

Develop guidelines, in conjunction with analytics, security, and legal teams, on appropriate usage of synthetic data.

- Educate the internal stakeholders through training programs on the benefits and limitations of synthetic data and institute guardrails to mitigate challenges (such as user skepticism, inadequate data validation, and improper feature engineering).
- Conduct a POC to verify vendor claims and validate use case fit. Choose vendors that can generate realistic synthetic datasets for your use cases, provide tools to measure the effectiveness of synthetic datasets, and provide privacy filters to comply with regulations and internal compliance mandates.
- Measure and communicate the business value, success and failure stories of synthetic data initiatives, as this creates realistic expectations on the art of what's possible and provides opportunities for continuous exploration.

According to Gartner, by 2025, the use of synthetic data and transfer learning will reduce the volume of real data needed for machine learning by 70%.

By 2025, synthetic data will reduce personal customer data collection, avoiding 70% of privacy violation sanctions.

Synthetic Data in A.I.

Synthetic data can be an effective supplement or alternative to real data, providing access to annotated data to build accurate, extensible A.I. models. Enterprise architecture and technology innovation leaders should evaluate its benefits, risks, use cases, and tech ecosystem to reap business value.

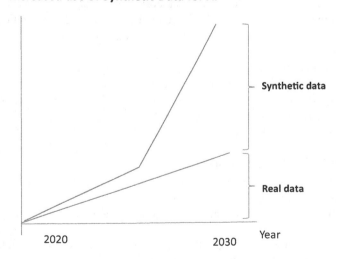

Increased use of Synthetic Data for AI

Source: Adapted from Gartner

Data is the lifeline for digital businesses. However, getting access to real-world data that is of high quality (i.e., clean, well-labeled, and audited for bias) is often challenging for enterprises. Synthetic data can address this challenge to enable faster, accurate, and responsible A.I. initiatives.

Synthetic data is a class of data that is artificially generated. It can be used to train A.I. models for scenarios such as:

Use cases for which data must be guaranteed to be anonymous or for which privacy must be preserved (such as with uses of medical data).

- Augmentation of real data, especially where the cost of data collection is high. There is a need to balance class distribution within existing training data (such as with population data).
- Emerging A.I. use cases for which limited real data is available.

Synthetic data is critical, since it can be generated to meet specific needs or conditions that are not available in real data, which makes it potentially context-aware, domain-specific, and privacy-enhanced. We believe that synthetic data is important for the future of A.I. because it solves one of the most pervasive and critical challenges that A.I. systems face today—the lack of domain-specific, well-labeled, high-volume data at a reasonable cost.

Description

Synthetic Data is a class of data that is artificially generated (i.e., not obtained from direct observations of the real world). Data can be generated using different methods, such as statistically rigorous sampling from real data, semantic approaches, generative adversarial networks, or by creating simulation scenarios where models and processes interact to create completely new datasets of events.

While there is a lot of hype around the promise of synthetic data recently, it isn't a completely novel idea. Synthetic data has been around for decades and has been used in applications such as computer games and scientific simulations. However, the recent advancements in computing power coupled with the advent of generative adversarial networks (GANs) have been a game changer in our ability to generate faster, cheaper, and more accurate synthetic data.

Synthetic data can be generated using several techniques, such as:

Statistical Distribution: Simple ways to generate synthetic data include observing the statistical distribution of real data and replicating the same through discrete or joint distributions to produce similar data. This can be an effective technique for simple and small-scale use cases involving tabular data.

- Variational autoencoders (VAEs): VAEs are a form of neural net. VAEs consist of an encoder and decoder. The encoder takes objects and compresses them into more condensed representations while retaining the main features. These representations can then be mapped onto a two-dimensional space where similar objects are clustered. New objects are generated by decoding a point in the dimensional space, say, between two objects. For example, a VAE could create an image that looks like a mix of a drone and a hovercraft. VAEs are relatively easy to implement and train.

However, if the original data is highly heterogeneous, VAEs can suffer from reconstruction errors.

- Generative adversarial networks (GANs): GANs are a form of neural net, where two neural networks are trained in an adversarial fashion. A generator generates the data, while the discriminator evaluates whether it's fake or real. When both networks are trained together, the discriminator needs to learn from patterns in real data, where the generator learns to outsmart the discriminator by producing more realistic samples from its random input. The advantage of GANs is their ability to learn the characteristics of "real" data quickly and iterating faster toward accurate representation. GANs are specifically powerful with unstructured data, such as images, although they may be more complex to train.

Synthetic data can include both structured and unstructured data. The most common forms of synthetic data include:

Synthetic data within enterprises can be used in a variety of ways—either fully synthetic, where there is no real data or in a hybrid manner (more common); where the real data is augmented or replaced with synthetic data; or where synthetic data is used to enhance class distribution and provide adequate quantity of well-labeled data.

Benefits and Uses

While synthetic data is not quite the panacea it is painted to be in the popular media, there are real, tangible benefits to its use in the data pipeline and in product development, such as:

Others: There are other techniques, such as gaming engines, and physics-based approaches for generating synthetic datasets.

- Tabular data: This form of synthetic data is structured and stored in a table in rows and columns. This mimics structured data stored in data warehouses and can also include forms such as time series data.
- Text: Text-based synthetic data has been challenging historically due to massive amounts of pretraining needed and the contextual aspects of natural language.

However, recent advancements in large language transformer models, such as BERT and GPT-3, have made text-based synthetic data possible. These models are massively pretrained on large datasets, including public repositories such as Wikipedia and Project Gutenberg books library, which enables better accuracy and cross-domain applications.

- Unstructured data: This form of synthetic data includes images, audio, and videos.

Use cases often include generating images or sounds of people, where the individuals aren't real for privacy preservation. This is one of the fast-growing use cases for next-generation A.I. applications, such as self-driving cars, geolocation services, healthcare patient images, and cashier-less stores.

Synthetic data within enterprises can be used in a variety of ways—either fully synthetic, where there is no real data or in a hybrid manner (more common); where the real data is augmented or replaced with synthetic data; or where synthetic data is used to enhance class distribution and provide adequate quantity of well-labeled data.

Benefits

Increased accuracy of ML models. Real-world data is happenstance and does not contain all permutations of conditions or events possible in the real world. Synthetic data can counter this by generating data at the edges or for conditions not yet seen.

More permutations of event data and the fact that synthetic data can be labeled automatically make for more accurate models. Today's state of the art in computer vision and natural language use cases is to use synthetic data in conjunction with real data to train models using transfer learning.

- A faster data pipeline. By switching to synthetic data, you can speed up (or avoid) internal processes, lengthy contractual efforts, legal blockers, or hosting challenges.
- The ability to experiment safely. Synthetic data "unlocks" signals in private and sensitive data that otherwise could not be examined. It also creates new opportunities to use cloud services or multi-party analytics in an effective way.
- A reduction of costs. Synthetic data reduces the cost of time and money.

Use case	Comment
Pooled and shared data	Sharing in an eco system
Open up external sharing	Expanding collaboration
Usage for evaluations	Easy to provide externally
Test data	Better coverage
Cloud adoption	Reduces risks
Data monetization	Potential opportunity
Combat data losses	Not regulated data

Source: Adapted from Gartner

Risks

While synthetic data techniques can score quite highly for cost-effectiveness and privacy, they do have risks and limitations, such as:

Automotive: Testing robotic and automotive systems is slow and costly. Synthetic data allows the automated vehicle (or its digital twin counterpart) to explore a dynamic environment safely and quickly.

- Healthcare: Share data with external parties but still maintain patient confidentiality (e.g., in clinical trials).
- Retail: Autonomous check-out systems, cashier-less stores, analysis of customer demographics, and improving inventory management are some examples of synthetic data usage in retail.
- Defense: The power of synthetic data in defense is its ability to provide training data for even the rarest occurrences, which enhances risk assessment and threat mitigation capabilities.
- The quality of synthetic data often depends on the quality of the model that created it and the input "seed" dataset.
- If seed datasets change, it is necessary to regenerate synthetic data using the new characteristics for it to enable meaningful model accuracy.
- Using synthetic data requires additional verification steps, such as the comparison of model results with human-annotated, real-world data, to ensure the fidelity of results.
- Beyond the technology challenges, user skepticism might be a hard challenge for synthetic data to overcome, as users may perceive it to be "inferior" or "fake" data.
  As synthetic data gains broader adoption, more questions will be posed on the openness of the data generation techniques and the efficacy of complete privacy guarantee, particularly in sensitive use cases, such as clinical trials or demographic surveys.
- If fringe or edge cases are not part of the seed dataset, they will not be synthesized. This means the handling of such borderline cases must be carefully accommodated.

Alternatives

Real data is the obvious alternative to synthetic data. There are use cases where the complexity and inability to prove the veracity of synthetic data may lead to simply using real data. Regulators are just now waking up to the benefits and risks of using synthetic data and may nudge organizations toward not using synthetic data for some scenarios. In privacy preservation use cases, techniques such as data masking and differential privacy may be deemed as alternatives to synthetic data.

Synthetic data is still nascent, with most organizations being either unaware of it or merely experimenting with it. While it holds tremendous potential, whether it can deliver substantial business benefits for a variety of enterprise use cases is yet to be seen and proven.

SYTHESIZING DATA

Example of synthesized data:

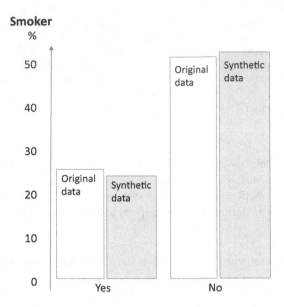

Source: Adapted from Chainalysis.com

An Example of Synthesized Data:

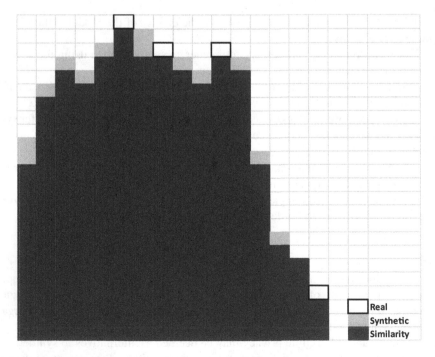

Source: Adapted from Statice

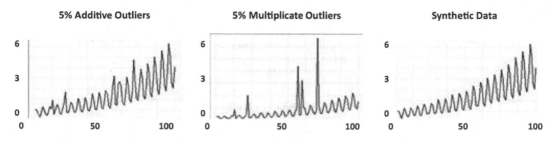

Source: Adapted from Statice

A BROAD DEFINITION OF PETS

Three general categories: algorithmic, architectural, or augmentation based include:

Algorithmic PETs include:

1. Homomorphic encryption
2. Differential privacy
3. Zero-knowledge proofs

Architectural PETs include:

1. Federated learning
2. Multi-party computation

Augmentation PETs include:

1. Synthetic Data
2. Digital twinning

Algorithmic PETs protect privacy by altering how data is represented (e.g., encryption, summary statistics) while still containing the necessary information to enable use. They provide mathematical rigor and measurability to privacy. Unlike algorithmic PETs, Architectural PETs are grounded in the structure of data or computation environments.

The focus is on the confidential exchange of information among multiple parties without sharing the underlying data. Augmentation PETs protect privacy by using historical distributions to direct the generation of realistic data that augments existing data sources. Augmentation PETs can enhance small datasets or generate fully synthetic datasets, including multiple interrelated datasets constitutive of a simulated system, which can augment the overall range of useful and available datasets.

Although we arrange the landscape of PETs into different categories, it is important to note that they are often used in combination to fill privacy, security, or data sovereignty needs as the use case requires.

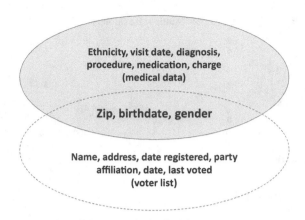

Source: Adapted from Statice

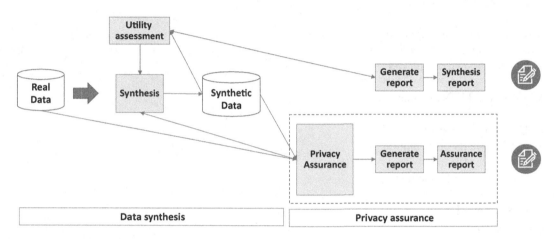

Source: Adapted from Statice

DIFFERENTIAL PRIVACY

Global (or centralized) differential privacy involves the "aggregator" having access to the real data. Each user sends data to the aggregator without noise. The aggregator then applies a differentially private mechanism by adding noise to the output (e.g., a response to a database query). The noise is added only once, at the end of the process, before sharing it with a third party. The main disadvantage of this approach is the requirement for the central aggregator to access the real data. All users must trust the aggregator to act appropriately and protect the privacy of individuals.

Source: Adapted from ICO UK

Global differential privacy was used by the U.S. Census Bureau when collecting personal data from individuals for the 2020 U.S. Census to prevent matching between an individual's identity, their data, and a specific data release. The U.S. Census Bureau was considered a trusted aggregator. In other words—the data was handled in line with the expectations of the participating individuals with robust controls in place. Local differential privacy involves the individual users applying the mechanism before sending anything to the aggregator. Noise is added to the individual (input) data points.

The aggregator receives "noisy" data—this addresses the trust risk of global differential privacy, as the real data is not shared with the aggregator. Since each user must add noise to their own data, the total noise is much larger than global differential privacy. Local differential privacy requires many more users to get useful results. The key difference between the two models is that the global model leads to more accurate results with the same level of privacy protection, as less noise is added.

Source: Adapted from ICO UK

Example, A smartphone provider, wants to know the average number of minutes an individual uses their device within a given month without revealing the exact amount of time.

The diagram below shows the difference between a real-world computation (where a specific individual's data is included in the processing) and an opt-out scenario (where the individual's data is not included). Epsilon (ε) is the maximum distance between a query on a database (real-world computation) and the same query on a database with a single entry added or removed. Small values of ε provide very similar outputs when given similar inputs and therefore provide higher levels of privacy as more noise is added. Therefore, it is more difficult to distinguish whether an individual's data is present in the database.

Large values of ε allow less similarity in the outputs, as less noise is added, making it easier to distinguish between different records in the database. Practical applications using local D.P. often use higher values of epsilon than global D.P. due to the higher amount of noise required. If anonymous information is required as output, epsilon can be set such that the relative difference in the result of the two scenarios is so small that it is unlikely anyone could single out or infer, with confidence, anything about a specific individual in the input.

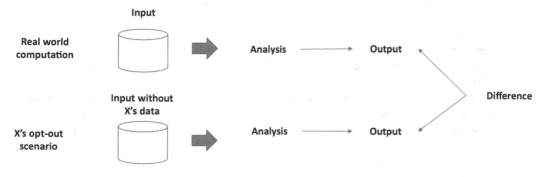

Source: Adapted from ICO UK

How does differential privacy assist with data protection compliance? Differential privacy can be used to anonymize data for other purposes, providing an appropriate level of noise is added. Anonymous aggregates can be generated from personal data, or it can be used to query a database to provide anonymized statistics. Both models of differential privacy are able to provide anonymous information as output, providing a sufficient level of noise added to the data. Local differential privacy adds noise to the individual (input) data points to provide strong privacy protection of sensitive attributes.

As the noise is added to each individual contribution, this will result in less accurate, lower utility data than global differential privacy. Any original data retained by the aggregator in the global model or the individual parties in the local model would be personal data in their hands. This also applies to any additional information that may reidentify. However, in either model, the output may not be personal data in the hands of another party. What do we need to know about implementing differential privacy? Using differential privacy can result in poor utility due to noise addition. It is challenging to generate differentially private outputs that provide strong protection and good utility for different purposes. Differential privacy can be useful in the context of statistical analysis and broad trends rather than detecting anomalies or detailed patterns within data.

SUMMARY

We discussed synthetic data, generating microdata artificially, synthetic data in A.I., and synthesising data.

NOTES

1. D. J. Power (10 March 2007). "A Brief History of Decision Support Systems, version 4.0". DSSResources.COM. Retrieved 10 July 2008.
2. Dedić N. & Stanier C. (2016). "Measuring the Success of Changes to Existing Business Intelligence Solutions to Improve Business Intelligence Reporting" (PDF). Measuring the Success of Changes to Existing Business Intelligence Solutions to Improve Business Intelligence Reporting. Lecture Notes in Business Information Processing. Lecture Notes in Business Information Processing. Vol. 268. Springer International Publishing. pp. 225–236. doi:10.1007/978-3-319-49944-4_17. ISBN 978-3-319-49943-7.
3. Henschen, Doug (4 January 2010). "Analytics at Work: Q&A with Tom Davenport" (Interview). Archived from the original on 3 April 2012. Retrieved 26 September 2011.
4. Jump up to:a b c Blumberg, R. & S. Atre (2003). "The Problem with Unstructured Data" (PDF). D.M. Review: 42–46. Archived from the original (PDF) on 25 January 2011.
5. Miller Devens, Richard (1865). Cyclopaedia of Commercial and Business Anecdotes; Comprising Interesting Reminiscences and Facts, Remarkable Traits and Humors of Merchants, Traders, Bankers Etc. in All Ages and Countries. D. Appleton and company. p. 210. Retrieved 15 February 2014. business intelligence.
6. [Ashmead et al., 2019] Ashmead, R., Kifer, D., Leclerc, P., Machanavajjhala, A., and Sexton, W. (2019). Effective Privacy After Adjusting for Invariants with Applications to the 2020 Census.
7. [94th Congress of the United States of America, 1975] 94th Congress of the United States of
8. [Abowd et al., 2019a] Abowd, J., Ashmead, R., Simson, G., Kifer, D., Leclerc, P., Machanavajjhala, A., and Sexton, W. (2019a). Census topdown: Differentially private data, incremental.
9. "A smarter way to jump into data lakes". McKinsey. 1 August 2017.
10. [Abowd et al., 2019b] Abowd, J., Kifer, D., Moran, B., Ashmead, R., and Sexton, W. (2019b).
11. [Abowd, 2018a] Abowd, J. M. (2018a). Staring-down the database reconstruction theorem. In
12. [Abowd, 2018b] Abowd, J. M. (2018b). The U.S. Census Bureau Adopts Differential Privacy. In
13. A.I. in cybersecurity, https://swisscognitive.ch/2021/12/10/the-artificial-intelligence-trajectory-an-outlook-of-2022/
14. America (1975). P.L. 94-171: Redistricting Data.

15. "Are Data Lakes Fake News?". Sonra. 8 August 2017. Retrieved 10 August 2017.

16. [Ashmead et al., 2019] Ashmead, R., Kifer, D., Leclerc, P., Machanavajjhala, A., and Sexton, W.

17. [Asi and Duchi, 2020] Asi, H. and Duchi, J. C. (2020). Instance-optimality in differential privacy

18. "Business Analytics vs Business Intelligence?". timoelliott.com. 9 March 2011. Retrieved 15 June 2014.

19. Census TopDown Algorithm: Differentially Private Data, Incremental Schemas, and Consistency

20. Cloud Standards Customer Council 2017, Cloud Customer Architecture for Big Data & Analytics.

21. Cloud Standards Customer Council 2017, Data Residency Challenges.

22. Data Mining, pages 2867–2867.

23. Data, machine learning and chaos. https://swisscognitive.ch/2021/12/08/faster-smarter-approach/

24. David Jensen (2004). "6. Using Scripts". Proximity 4.3 Tutorial.

25. "Decoding big data buzzwords". cio.com. 2015. B.I. refers to the approaches, tools, mechanisms that organizations can use to keep a finger on the pulse of their businesses. Also referred by unsexy versions -- "dashboarding", "MIS" or "reporting".

26. Evelson, Boris (21 November 2008). "Topic Overview: Business Intelligence".

27. Evelson, Boris (29 April 2010). "Want to know what Forrester's lead data analysts are thinking about B.I. and the data domain?". Archived from the original on 6 August 2016. Retrieved 4 November 2010.

28. "Experimental Characteristics Study of Data Storage Formats for Data Marts Development within Data Lakes". Retrieved 18 September 2021.

29. G. Zyskind, O. Nathan, and A. Pentland. Enigma: Decentralized computation platform with guaranteed privacy. CoRR, abs/1506.03471

30. H P Luhn (1958). "A Business Intelligence System" (PDF). *IBM Journal of Research and Development*. 2 (4): 314–319. doi:10.1147/rd.24.0314. Archived from the original (PDF) on 13 September 2008.

31. http://standards.iso.org/ittf/PubliclyAvailableStandards/c060544_ISO_IEC_17788_2014.zip

32. http://www.cloud-council.org/deliverables/cloud-customer-architecture-for-big-data-andanalytics.htm

33. http://www.cloud-council.org/deliverables/data-residency-challenges.htm

34. https://www.frontiersin.org/articles/10.3389/fpubh.2022.814163/full

35. https://www.r-bloggers.com/2019/01/generating-synthetic-data-sets-with-synthpop-in-r/

36. https://www.tetrate.io/

37. ISO 17788 Cloud Computing Overview and Vocabulary.

38. Joint Statistical Meetings, Vancouver, BC.

39. Jump up to:a b c Rao, R. (2003). "From unstructured data to actionable intelligence" (PDF). I.T. Professional. 5 (6): 29–35. doi:10.1109/MITP.2003.1254966.

40. Kobielus, James (30 April 2010). "What's Not B.I.? Oh, Don't Get Me Started....Oops Too Late...Here Goes..." Archived from the original on 7 May 2010. Retrieved 4 November 2010. "Business" intelligence is a non-domain-specific catchall for all the types of analytic data that can be delivered to users in reports, dashboards, and the like. When you specify the subject domain for this intelligence, then you can refer to "competitive intelligence", "market intelligence", "social intelligence", "financial intelligence", "H.R. intelligence", "supply chain intelligence", and the like.

41. L-diversity: privacy beyond k-anonymity, https://ieeexplore.ieee.org/document/1617392

42. Power, D. J. "A Brief History of Decision Support Systems". Retrieved 1 November 2010.

43. Proceedings of the 24th ACM SIGKDD International Conference on Knowledge Discovery &

44. schemas, and consistency with public knowledge. U.S. Census Bureau.

45. Springer-Verlag Berlin Heidelberg, Springer-Verlag Berlin Heidelberg (21 November 2008). Topic Overview: Business Intelligence. doi:10.1007/978-3-540-48716-6. ISBN 978-3-540-48715-9.
46. Technical report, Technical Report. U.S. Census Bureau.
47. What Is Blockchain Sharding?, https://changelly.com/blog/what-is-sharding/#:~:text=%E2%80%9CSharding%20is%20a%20database%20partitioning%20technique%20that%20will,is%20not%20the%20prerogative%20of%20the%20Ethereum%20network

Appendix C: API Security

INTRODUCTION

We will discuss APIs the mechanism for data access, Best practices for secure design, API discovery and cataloging, Best practices for authentication and authorization, and immutable infrastructure.

WHAT YOU NEED TO DO TO PROTECT YOUR APIS

Key Challenges

- Attacks and data breaches involving poorly secured application programming interfaces (APIs) are frequently occurring.
- Protecting web APIs with general purpose application security solutions alone continues to be ineffective. Each new API represents an additional and potentially unique attack vector for your systems.
- API threat protection technologies are making progress but aren't fully mature yet. They lack in areas, including automated discovery and API classification.
- Modern application architecture trends—including mobile access, microservice design patterns, and hybrid on-premises/cloud usage—complicate API security since there is rarely a single "gateway" point at which protection can be enforced.

RECOMMENDATIONS

As part of your application and product portfolio governance:

- Discover your APIs before attackers discover them by analyzing mobile and web applications. You cannot secure what you cannot find or categorize. Quantify the threats by uncovering hidden APIs and documenting API usage.
- Use a combination of API management and web application firewalls to protect APIs, in conjunction with identity infrastructure. When these do not provide sufficient protection for APIs you have categorized as high risk, add specialist API security products.
- Adopt a continuous approach to API security across the API development and delivery cycle, designing security into APIs. Include API security testing and the creation and application of reusable API security policies.

    Use a distributed enforcement model to protect APIs across your entire architecture, not just at the perimeter.

APIs are used for integration between applications, to enable modern web and mobile experiences, and to deliver new digital business as public APIs in partner ecosystems. APIs enable all these benefits by allowing developers to access application functionality and to send and receive data using familiar web technologies, particularly HTTP, JSON, and XML. However, the benefits which APIs bring in opening access to data and application functionality naturally also bring security concerns.

These incidents have raised awareness of API vulnerabilities. Reflecting this, Gartner has noted a 30% year-on-year increase in client inquiries related to API security. Furthermore, Gartner's survey "API Usage and Its Role in Digital Platform Growth" found that API security ranked in the top three challenges to API strategy for 50% of respondents, followed by lack of skills and lack of API standards:

Top Challenges of API Security Strategy

Area	%
Security Concerns	19
Lack of Skills	19
Lack of API standard	15
Missing Roles	14
Immature Tooling	11
Other	7

Source: Adapted from Gartner

API Security Consists of API Protection and API Access Control

	API Threat Protection	API Access Control
Key functionality	Content validation	Authication and authorization
Key technology	Attack signature	Oath, OpenID Connect, JSON Web Tokens
Products	WAF	API management, access managementw, IDaaS

Source: Adapted from Gartner

Unfortunately, no tools will automatically discover all your APIs, except in narrow cases such as those built in a Kubernetes container environment (e.g., TIBCO Software's API Scout) or on certain cloud platforms (e.g., Data Theorem's API Discover). However, some organizations already have an API platform team or other similar API governance group to manage their API portfolio. I

After discovering your APIs, the next step is to categorize your APIs. Use criteria such as those shown in this table:

Exposure	Business Context	Technology
Type of client	Data sensitive	Platform
Scope	Product owner	Update cycle
Location	Business goal	DevOps

This categorization allows the security profile of your APIs to be measured. Following discovery and categorization, identify your APIs' vulnerabilities. To secure APIs, it is important to be aware of the ways in which your APIs can be breached. The most common API vulnerability paths are shown in Figure 3 and described below.

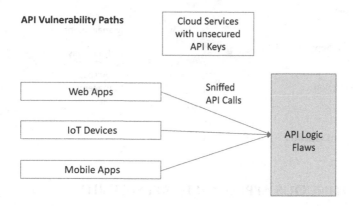

Source: Adapted from Gartner

1. Unsecured API keys in repositories and storage. API keys or other keys, such as SSH keys or SSL/TLS private keys, may be discovered in cloud-based storage such as Amazon S3.
2. Hardcoded API keys in applications. API keys or other credentials may be hardcoded in web and mobile applications.
3. API logic flaws. APIs may have bugs or other logic flaws which can be exploited.
4. Sniffed API calls. API traffic may be sniffed through a man-in-the-middle (MITM) approach.

So-called "shadow APIs"—which are unadvertised, unused, no-longer used, sample, or prototype APIs—may suffer from the flaws listed above

It is likely that your organization already has some infrastructure already in place which can help address API security. This includes:

- API management. API management products consist of API gateways and customizable API developer portals. Use "Critical Capabilities for Full Life Cycle API Management" to compare
  API management products on their API protection and API access control capabilities.
- Web application firewalls. Web application firewalls include some API threat protection in the form of content threat detection and message validation against OAS (formerly Swagger) schemas.
- Access management. These include on-premises access management software and cloud-based IDaaS (identity as a service). Some vendors in this category provide API access control.
- In-app protection. These products protect mobile applications from attacks including "API scraping", whereby APIs are maliciously useds.
- Specialist API Security tools. Various API security tools have emerged. These tools provide a variety of solutions, from discovery and security testing, to security configuration and threat mitigation, including acting as a gateway or proxy.

Infrastructure Providing API Security

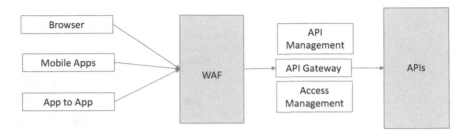

Source: Adapted from Gartner

ADOPT A CONTINUOUS APPROACH TO API SECURITY

Apply API security throughout the API life cycle, including application security testing (AST) at design and implementation time (see "How to Integrate Application Security Testing Into a Software Development Life Cycle").

But be aware that support for API security testing varies among AST vendors. For a comparison of the API security testing capabilities of AST vendors, see "Critical Capabilities for Application Security Testing". Some new API security vendors address API security testing, including 42Crunch, which provides tooling to perform security assessment and hardening of OAS (OpenAPI specification) definitions.

Good API security also requires change control throughout the entire application life cycle. For example, application security testing is performed whenever an API change is made during development. Undocumented changes to APIs can also have serious implications to the availability and security of the overall system (e.g., some protections may stop working as expected if the API changes).

USE A DISTRIBUTED ENFORCEMENT MODEL TO PROTECT APIS ACROSS YOUR ENTIRE

Architecture, Not Just at the Perimeter API gateways have traditionally been used to secure APIs. Recently, web application firewall (WAF) vendors have added some support for API threat protection. Even so, a purely perimeter-based "API gateway and WAF" defense strategy is not adequate to secure APIs. This is due to several factors.

- Mobile devices that provide access to APIs through mobile applications, which can be tampered with or reverse engineered to attack an API.

API Security in a Service Mesh Environment

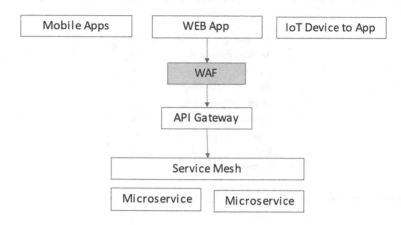

Source: Adapted from Gartner

CONFIDENCE IN CLOUD CONTINUES TO GROW

By 2023, 70% of all enterprise workloads will be deployed in cloud infrastructure and platform services, up from 40% in 2020 according to Gartner.

Through 2025, more than 99% of cloud breaches will have a root cause of preventable misconfigurations or mistakes by end users.

OBSTACLES

- Trust is slow to build and quick to evaporate, wildly when experimental technology like confidential computing is paired with occasional hardware vulnerabilities.
- Because the technology is new and novel, and it touches sensitive data, potential clients have a hard time identifying valid use cases for their business.
- Confidential computing can provide such protection now. Be mindful of the potential performance impacts and the extra cost. IaaS clandestine computing instances (whether SGX-based or otherwise) will cost more to run.
- Confidential computing isn't usually plug-and-play, and should be reserved for the highest-risk use cases. Depending on the vendor, it can require a high level of effort but offers diminishing marginal security improvement over more pedestrian controls like TLS, MFA, and customer-controlled key management services.

APIS ARE THE MECHANISM FOR DATA ACCESS

What Mechanisma Do You Use to Document and Inventory Your API?

Postman	40
API mgmt platform	34
Swagger	28
Application scanning	23
Open API Generator	20
Config mgmt database	18
ReDoc	8
Other	8
DapperDox	4

Source: Adapted from Salt Security

Secure design and development surface and risk posture to help prioritize the wide range of API security activities that must be accounted for.

BEST PRACTICES FOR API DISCOVERY AND CATALOGING

1. Discover non-production environments, not just production: it's critically important that you track lower backgrounds, including QA, UAT, staging, SIT, and pre-production, in addition to your production environments. Attackers know that non-production domains often have fewer relaxed or no security controls, yet APIs in those environments may still allow access to similar sets of functionality and data.

Security Testing

The top three recommendations for security testing include:

1. Statically analyze API code automatically as part of version control and CI/CD
2. Check for known vulnerable dependencies in your API code
3. Dynamically analyze and fuzz deployed APIs to identify exploitable code in runtime

Often viewed as the backbone of an application security program, security testing is a significant focus area of many organizations' API security strategies. The emphasis on investing in security testing tooling and integrating it as part of development and release processes has only grown as industry has pushed the ideal of shiftleft more heavily. While it is possible to scan for certain types of security issues automatically, mainly known vulnerabilities in published software, this type of scanning is less useful for the world of APIs.

Traditional scanning technologies struggle with parsing custom developed code, since design patterns and coding practices vary per developer. As a result, organizations often struggle with high false-positive and false-negative rates. No scanner is adept at parsing business logic, which also leaves organizations exposed to major forms of API abuse.

Use traditional security testing tools to verify some aspects of an API implementation such as well-known misconfigurations or vulnerabilities, but you must operate these tools with awareness of the limitations. Traditional testing tools often fail to identify flaws, or zero-day vulnerabilities, in the application and API code you create.

BEST PRACTICES FOR SECURITY TESTING INCLUDE

Repurpose vulnerability scanning to identify API infrastructure: most organizations have established vulnerability assessment and vulnerability management (VA/VM) scanning capabilities. These services are helpful for identifying some misconfigurations and well-known vulnerabilities, typically reported as common vulnerabilities and exposures identifiers (CVE IDs), but this information applies only to published software. For custom API development or integration work, vulnerability scanning benefits are limited.

These scanning services can still be helpful in identifying exposed servers or workloads that may be listening on well-known TCP ports like 80 and 443 for API requests. Bear in mind that API services may also be configured to listen on other TCP ports, so scanning more extensive port ranges is advisable.

Vulnerability scanners should also support ephemeral and containerized environments to adequately assess API hosting infrastructure.

Run fuzzing and dynamic testing against deployed APIs: absent code scanning, the other approach to testing custom APIs is the use of fuzzers and dynamic application security testing (DAST) tools. Fuzzers are challenging to configure correctly and require subject matter expertise to run effectively. However, fuzzing typically results in more thorough testing and identifying a wide range of exploitable conditions in code.

The time it takes for a fuzzer to run to completion can be unpredictable, and subsequent runs can produce different results due to the number of variables in play. DAST fairs are slightly better, since tools, particularly commercialgrade options, are designed to be easier to start with. When automating the scanning of APIs with DAST, you will need API schema along with historical traces of an application session or automation scripts like Selenium or Appium to drive the scanner.

While DAST scanners can be effective with traditional web application designs, they will often fail to understand how to exercise APIs. It is common to see a DAST scan run for a few minutes and return trivial results because the scanner wasn't configured properly to navigate API functionality in the correct sequence.

Check for known vulnerable code dependencies: similar to VA/VM where the goal is identifying CVE-IDs, dependency analyzers and software composition analysis (SCA) scanners can place known vulnerable open-source software packages and third-party libraries in API source code, infrastructure-as-code, and container images that all play a part in the complete systems that run APIs. Quickly identifying these known vulnerable dependencies helps knock out a wide range of potentially exploitable code that inevitably becomes part of your running APIs and serving infrastructure. Run these dependency analysis tools during code commits, in build, in delivery, and continuously.

API infrastructure may be mutable depending where your organization is at with DevOps maturity and pursuit of infrastructure automation. New vulnerable dependencies may be inadvertently introduced making it crucial to run these checks continuously.

Pentest APIs periodically or as mandated by regulation: penetration testing, specifically application-scoped and API-scoped engagements, involves a mixture of automated and manual testing techniques. It should be handled by those with appropriate subject matter expertise. If a pentesting firm is offering junior level testers or running VA scanners to analyze your most critical APIs, look elsewhere.

The interval at which you should or must perform pentests is sometimes outlined by corresponding regulation. Absent compliance or regulatory requirement, it is advisable to coordinate pentest engagements quarterly, semi-annually, or annually for your most critical or exposed APIs.

Augment testing further with bug bounties if you want more assurance: some organizations also opt to augment their security testing capacity further with bug bounty programs that are public or private, and possibly coordinated through a crowd-sourced platform. Bug bounty programs can be the subject of debate, and bounty services often provide no guaranteed testing methodology as typically seen with a qualified pentesting firm.

Typically, you pay for results, not the engagement and testing activity itself. Still, using the "power of the crowd" continuously with bug bounties can be helpful in uncovering API issues that even the most seasoned security experts are unable to find.

API MEDIATION AND ARCHITECTURE

The top three recommendations for API mediation and architecture include:

1. Mediate APIs to improve observability and monitoring capabilities
2. Use mediation mechanisms like API gateways to enforce access control
3. Augment your mediation mechanisms with API security tooling that can provide context

While it's possible to directly expose an API via a web or application server, this practice is less common in typical enterprise architectures. API mediation can be achieved through a number of other mechanisms as well, including network load balancers, application delivery controllers, Kubernetes ingress controllers, sidecar proxies, and service mesh ingresses. Design patterns like API facade and frontend for backends involve putting a proxying mediation layer "in front of" APIs. Typically, this design pattern is achieved by deploying API gateways that function as reverse proxies, forward proxies, or both.

API management suites and integration platforms also make use of API gateways to enable their functionality and enforce policies. Mediation provides a wide range of benefits, including improved visibility, accelerated delivery, increased operational flexibility, and improved enforcement capabilities, particularly when it comes to API access control.

BEST PRACTICES FOR API MEDIATION AND ARCHITECTURE INCLUDE

1. Mediate APIs to improve observability and monitoring: by virtue of positioning within enterprise architecture, API gateways are deployed in various spots of a network topology and application architecture to mediate inner and outer APIs.
2. Collectively, all these API gateway instances "see" how API callers are consuming your exposed, outer APIs, and how those requests traverse into internal APIs as well as microservices. Rarely is there one gateway unless it is a monolithic design or enterprise service bus type deployment. Harvest telemetry from your API gateways to improve your monitoring capabilities and create amplifying effects for your non-security and security initiatives.
2. Mediate APIs to enforce access control: API gateways are foundational for providing traffic management, authentication, and authorization mechanisms.
3. Adopt API management for non-security use cases: organizations sometimes reach a tipping point where they have too many APIs or too many API gateway deployments that lack standardization and centralization. To bring order to the chaos, organizations will often opt for an APIM offering that brings a broader range of lifecycle capabilities, including features to support monetization of APIs, partner enablement, developer self-service, quote management, access control policies, operational workflow, publishing control, and centralized logging. The APIM offering enables and enforces these features via API gateway deployments.
4. Augment API mediation technologies with security-focused controls: organizations historically frontend their mediation layer with web application firewalls (WAF). This approach can provide a level of protection from general web injection attacks, protect partner or developer self-service portals in the API management (APIM) suite, and protect backend database services used to power the APIM itself. Some APIM offerings also offer lightweight threat protection that are essentially message filters. Much like WAFs, these APIM

and API gateway threat protection filters can be helpful in blocking some forms of injection, including XML or JSON injection, but rules are typically too static, generic, or not maintained by the vendor.

You should look to purpose-built API security offerings that can provide full lifecycle security and API context rather than repurposing traditional controls like WAF.

DATA SECURITY

The top three recommendations for data security include:

1. Use encryption selectively and transport protection suffices for most use cases
2. Avoid sending too much data to clients and relying on the client to filter data
3. Adjust for threats like scraping or data inference where encryption is not a mitigation protect organizations from attacks where the data storage is targeted directly. If your API is designed to only send encrypted payloads as an additional level of encryption beyond transport protection, attackers will still attempt to extract unencrypted data elsewhere, such as in memory, from client storage, or other positions within network topology. These encryption approaches also do not protect the organization from cases where an attacker obtains a credential or authorized session since the data will be decrypted for them when accessed through an API.

BEST PRACTICES FOR DATA SECURITY INCLUDE

1. Use encryption selectively or as mandated by regulation: history is riddled with many failed crypto implementations and misconfigurations that were exploited by attackers. Key management is already a complex endeavor, but matters only get worse in the world of automation and API communication where time is of the essence and prompting for crucial material is a non-starter. As a result, application teams sometimes make the mistake of storing key material in unsecured locations, such as in code, in client-side storage, or in general purpose cloud storage, all of which are frequently harvested by attackers.
2. Transport protection should suffice for most business and security cases: most organizations have a hard enough time implementing TLS. Encrypting message bodies or payloads on top of encrypted transport can be overkill. This added layer of encryption requires a high level of effort to do effectively, not to mention that it can also add latency or can create integration headaches with other systems. More often than not, attackers defeat such mechanisms by harvesting exchanged key material that the client needs in order to encrypt and decrypt data from backend APIs.

    Eighty-five percent of organizations lack confidence that they know which APIs expose sensitive data based on results from the exposures of sensitive data can lead to significant regulatory penalties, large-scale privacy impacts, and brand damage.
3. Always use well-vetted algorithms and encryption libraries: many implementation details of encryption are essential to get "right" to avoid incidents such as salt sizes, rounds of salting, initialization vectors, key sizes, and more. These considerations also vary for symmetric encryption and asymmetric encryption. NIST provides some guidance on encryption, but you will also need to augment with specifics related to your technology stack. Guidance evolves over time as new encryption exploits surface or weaknesses are uncovered in cipher suites.

    You must also correctly maintain encryption tooling and code libraries since flaws can be uncovered over time, such as OpenSSL and the Heartbleed bug. This best practice is not just a developer problem since encryption tooling and libraries are used in many layers of the technology stack.

4. Avoid sending too much data to API clients: backend APIs are sometimes designed to serve up a great deal of data in responses to API calls, and it becomes the duty of the frontend client code to filter out what should be visible based on the goals of the user experience (UX) or permission levels. This design pattern goes against API security best practice since that data is evident by observing API requests and responses. Attackers commonly reverse engineer frontend code and sniff API traffic directly to see what information is actually being transmitted. The issue ranks as one of the OWASP API Security Top 10 as API3:2019 Excessive Data Exposure because it is so commonplace. Don't send too much data, particularly sensitive or private data, to front-end clients and always presume that they are compromised. Filter data appropriately in the backend and ship only the data that is necessary for that particular API consumer.

5. Plan for risks of scraping, data aggregation, and data inference: a few pieces of data may be innocent, but when data is collected and aggregated at scale, the situation becomes much more precarious. The resulting data sets quickly become privacy-impacting and brand-damaging. No quick fixes exist for these data security and privacy risks. Mitigation requires a combination of many techniques like limiting how much private data you collect in the first place, using rate limiting effectively, and limiting how much information you send to API clients.

Attackers will use automation to their advantage to scrape and aggregate data in large volumes. Attackers employ a plethora of tooling, including intercepting proxies, debuggers, Python scripting, and command line clients like cURL and HTTPie. Scraped data is also useful in other attack techniques, such as brute forcing, credential stuffing, phishing, and social engineering. To detect and stop abnormal API consumption like scraping, you will need to seek API security tooling that continuously analyzes API telemetry, analyzes behaviors, and identifies anomalies.

BEST PRACTICES FOR AUTHENTICATION AND AUTHORIZATION INCLUDE

1. Authenticate and continuously authorize API consumers: access control has always involved authentication and authorization. Authentication (AuthN), consists in identifying the requester of a given function or resource and challenging that entity for authentication material or credentials. Approval (AuthZ) involves verifying whether that authenticated entity actually has permission to exercise a role or read, write, update, or delete data.

2. Traditionally, both were handled at the start of a session. In the web world, and by extension, APIs, sessions are stateless. The operating environments of backends and frontends are not guaranteed and are often ephemeral. Increasingly, settings are also prone to integrity issues or compromise, hence the rise of zero-trust architectures. As a result, you must continuously verify whether a user or machine identity should have access to a given resource and always presume the authenticated session might be compromised.

3. This approach requires analyzing behaviors of a given session for an API consumer and potentially terminating that session, requiring step-up authentication or blocking access as appropriate.

Ninety-five percent of API exploits happen against authenticated APIs based on data from the Salt Security API Protection Platform, as detailed in the Q3 2021 State of API Security report. Attackers regularly circumvent access controls and hijack authenticated sessions, spotlighting the fact that API security strategy must focus on more than just authentication and authorization.

4. Use modern authentication and authorization protocols: use newer authentication protocols like OpenID Connect and authorization protocols. Using sufficient authentication

token lengths and entropy are also critically important to mitigate the risk of session guessing or brute forcing. JSON Web Tokens (JWT) are a popular choice as a token format within OAuth2.

5. Two-factor authentication (2FA) should also be in your arsenal for authenticating users that consume APIs. 2FA challenges are delivered through email, SMS, or Time-based One-time Password (TOTP) authenticator apps. Certificate-based authentication is more common for machine-to-machine communication and automation scenarios where it is not technically feasible to prompt for authentication material. Mutual TLS (mTLS) is also prominent for microservice authN and authZ as seen within Kubernetes and service mesh. Never rely on mechanisms like basic authentication or digest authentication. Attacks against these older authentication mechanisms are well documented, and they are trivial for attackers to defeat.

   Don't rely on API keys as authentication: API keys are commonplace in the world of APIs, and they are frequently seen as a means of connecting partners, connecting client apps to backend APIs, and enabling machine-to-machine (or direct API) communication. API keys are easily harvested by attackers through reverse engineering client-side code and sniffing network traffic if keys traverse unprotected networks and the Internet. API keys alone are not an acceptable form of authentication and should be used primarily as a form of version control. If you rely on API keys, ensure that you monitor consumption, generate new API keys, and revoke old API keys or API keys of malicious consumers appropriately. Realistically, API keys should be paired with additional authentication factors such as certificates or other authentication material.

6. Set reasonable idle and max session timeouts: idle session timeout controls how long a given session with the backend can stay live without receiving requests from the client until a user or machine is required to re-authenticate. Max session timeouts control the total time a session can be live with the backend, regardless of whether the session is active or idle. Idle session timeout recommendations range anywhere from 5 to 30 minutes, depending on the exposure of the API, business criticality, and data sensitivity.

7. Max session timeouts are usually in the range of a few hours or days. Some organizations opt for shorter session lifetimes, but such an approach requires a trade-off with UX since you will be forcing users to re-authenticate more frequently. You must consider these lifetimes for all session identifiers, authentication tokens, and refresh tokens throughout the technology stack. The intent of controlling session timeouts is to reduce the time window for attackers to steal session identifiers and hijack authenticated sessions. Active session identifiers and authentication tokens are just as valuable to an attacker as an original credential and can easily be used to obtain access to API and data.

8. Weigh the pros and cons of session binding: binding IP addresses of API consumers to session cookies and authentication tokens can provide some security benefits. If a bound session identifier or authentication token is stolen by an attacker, and the attacker attempts to reuse that authenticated session from another machine with a different IP address, the API request will be blocked since the request isn't coming from the original IP address. Session binding has the unintended side effect of limiting mobility. If a given API consumer uses multiple machines or mobile devices typically, they can be forced to authenticate excessively, which becomes damaging to UX.

9. Use additional secrets in authorization flows and nonces in requests: adding additional secrets in authentication flows helps reduce the risk of token interception and replay attacks.

10. OAuth2 provides this type of protection with a proof key for code exchange (PKCE). If you are using OAuth for authentication in your mobile app, consider employing PKCE to mitigate the risk of token interception and replay attacks. PKCE is also slated to become mandatory in OAuth 2.1. Using nonces in requests also helps reduce the risk of message

replay attacks and cross-site request forgery (CSRF) attacks. You can also use one of the many implementations of anti-CSRF mechanisms within code libraries and frameworks. It's often simply a matter of ensuring you've enabled the tool.

API Security with SAML Identity Provider

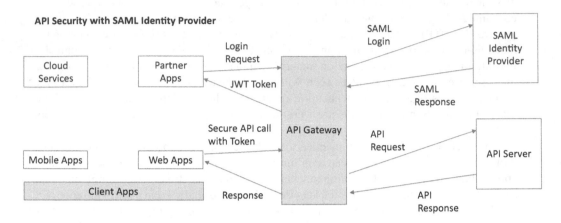

Source: Adapted from API Security Miniorange

IMMUTABLE INFRASTRUCTURE

Immutable infrastructure is a process pattern (not a technology) in which the system and application infrastructure, once deployed into production, is never updated in place. Instead, the infrastructure and applications are simply replaced by the development pipeline when required changes. Why This Is Important Immutable infrastructure ensures that the system and application environment are accurately deployed and remain in a predictable, known-good-configuration state. It simplifies change management, supports faster and safer upgrades, reduces operational errors, improves security, and simplifies troubleshooting. It also enables rapid replication of environments for disaster recovery, geographic redundancy, or testing. This approach is easier to adopt and often applied with cloud-native applications.

SUMMARY

We discussed that APIs are the mechanism for data access, Best practices for secure design, API discovery and cataloging, Best practices for authentication and authorization, and Immutable Infrastructure.

NOTES

1. Varia, Jinesh: Migrating Existing Applications to the AWS Cloud. Amazon Web Services, October
2. V2.0. http://www.cloud-council.org/deliverables/security-for-cloud-computing-10-steps-to-ensure success.htm
3. NIST Special Publication 800-88.
4. NIST Special Publication 800-175B.
5. ISO/IEC 20889. https://www.iso.org/standard/69373.html
6. https://www.schneier.com/crypto-gram-0907.html
7. https://www.owasp.org/index.php/Top_10_2013-Top_10
8. https://www.owasp.org/index.php/Secure_SDLC_Cheat_Sheet
9. https://www.owasp.org/images/0/08/OWASP_SCP_Quick_Reference_Guide_v2.pdf
10. https://nvlpubs.nist.gov/nistpubs/Legacy/SP/nistspecialpublication800-145.pdf

11. https://kubernetes.io/
12. https://hbr.org/2012/12/who-can-fix-the-middle-skills-gap
13. https://googleprojectzero.blogspot.com/2015/03/exploiting-dram-rowhammer-bug-to-gain.html
14. https://gdpr.cloudsecurityalliance.org/wpcontent/uploads/sites/2/2017/11/EU_GDPR_Impact_for_BusinessesEstablished_Outside_the_EU_and_EEA.pdf
15. https://datatracker.ietf.org/doc/rfc6749/
16. http://www.redbooks.ibm.com/redbooks/pdfs/sg248011.pdf
17. http://www.oreilly.com/programming/free/migrating-cloud-native-application-architectures.csp
18. http://www.nist.gov/itl/cloud/upload/NIST_SP-500-291_Version-2_2013_June18_FINAL.pdf
19. National Institute for Standards and Technology (2011): NIST Cloud Computing Standards Roadmap.
20. http://www.nist.gov/itl/cloud/upload/NIST_SP-500-291_Version-2_2013_June18_FINAL.pdf
21. https://www.opencontainers.org/
22. National Institute for Standards and Technology (2011): Special Publication 500-292 NIST
23. Cloud Computing Reference Architecture.
24. http://ws680.nist.gov/publication/get_pdf.cfm?pub_id=909505
25. Cloud Standards Customer Council (2015). Practical Guide to Platform as a Service.
26. http://www.cloud-council.org/deliverables/practical-guide-to-platform-as-a-service.htm
27. Moore's Revenge' is upon us and will make the world weird, Mark Pesce, The Register. https://www.theregister.co.uk/2018/06/04/moores_revenge/ [2] 2017 State of Application Security: Balancing Speed and Risk, Jim Bird, SANS. Available at: https://www.sans.org/reading-room/whitepapers/analyst/2017-state-application-security-balancing-speed-risk-38100
28. https://csrc.nist.gov/publications/detail/sp/800-163/rev-1/final
29. https://github.com/OWASP/owasp-mstg
30. https://cheatsheetseries.owasp.org/cheatsheets/Unvalidated_Redirects_and_Forwards_Cheat_Sheet.html
31. https://cheatsheetseries.owasp.org/cheatsheets/REST_Assessment_Cheat_Sheet.html
32. https://cheatsheetseries.owasp.org/cheatsheets/Abuse_Case_Cheat_Sheet.html
33. https://cheatsheetseries.owasp.org/cheatsheets/Abuse_Case_Cheat_Sheet.html
34. https://www.threatmodelingmanifesto.org/
35. https://csrc.nist.gov/publications/detail/sp/800-163/rev-1/final
36. https://cheatsheetseries.owasp.org/cheatsheets/Web_Service_Security_Cheat_Sheet.html
37. https://cheatsheetseries.owasp.org/cheatsheets/Web_Service_Security_Cheat_Sheet.html
38. https://cheatsheetseries.owasp.org/cheatsheets/XML_Security_Cheat_Sheet.html
39. https://cheatsheetseries.owasp.org/cheatsheets/XML_External_Entity_Prevention_Cheat_Sheet.html
40. https://content.salt.security/thanks-api-security-best-practices.html

Appendix D: Blockchain Architecture and Zero-Knowledge Proof

INTRODUCTION

We will discuss how blockchain technology could change the way enterprises conduct business and transactions with business partners and how blockchain technology can reduce operational costs and friction, and create immutable transaction records.

REDUCE OPERATIONAL COSTS AND FRICTION

Blockchain technology could change how enterprises conduct business transactions with business partners.

Blockchain technology and architecture can reduce operational costs and friction, and create immutable transaction records.

Record Keeper   Efficiency Play   Digital Asset Market   Blockchain Disruptor

Source: Adapted from Gartner

CLOUD CUSTOMER ARCHITECTURE FOR BLOCKCHAIN

Blockchain technology can be viewed from different perspectives:

1. From a business perspective, for transferring value, assets, or other entities between willing and mutually agreeing on participants, ensuring privacy and control of data to stakeholders
2. From a legal perspective, the transactions are validated
3. From a technical perspective, cryptography is used to ensure security, authenticated and verifiable.

BLOCKCHAIN BASICS

Blockchain transactions are permanently recorded in append-only blocks to the ledger. All the consensually confirmed and validated transaction blocks are linked from the genesis block to the most current block.

HIGH-LEVEL VIEW OF A BLOCKCHAIN

The figure shows the basic components of the blockchain.

COMPONENTS OF A BLOCKCHAIN

Blockchain Layer	Transaction ledger
	Consensus algorithm
	Peer-to-peer network
Internet Layer	TCP/IP

A blockchain system consists of nodes that communicate to validate transactions.

The agreement process is called consensus, and several different algorithms have been developed for this purpose.

Encryption is used to secure the Blockchain itself and the transactions and provides integrity on messages from users or between nodes, and ensures authorized entities only perform operations.

Blockchain Reference Architecture
Runtime flow

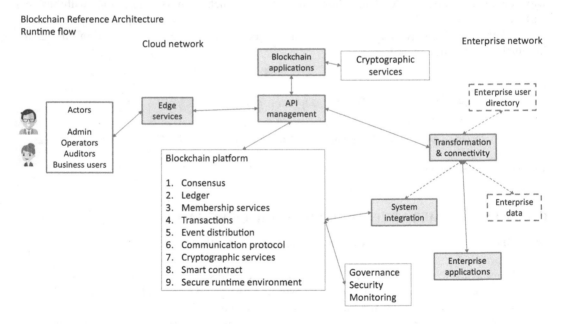

Source: Adapted from Cloud Standards Customer Council

Key Characteristics Blockchain
The following are the characteristics of Blockchain systems:

1. Cryptography
2. Immutability so transactions cannot be deleted or altered
3. Provenance
4. Decentralized computing infrastructure
5. Distributed transaction-processing platform
6. Decentralized database
7. Shared and distributed accounting ledger

8. Software development platform
9. Cloud computing
10. Peer-to-peer network
11. Wallet that includes identities, passwords, certificates, and encryption keys.

RUNTIME FLOW

Blockchain Reference Architecture
Runtime flow

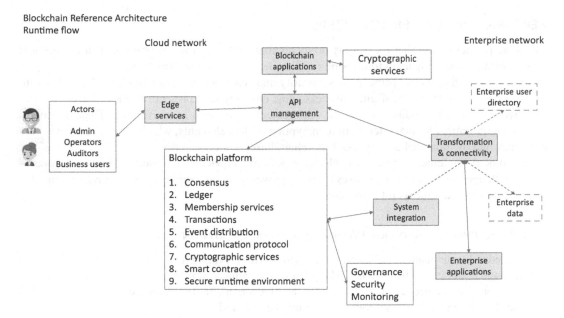

Source: Adapted from Cloud Standards Customer Council

Cloud Deployment Considerations
Scalability and Elasticity
The transaction volumes can be very large, and de-provision computing resources on demand as workloads change and clouds can make up some of the different demands.
Data Bandwidth
Public and private clouds need to be optimized for handling large data sets.
Data Sovereignty
The physical location could be regulated, with the regulations varying from country to country.
Resilience
Resilience should not rely on single components.

SECURITY

As more data is collected, requirements for governance and security increase and data privacy is increasingly important.

The cloud generally allows for faster deployment, and hybrid systems offer unique application governance features: where Software can be centrally maintained with in-house data to meet jurisdictional policies.

DECENTRALIZED IDENTITY (DCI)

Distributed ledger technologies and DCI

Decentralized identity (DCI) leverages, for example, blockchain to establish trust in identities. Online and mobile identities continue to be fragmented due to service providers requiring consumers to create individual identities for each service. DCI offers an alternative approach to ease the use of problems with traditional, fragmented, digital identity approaches.

ZERO-KNOWLEDGE PROOFS (ZKPS)

ZKPs are privacy-preserving messaging protocols that enable entities to prove that information is correct without requiring them to transmit or share the underlying information.

Due to cyber threats and privacy laws, security and risk management (SRM) leaders must support use cases that enable the digital business while ensuring data protection. ZKPs enable entities to prove information validity without the requirement to transmit sensitive data. These protocols limit the requirement for mass decryption/encryption of data elements, which benefits the network's efficiency and the potential adoption of blockchain-based systems.

A protocol implementing zero-knowledge proofs of knowledge is based on input like one or more challenges such that the responses from the prover to avoid a replay of it to convince someone else that they possess the secret information.

How Blockchain Technology Works—Asymmetric Encryption

Distributed ledger technology relies on using asymmetric cryptography to sign messages and encrypt data through a private/public key pair. The private keys, which allow a given entity to transact with the assets or virtual currency allocated to it in the blockchain, are typically stored in what is called a wallet. In a given wallet, there could be multiple keys stored.

Overview of a Blockchain—Workflow

- Step 1: Users sign off on transactions from their wallet application, attempting to send certain crypto from them to someone else.
- Step 2: The transaction is picked up by the blockchain network and inserted into a pool of unconfirmed transactions. This pool is a collection of all the transactions on that network that have not been confirmed yet.
- Step 3: Miners on the network select transactions from the pool of unconfirmed transactions and collect them in a block.
- Step 4: When a miner has filled up its block with transactions, it will start to try and solve a complicated mathematical problem that is unique to that block all together.

    The mathematical problem every miner faces when trying to enter a blockchain block is finding a hash output for the data in its block that starts with a certain amount of zeros.

    The data inside a block as the hash input (a string of data). When this input is hashed, it gives a hash output (32-digit string).

    Miners repeatedly change a part of the data inside their block called the nonce. Because the nonce changes all the time, the input data for the hash function also change, leading to different hash outputs. Eventually, the miner hopes to find an input string (string of block data and the nonce) that hashes to an eligible output string (that starts with an amount of zero's).

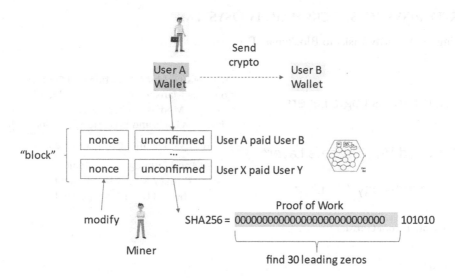

- Step 5: The miner that finds a solution sends his "proof of work", aka the solution, to the other miners.
- Step 6: The other miners verify if the work has resulted in the correct solution.
  - Before other nodes agree that the block can be added to the blockchain, they will run another check on the transactions in the corresponding block first.
  - According to the blockchain, if all transactions are still valid, the other miners will agree, and a "consensus" is reached.
- Step 7: If most miners reach consensus, the block gets added to the blockchain.

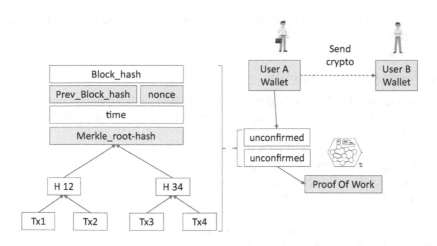

Sharding and Pruning

The possibility that only specific transactions are to be verified by specific nodes (validators) is called Sharding. It could also introduce a significant fault (i.e., reversion of subsequent transactions) if a specific subset of validators were to wrongly validate transactions to which other members of that same blockchain refer. This is due to the fact that communication between shards will require the use of transaction receipts from one shard to communicate with the next.

SECURITY RISKS TO BLOCKCHAIN ECOSYSTEMS

Evaluating the Security Risks to Blockchain Ecosystems

Business Logic Layers	Business Problem Definition and Contracts
	Consortia Management - Decentralized Trust Models - Public / Private
	Business Logic and Execution / Resiliency
Risk and IAM Process Layers	Risk Management and Compliance
	IAM and Cryptographic Architecture
Technology / IT Layers	Threat / Node Management
	Physical Layer Management

Source: Adapted from Gartner

PROBLEM AREAS

Problem Area 1

- When using blockchain, the user's private key is regarded as the identity and security credential generated and maintained by the user instead of third-party agencies.
- Each user has their own pair of public keys and private keys. These are two secure cryptographic keys that allow limited interaction with the system.
- The attacker can use social engineering to steal private keys from the user's machine.
- An attacker who obtained encryption keys to a dataset would be able to read the underlying data, can plant malware, and/or misuse the sender's data asset.

However, if the signing/private key is secured, they will not be able to modify the data or disrupt the blockchain ecosystem.

CHALLENGE–SMART CONTRACT SECURITY

- Smart contracts (also known as digital contracts) help you exchange money, property, shares, or anything of value in a transparent, conflict-free way while avoiding the services of a middleman.
- These self-executing contracts are with the terms of the agreement between sender and receiver being directly written into lines of code. The code and the agreements contained therein exist across a distributed, decentralized blockchain network.
- Hackers steal cryptocurrencies by exploiting code flaws in smart contracts. DAO is a classic example.
- In June 2016, an attack on the DAO16 took place, an investment vehicle created on the Ethereum network and operated as a smart contract. Over $59m in Ether17 was stolen by an unknown source from the wallet controlled by the program on behalf of all investors.

CHALLENGE–CONSENSUS PROTOCOL SECURITY

The system allows multiple participants to submit new inputs to a distributed ledger. Consensus is then used to determine which state of the database is considered valid over time. This is in contrast to a traditional database, where multiple participants submit new inputs, and one counterparty is relied on to provide the valid state of the database.

Types of Consensus Protocol

Proof of Work: Uses computational power to validate new blocks of data. To participate in this scheme, participants must collate transactions within a single block and then apply a hash function with some additional metadata.

Proof of Stake: Unlike Proof of Work, Proof of Stake relies on proving the user is invested in the underlying token of the value of the network being mined rather than being the owner of a large amount of computing power

Ripple Protocol: All participants then vote on valid transactions to be included in the ledger. Transactions that meet the 80% threshold of "yes" votes are included within the following last closed ledger state.

Proof of Elapsed Time: Intel has devised a means of establishing a validation lottery that takes advantage of the capability of its CPUs to produce a timestamp cryptographically signed by the hardware. Whoever in the chain has the next soonest timestamp will be the one to decide which transactions will be a part of the next block in the chain. This consensus method is more energy efficient than Proof of Work and, therefore, more adapted to IoT devices.

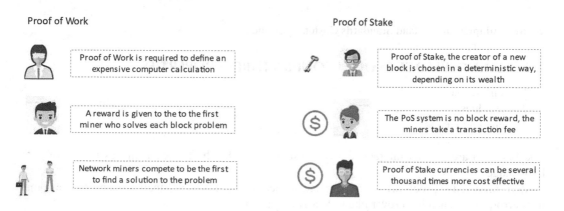

Proof of Work
- Proof of Work is required to define an expensive computer calculation
- A reward is given to the to the first miner who solves each block problem
- Network miners compete to be the first to find a solution to the problem

Proof of Stake
- Proof of Stake, the creator of a new block is chosen in a deterministic way, depending on its wealth
- The PoS system is no block reward, the miners take a transaction fee
- Proof of Stake currencies can be several thousand times more cost effective

SOLUTION AREAS

Secure Transaction Ledgers

Use different keys to sign and encrypt in a secure wallet to prevent an attacker can steal the private keys from the user's machine.

Use tokenization or encryption for securing the transactional/key element data in each block created / transmitted in a blockchain ecosystem.

Use log analytics and data discovery for predictive analytics.

Blockchain technology has the potential to have a major impact on how institutions process transactions and conduct business.

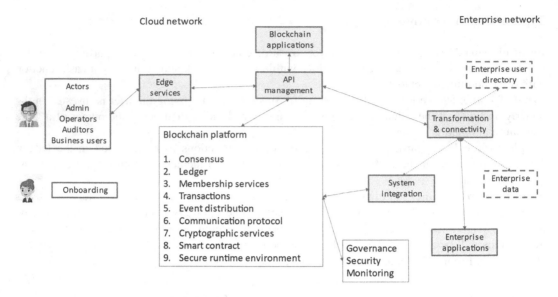

Source: Adapted from Cloud Standards Customer Council

A ZERO-KNOWLEDGE PROOF REQUIRES THREE PROPERTIES

1. Completeness
2. Soundness
3. Zero-knowledge

The first two are general interactive proof systems, and the third is what makes the proof zero-knowledge.

Zero-knowledge proofs are not mathematical because there is some small probability, the soundness error, that a cheating prover like with a Turing machine.

APPLICATIONS

One application is in authentication systems to enforce honest behavior while maintaining privacy. Another one is in potential nuclear disarmament talks. To verify that an object is indeed a nuclear weapon without recording, sharing, or revealing the internal workings, which might be secret. Zero-knowledge proofs are used in Zerocoin, Zerocash, and Zcash.

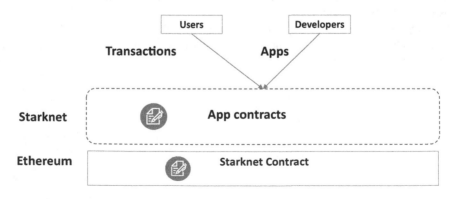

Source: Adapted from Starkware

SNARKs vs STARKs

Conflict existing between new technologies and similar technologies has always come to market around the same time to seek similar results and both the SNARK and STARK camp are interesting.

Two approaches are zk-SNARKs and zk-STARKs. They are different zero-knowledge technologies, from a cultural and technical perspective, and are noninteractive.

The tables show high-level differences between the two technologies:

	SNARK	STARK	Bullet proofs
Starkware and ZK proofs	zk-SNARK stands for zero-knowledge succinct non-interactive argument of knowledge	zk-STARK stands for zero-knowledge scalable transparent argument of knowledge	
zero-knowledge technologies are non-interactive	non-interactive	non-interactive	
Alorithmic complexity: prover	O(1)	O(N)	O(N*log(N))
Alorithmic complexity: verifier	O(1)	O(log(N))	O(N)
Txn size	46kB	1kb	1kb
Etherum verification gas cost	600k	2.5M	
Trust setup required	Yes	non-interactive	No
Post-quantum secure	No	Yes	
Crypto assumptions	Strong	Collision resistant hashes	Discrete log

Source: Adapted from Consensys

SNARKs

One question is whether there is a backdoor into elliptic curve random number generators. The algorithm as a whole generally remains secure. Side-channel attacks can be mitigated through several techniques, but Quantum attacks are more concerning.

Since based on elliptic curves, zk-SNARKs need a trusted setup as a starting with the generation of keys.

SNARKs many require 24% of that gas that STARKs will need. SNARKs is cheaper for the end-user and smaller than STARKs with smaller on-chain data.

STARKs

STARKs have far larger proof sizes than SNARKs, which means that verifying STARKs takes more time than SNARKs and also leads to STARKs requiring more gas.

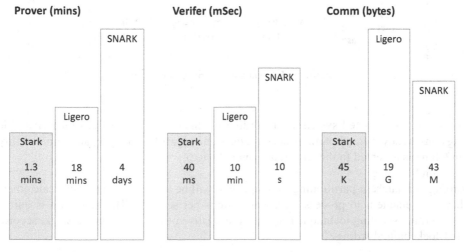

Source: Adapted from Starkware

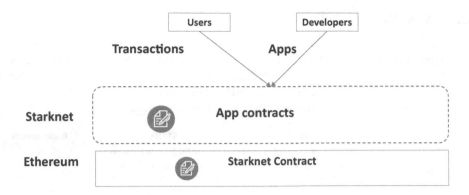

Source: Adapted from Starkware

SMART CONTRACTS MARKETPLACE

Smart Contracts Marketplace

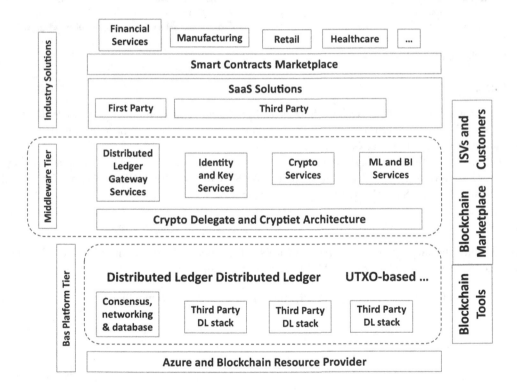

A blockchain is a distributed system for recording the history of transactions on a shared ledger, providing consistency (i.e., all participants have the same view of the ledger) and immutability (i.e., once something is accepted to the ledger, it cannot change).

Blockchain Sharding

"Sharding is a database partitioning technique that will be used to dramatically scale ethereum's blockchain and enable it to process more transactions per second." The definition is quite accurate. However, the sharding technique is not the prerogative of the Ethereum network, according to "What Is Blockchain Sharding?"

BLOCKCHAIN WITH PRIVATE DATA

In many application scenarios, we would like to use a blockchain architecture in a setting where some information is private to some participants and should not be seen by others. Some examples of applications that require dealing with private data include the following:

RUNNING MEDICAL STUDIES

Consider multiple hospitals that want to jointly run statistics on patient treatment data, for example, the success rate of a treatment option for patients with some rare condition. The data is private, so the hospitals cannot share it, and the condition is sufficiently rare that a simple redaction of PII is not sufficient.

DETECTING INSURANCE FRAUD

For another example, imagine an insurance market in which insurers want to pool their data together to detect fraud.

SOLUTION

Encryption for Blockchain Smart Contracts

Encryption and Tokenization Service for Blockchain Smart Contracts

Stack integration

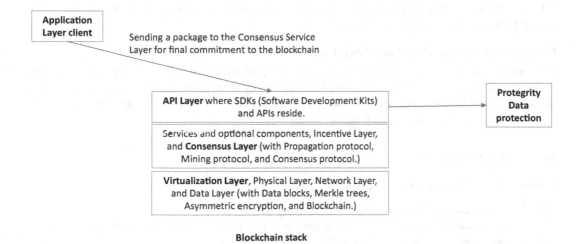

Blockchain stack

DATA ENCRYPTED WITH MULTIPLE KEYS

Encryption Service for Blockchain Smart Contracts

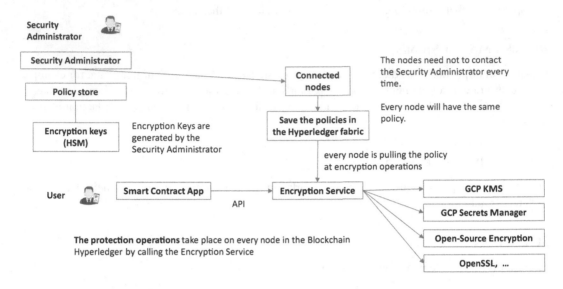

SECURE MULTIPARTY COMPUTATION

"Supporting Private Data on Hyperledger Fabric with Secure Multiparty Computation" uses secure-MPC protocols to support private data on Hyperledger Fabric, integrating the execution of the secure-MPC protocol as part of the smart contract.

Data Encrypted with Their Own Secret Key

The parties store their private data on the ledger, encrypted with their own secret key. When private data is needed in a smart contract, the party that has the key decrypts it and uses the decrypted value as its local input to the secure-MPC protocol. This allows the smart contract to depend on any combination of public and private data from the ledger.

SMART CONTRACTS

BUSINESS OBJECTIVES OF SMART CONTRACT

What are the goals of the smart contract that is being developed?

We must consider the goal or purpose of the smart contract we are considering. The number of higher-order objects we must consider will be tied to the use case.

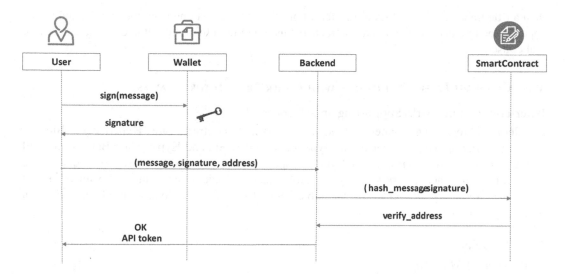

Source: Adapted from Drecom

Who Are Your End Users?

Why do we want to know how the users of your smart contract are? Because we want to understand what behaviors we can attribute to a particular demographic, cultural, or sentimental marker. If we know the types of behaviors to expect of our users, we may be able to mitigate for those behaviors or at the least baseline those behaviors to unlock additional value from the knowledge of our users. Additionally, we need to understand if we are dealing with a cross-border transaction and the associated treaty, statutory, regulatory, and case law that affects the parties involved in each jurisdiction. Also, the end users' basic technical understanding of smart contracts will drive how smart contracts will be received. Suppose an end user understands the efficiencies gained through the use of a smart contract, as well as the associated legal and technical risks. In that case, they will be better suited for adopting a smart contract for their use case.

Does Your Smart Contract Transact Currency?

If your smart contract transacts currency, there are additional legal considerations to take into account, such as compliance with Know Your Customer (KYC) and Anti Money Laundering (A.M.L.) regulatory requirements. Cross-border transactions involving currency (including cryptocurrencies) must comply with international law and all specific legal requirements from any governmental entity that may have jurisdiction over the matter. This may include required reporting to tax authorities about any capital gains around the sale or transfer of any cryptocurrency.

Does Your Smart Contract Transfer Asset Titles?

Asset transfers may be governed by international, national, state/province, and even local jurisdictional laws. One of the primary items to consider when working with blockchain smart contracts is whether the transfer of title can be accomplished via blockchain solutions such as Hyperledger Fabric and whether such a transfer is supported by the relevant statutes and regulations treaty or local law. There also needs to be a consideration of the broader legal picture of how asset titles are transferred. In the case of real estate transactions in the United States, if an automated blockchain smart contract were to transfer title without first checking to make sure that the individual was not on active duty with one of the branches of the military or that the individual had not filed for bankruptcy protection under the United States Bankruptcy Code, that automatic transfer would be in violation of the federal laws of the United States and the parties and counsel would likely be subject to sanction and legal penalties. Additionally, in real estate law, there is the concept of a bundle of rights, and when a title transfer occurs, does it transfer all of the rights or just one from the bundle, and is that properly documented via the smart contract. If this is not done correctly, this can result in severe legal consequences.

SMART CONTRACT LAYER'S INTERACTION WITH OTHER ARCHITECTURAL LAYERS

Hyperledger Frameworks Supporting Smart Contracts

Hyperledger blockchain frameworks supporting smart contracts are Hyperledger Burrow, Hyperledger Fabric, Hyperledger Iroha, Hyperledger Sawtooth, and Hyperledger Besu. Across all these frameworks, the smart contract layer is responsible for processing transaction requests and determining if transactions are valid by executing business logic. Each framework supports smart contracts in a slightly different way. The table below lists the smart contract implementations in Hyperledger Frameworks.

Threat Modeling

What Is Threat Modeling?

Threat modeling is a process of identifying potential vulnerabilities and weaknesses in a system that could be exploited by an attacker (in other words, an attacker with an intent and a capability that can exploit a vulnerability is what we call a threat). The vulnerabilities, weaknesses, and other risks can then be addressed by using mitigations, architecting them out, accepting them, adding compensating controls, etc. Technical threat modeling usually (but not always) involves the creation of a data-flow document (DFD).

Please note that while this article is focused on technical threat modeling of information systems, it can also be applied to other systems and security, such as physical buildings, locks, and even abstract things like business processes.

Why Create a Threat Model?

A threat model allows you to identify potential vulnerabilities and weaknesses, from architectural issues all the way down to operational levels. Once threats are identified, you can then deal with them structured and methodically. There are several reasons threat models are now more important than ever:

1. Systems are more complex now, 20 years ago, a web application was composed of 5-10 parts typically (a three-tier architecture, authentication, logging, connection to a handful of other systems, etc.), nowadays, a web app like "Netflix" or "eBay" has thousands of complex components and integration literally with dozens or hundreds of external systems (payment, orders, shipping, often from multiple providers, etc.)
2. We need to be able to validate that the model actually reflects reality, especially as things change over time. This means you need it written down, ideally in a way that can be shared easily with multiple people (operations, auditors, etc.) and supports versioning, collaboration, and so on.
3. Threat models can be created and applied not just at design time but both prior to design (e.g., initial scope of work phase) and post-design, during development, deployment, operations, and end-of-life.
4. There is now tooling for some specific use cases (mostly web applications and mobile applications) that can be used to simplify and speed the process up significantly.

Once you have a threat model, you can now look at the following activities:

1. With a good threat model, you can examine the system for weak points or vulnerable areas that may need additional work, and you can maximize the R.O.I. of your time and effort

2. You can make better predictions based on proposed changes ("what happens if we supplement passwords with 2FA, what happens if we make it mandatory?") with a greater degree of certainty

3. You can map (sometimes automatically, depending on the tooling) compliance standards and regulations to your threat model, for example, identify what parts of the model G.D.P.R. might apply to, such as account creation, data backups, etc.

4. Tools exist now that allow you to attach weightings (such as C.V.S.S. vulnerability scores) and values (such as the need for AIC/CIA) to various aspects of the system, which can also help guide spending on security efforts

5. Tooling now exists that can create a threat model that also has real-world information like Software and versions used. When vulnerability (e.g., C.V.E., vendor advisories), data is released that affects your system, it can be flagged. This can generate reports on the severity and importance of applying fixes or otherwise dealing with vulnerabilities

> Isn't a threat model just a DFD (Data Flow Diagram) with some added vuln info?
> Short answer: Yes.
> Longer answer: many existing systems do not have a good DFD (Data Flow Diagram), one that is up to date, or one that reflects the operational realities of how it now behaves and works.
> When should you create a threat model?
> Ideally, you would create a threat model at the beginning of the lifecycle when you are designing the system. This would allow you to make informed design choices and potentially create a more secure system.

However, not all is lost if you have an existing system without a good threat model. Threat modeling is also extremely valuable for existing systems, as it allows you to better understand them by looking at assumptions and the actual as built and operated system and making sure they are still correct. This section needs a major rewrite but in major terms, boils down to:

- You want to support pre-system architecture threat modeling, helping to inform decisions like whether or not you will handle payments or simply outsource it entirely. Using a PaaS or an IaaS early on can provide significant value

- You want to support the system during the major formative stages, such as architecture, development, and deployment. This is where most threat modeling focuses currently

- You want to support the system through the rest of the lifecycle, operations, end of life, etc. Also, it should be noted that most systems are not static and have review and modification phases

- Your threat modeling strategy needs to deal with entirely new classes of attacks that may not have existed when you started. In other words, you'll need to be able to deal with unknown unknowns that become known in the future, failure to do so leaves you exposed

- You need to account for how modern systems are built. This means broad and deep supply chains in both software terms (libraries, etc.) and service terms (IaaS, PaaS, SaaS, etc.)

Threat Modeling Basics

A threat model is only as good as its understanding and representation of the underlying system(s). In general, a threat model starts with the high-level DFD (Data Flow Diagram) of the system, followed by the data flows and then add things such as possible user actions and interactions with external systems. Alternatively, you can work bottom-up. This is an especially effective technique for dealing with existing systems where you may no longer know the original assumptions/data flow architecture.

While you can look at only the surface of a system (e.g., publicly exposed components) and create a threat model from that, it is far more valuable to understand and include the underlying system. Does the system use SQL? NoSQL? Is there caching? A single point of failure? A load balancer?

One major challenge in threat modeling is striking a balance between having necessary details, abstracting things away that are less important or unimportant, and simply being a distraction.

Shostack's 4-Question Frame for Threat Modeling

Adam Shostack has developed a simple set of four questions that help frame threat modeling:

- What are you building?
- What can go wrong with it once it's built?
- What should you do about those things that can go wrong?
- Did you do a decent job of analysis?

Combining Threat Modeling with the OODA loop

Essentially most decision-making processes can be dealt with using the OODA loop model:

$$Observe > Orient > Decide > Act$$

However, like most decision-making, there are nuances to threat modeling that can be applied to make it more effective.

Threat modeling process overview

Most threat modeling methodologies, be they risk-based, application-based, asset-based, privacy-based, etc., share several traits in common:

1. Define business objectives/requirements
2. Define the scope of threat model coverage
3. Identify assets and create architecture diagrams, Dataflow Diagrams (DfD)
4. Identify weaknesses, vulnerabilities, and threats
5. Analyze risk and impact
6. Mitigation, remediation, and so on

Several of the threat modeling methodologies essentially include all the above steps (e.g., P.A.S.T.A.), and several only address specific steps (STRIDE, for example, helps identify weaknesses, vulnerabilities, and threats).

Define Business Objectives/Requirements

Realistically, if your project hasn't started with defining business objectives and requirements, then it's doomed to failure. This is an integral part of any project, but I sadly feel it must be mentioned, as it is often not as clearly documented as it should be or has been subject to changes that are not documented. It is critical to get a current copy of the business objectives and requirements and a commitment that any ongoing updates or changes are communicated quickly to the threat modeling team as it impacts all aspects of the threat model.

One note: due to the distributed and multi-organizational nature of many Blockchain and Smart Contract projects, it should be noted that different organizations may have different requirements. This is guaranteed to be true if the project is international in scope due to different regulatory and legal environments.

Define the Scope of Threat Model Coverage

Once you have the business objectives and requirements, you'll be able to do a rough scope/architecture plan. This is a good point to decide how far down the rabbit hole you want to go. For example, you may decide to limit threat model coverage to the Smart Contracts and Blockchain network itself and limit coverage of the underlying computational infrastructure to the virtual machines, trusting that the provider of the actual hardware, network, and so on is secure. Alternatively, a more risk-averse threat model may also consider the hardware, networks, and even the infrastructure's power delivery and physical security.

If the threat model ignores components that are directly controlled, it should be noted why they are out of scope and what, if any, compensating measures are being considered, for example, it may be as simple as "Smart Contract security is not considered as a risk due to this specific project being a private Blockchain network with a governance model that includes mechanisms for deciding if a transaction is incorrect and must be undone".

In general, the threat modelling team should not Identify assets and create architecture diagrams, Dataflow Diagrams (DfD), and so on. This should be done by the group(s) actually creating and implementing the project, and the data should be shared with the threat modeling group. Especially as the project changes, the updated information must be communicated to the threat model group in a timely manner.

Suppose the threat modeling team is expected to Identify assets and create architecture diagrams, DfD. In that case, it will most likely be incorrect or incomplete (and certainly out of date) as they attempt to determine exactly what is being done. Additionally, it shows a lack of cooperation and support for the threat modeling effort that will cripple it, if not prevent it completely.

IDENTIFY WEAKNESSES, VULNERABILITIES, AND THREATS

In general, there are three types of weaknesses, vulnerabilities, and threats in Blockchain and Smart Contracts:

1. "Traditional" issues that have a traditional impact on Blockchain and Smart Contracts technology
2. "Traditional" issues that have a new and interesting impact on Blockchain and Smart Contracts technology
3. New issues specific to Blockchain and Smart Contracts technology

The first is relatively easy, for example, Blockchains and Smart contracts must run on some sort of computing infrastructure and network, so things like DNS security, operating system patches, and so on must be applied or else an attacker will be able to gain access through traditional attacks and then execute further attacks. This class of issue can generally be dealt with either directly or through the abstraction and implementation of policy such as "all computer infrastructure must conform to standard [X]" (PCI, SOC2, etc.).

The second issue is more interesting. There are many traditional vulnerabilities, such as integer overflows or improperly created cryptographic material, which has new and novel impacts on Blockchains and Smart contracts. For example, depending on the consensus algorithm in use, an attacker can leverage denial of service attacks to isolate parts of the Blockchain network and make subsequent attacks against voting systems or Proof-of-Work (PoW) much easier. The third class of attack is of real interest, and some research is going on here. Blockchains and Smart contracts present new and novel technological approaches, including new and novel attacks. For example, the support for multi-step atomic transactions such as "buy asset A on exchange Y and then sell asset A on exchange Z for asset B, all at current prices" can be combined with flash loans and price manipulation to create a situation where the attacker only has to put up several hundred dollars (in fees and loan costs) to leverage tens or even hundreds of thousands of dollars, a situation in which even a minor price manipulation (of less than a percent) can result in a windfall for the attacker.

One method to create a list of weaknesses, vulnerabilities, and threats is to essentially conduct a tabletop exercise and walk through what an attacker might want to do and how they might accomplish it. This allows the use of other existing assets, such as Persona-non-Grata and lists of existing vulnerabilities (https://csaurl.org/blockchain-vulnerabilities) and incidents (https://csaurl.org/blockchain-incidents).

ANALYZE RISK AND IMPACT

1. Similar to the "Identify weaknesses, vulnerabilities and threats", there is a wealth of traditional information but not a lot of Blockchain and Smart contract-specific information. Blockchains and Smart contracts have some very different behaviors, for example, backups. I have seen some people claim that backups are not required in a Blockchain world as long as you have a trusted copy of the genesis block (the root of the Blockchain) and the data, such as public keys, needed to validate it. But this ignores some common failures:

   a. You will want a backup of your data so you don't have to download all the records in the event of a failure. Recovery is much faster if you have most of the data locally on a nearline backup system.

   b. In the event of a major flaw in the Blockchains software, for example, that results in network-wide deletions or alterations, having trusted backups will be beneficial (and if you think your Blockchain software has no such flaws, I hope you are correct, but you may not be)

   c. In the event a transaction needs to be removed, and the network is rolled back (an uncommon but not impossible occurrence), it is probably a good idea to have a copy of the bad transactions for later forensics and investigation.

   d. We haven't even discussed non-committed data, such as transaction memory pools where pending transactions exist.

Backups are an integral part of I.T.. However, Blockchain changes this, especially as a Blockchain may be configured to have private records or records that are shared among a limited subset of the network. Some Blockchains (like Bitcoin) have a single global state that is public, and everyone has access to, and some, like HyperLedger, support much more complicated implementations with private data and semi-private data.

In line with this, Blockchain and Smart Contract technologies are still young and rapidly evolving. Additionally, they present complex, interrelated systems where it can be difficult to predict second and third-order effects from a risk or an impact on one aspect of the system. We have an additional bias in the data available. Public financial Blockchains that have been attacked and compromised cannot generally hide it (hey, who did this $600 million dollar transaction?), while private industry Blockchains do not generally share data about being attacked and compromised.

To complicate matters worse, there are various recovery options that may or may not be available. This can work, but now attackers are increasingly targeting cross-chain systems so that they can move their stolen tokens to other Blockchains where they cannot be easily recovered (if at all).

It should also be noted that of the A.I.C. triad of information security, you can recover Availability and Integrity (indeed, Blockchain can make this much easier), but recovering Confidentiality can be impossible (once it's out, it's out).

Be Aware of Blockchain Properties

Be careful about external contract calls, which may execute malicious code and change control flow.

Common Hyperledger Smart Contract Security Patterns and Vulnerabilities

Static code analysis tools have been determined to be effective at detecting Hyperledger vulnerabilities. The study did not discuss possible countermeasures for the attack examined but revealed that smart contract verification tools are able to detect most of the identified vulnerabilities.

In the International conference on principles of security and trust, N. Atzei, M. Bartoletti, and T. Cimoli, "A survey of attacks on Ethereum smart contracts (sok)", A survey of attacks on principles of security and trust.

A 2019 IEEE paper, "Potential risks of Hyperledger Fabric smart contracts", discussed several security risks in Hyperledger Fabric smart contracts that are attributed to Go and other general-purpose languages programming language that are used to write smart contracts in Hyperledger as opposed to domain-specific languages (DSLs) like Solidity

Using a relevant literature going back to 2019 three, (3) smart contract vulnerabilities in Hyperledger Fabric (Rich Queries, Pseudorandom Number Generators, and Global Variables) were selected. Smart contracts containing these vulnerabilities were deployed on a test network, and the vulnerable contract features were exploited. What was determined was that proposed countermeasures at a minimum mitigate the impact severity of these vulnerabilities.

https://repository.tudelft.nl/islandora/object/uuid:dd09d153-a9df-4c1b-a317-d93c1231ee28

A Closer Look at Two of the Vulnerabilities:

#1 Updates Using Rich Queries – Also Referred to as "Range Query Risk"

Exploit: Illegal value propagation

The default access controls provided with CouchDB are no good. If not changed, a malicious actor on the network could access a peer's CouchDB instance with little difficulty.

The attacker could then directly modify and control the world state perceived by that peer without invoking any ledger transactions.

The value has been modified from 300 to -1 through the CouchDB G.U.I. accessible on localhost:5984/ utils.

If combined with the rich queries vulnerability, illegal changes made in the state database can propagate to the ledger.

The attacker needs to modify the state database of a sufficient number of endorsing peers to pass consensus to propagate the change.

Countermeasures

Rich query methods like GetQueryResult should only be used for query transactions, including Hyperledger Fabric's own documentation because the query results are not verified in the validation phase.

Besides avoiding rich queries within update transactions altogether, the following design pattern can be adapted:

- Use rich query to retrieve the appropriate keys from the state database.
- Use a safe key-based query (e.g., GetState) to retrieve the latest committed values from the ledger.

This pattern was based on community discussions on the Hyperledger Fabric forums:

- Validating transactions including rich queries - https://lists.hyperledger.org/g/fabric/topic/validatingtransactions/74932404?p=

#2 Pseudorandom Number Generator

A secure random number generator (RNG) should be unpredictable. The outcome of invoking a smart contract must be deterministic. These conflicting properties make implementing secure RNGs in smart contracts a challenging problem.

An unpredictable RNG generates a new random number every time it is called. As a result, unpredictable RNG cannot be used in smart contracts; every endorsing peer will calculate a different random number and the contract will be non-deterministic.

- However, this makes the contract vulnerable to exploitation.

PRNGs generate number sequences by following a deterministic algorithm: Given the same input, or seed, the sequence output by the PRNG is the same every time it is run

Since all peers need access to the same seed, it must be available on the Blockchain.

- The seed will also be available to a potential attacker.
- If an attacker knows the seed used by the PRNG, he can predict the outcome and exploit the contract.

This PRNG vulnerability was implemented into a simple lottery smart contract (see code).

- The smart contract generates a random number using the math/rand PRNG seeded with the transaction timestamp on (line 5), which is the vulnerable feature of this contract.
- The number is hashed and stored on the ledger for future reference.

The participants can then invoke the contract to try and guess the random number to win the lottery.

The function used by the vulnerable lottery contract to generate the new winning number using a PRNG.

Exploit: Predicting the outcome

The transaction timestamp and the smart contract are available to everyone on the channel.

- A malicious participant can re-calculate the random number and predict the lottery with the information available on the ledger.

The ledger was inspected using Hyperledger Explorer (v1.1.5) to reproduce this scenario (see Image).

- Current Hyperledger Explorer (v1.1.8)
- CLI can also be used, but navigating to the relevant information can be difficult.

The winning number is hidden, but the timestamp used to calculate the number is visible.

- The attacker can then use the same PRNG method to re-calculate the winning number and invoke the contract to win the lottery.

COUNTERMEASURES

Passing seed as input – Transient data is not recorded on the ledger, so passing the seed as transient input data allows using a PRNG while keeping the seed secret from the blockchain.

- Moves the security issue from the smart contract to the invoking client.
    - The client becomes a single point of failure.
    - Client must generate and store the seed securely.
- If the client is compromised, the smart contract is also compromised.

CENTRALIZED ORACLES

The smart contract can then request the random number from a centralized oracle (without deterministic constraints) using a high entropy function to calculate the random number.

- Solution relies on third-party oracle being trusted and secure since it controls the outcome of the RNG.
- Relying on (centralized) trusted third party.
- If the oracle is compromised, so is the smart contract.

I.B.M.'S BLOCKCHAIN-BASED VACCINE PASSPORT

As international travel ramps up in parts of the world, Amadeus, a reservation system used by 474 airlines, has adapted I.B.M.'s digital health passport solution called I.B.M. Digital Health Pass. Instead of presenting paper-based certifications, travelers need only scan a Q.R. code sent by email at the gate. Travelers without smartphones can print a Q.R. code. The backend technology authenticates credentials against the requirements of each country—relieving agents from an onerous burden, given how frequently countries change travel restrictions as the pandemic evolves.

SUMMARY

We discussed how blockchain technology could change the way enterprises conduct business and transactions with business partners and how blockchain technology can reduce operational costs and friction, and create immutable transaction records.

NOTES

1. "Introducing Zero-Knowledge Proofs for Private Web attestation with Cross/Multi-Vendor Hardware". The Cloudflare Blog. 2021-08-12. Retrieved 2021-08-18.
2. https://qz.com/2036529/more-than-450-airlines-can-now-use-ibms-digital-health-pass/
3. "hPPPL and Princeton demonstrate novel technique that may have applicability to future nuclear disarmament talks - Princeton Plasma Physics Lab". www.pppl.gov. Archived from the original on 2017-07-03.
4. "Transparent Zero-Knowledge Proofs With Zilch". Medium. 2021.
5. Andrew, Munro (30 July 2019). "Zcoin cryptocurrency introduces zero knowledge proofs with no trusted setup". Finder Australia. Archived from the original on 30 July 2019. Retrieved 30 July 2019.
6. Aram, Jivanyan (7 April 2019). "Lelantus: Towards Confidentiality and Anonymity of Blockchain Transactions from Standard Assumptions". Cryptology ePrint Archive (Report 373). Retrieved 14 April 2019.
7. Bünz, B; Bootle, D; Boneh, A (2018). "Bulletproofs: Short Proofs for Confidential Transactions and More". IEEE Symposium on Security and Privacy. San Francisco, California: 315–334. doi:10.1109/SP.2018.00020. ISBN 978-1-5386-4353-2. S2CID 3337741. Retrieved 3 December 2020.
8. Bunz, Benedikt; Bootle, Jonathan; Boneh, Dan; Poelstra, Andrew; Wuille, Pieter; Maxwell, Greg (May 2018). "Bulletproofs: Short Proofs for Confidential Transactions and More". 2018 IEEE Symposium on Security and Privacy (S.P.): 315–334. doi:10.1109/SP.2018.00020.
9. Bünz, Benedikt; Fisch, Ben; Szepieniec, Alan (2020). "Transparent SNARKs from DARK Compilers". Advances in Cryptology – EUROCRYPT 2020. Springer International Publishing: 677–706. doi:10.1007/978-3-030-45721-1_24.
10. Dwork, Cynthia; Naor, Moni; Sahai, Amit (2004). "Concurrent Zero Knowledge". Journal of the A.C.M. 51 (6): 851–898. CiteSeerX 10.1.1.43.716. doi:10.1145/1039488.1039489. S2CID 52827731.
11. Eberhardt, Jacob; Tai, Stefan (July 2018). "ZoKrates - Scalable Privacy-Preserving Off-Chain Computations". 2018 IEEE International Conference on Internet of Things (iThings) and IEEE Green Computing and Communications (GreenCom) and IEEE Cyber, Physical and Social Computing (CPSCom) and IEEE Smart Data (SmartData): 1084–1091. doi:10.1109/Cybermatics_2018.2018.00199.
12. Feige, Uriel; Shamir, Adi (1990). Witness Indistinguishable and Witness Hiding Protocols. Proceedings of the Twenty-second Annual A.C.M. Symposium on Theory of Computing (S.T.O.C.). pp. 416–426. CiteSeerX 10.1.1.73.3911. doi:10.1145/100216.100272. ISBN 978-0897913614. S2CID 11146395.

13. Gabizon, Ariel; Williamson, Zachary J.; Ciobotaru, Oana (2019). "PLONK: Permutations over Lagrange-bases for Oecumenical Noninteractive arguments of Knowledge".

14. Goldreich, Oded (1985). "A zero-knowledge proof that a two-prime moduli is not a Blum integer". Unpublished Manuscript.

15. Goldreich, Oded; Micali, Silvio; Wigderson, Avi (1991). "Proofs that yield nothing but their validity". Journal of the A.C.M. 38 (3): 690–728. CiteSeerX 10.1.1.420.1478. doi:10.1145/116825.116852. S2CID 2389804.

16. Hurst, Samantha. "Zcoin Announces Rebranding to New Name & Ticker "Firo"". Crowdfund Insider. Archived from the original on 30 October 2020. Retrieved 4 November 2020.

17. Kosba, Ahmed; Papamanthou, Charalampos; Shi, Elaine (May 2018). "xJsnark: A Framework for Efficient Verifiable Computation". 2018 IEEE Symposium on Security and Privacy (S.P.): 944–961. doi:10.1109/SP.2018.00018.

18. Maller, Mary; Bowe, Sean; Kohlweiss, Markulf; Meiklejohn, Sarah (6 November 2019). "Sonic: Zero-Knowledge SNARKs from Linear-Size Universal and Updatable Structured Reference Strings". Proceedings of the 2019 ACM SIGSAC Conference on Computer and Communications Security. Association for Computing Machinery: 2111–2128. doi:10.1145/3319535.3339817. hdl:20.500.11820/739b94f1-54f0-4ec3-9644-3c95eea1e8f5.

19. Odendaal, Hansie; Sharrock, Cayle; Heerden, SW. "Bulletproofs and Mimblewimble". Tari Labs University. Archived from the original on 29 September 2020. Retrieved 3 December 2020.

20. Atzei, Nicola; Bartoletti, Massimo; Cimoli, Tiziana (2017), "A survey of attacks on Ethereum smart contracts" (PDF), 6th International Conference on Principles of Security and Trust (POST), European Joint Conferences on Theory and Practice of Software

21. Chen, Tai-yuan; Huang, Wei-ning; Kuo, Po-chun; Chung, Hao (6 August 2020). "Method for Generating Secure Randomness on Blockchain". Retrieved 28 August 2020.

22. CleanApp (January 21, 2019). "Crypto's Founding Fallacy: How Mistakes in the 'Smart Contract' Genesis Block Weaken the Whole Chain". Crypto Law Review.

23. Dawson, R., PegaSys, Baxter, M., & PegaSys. (2019, August 29). Announcing Hyperledger Besu. Hyperledger. https://www.hyperledger.org/blog/2019/08/29/announcing-hyperledger-besu

24. Drummer, Daniel; Neumann, Dirk (5 August 2020). "Is code law? Current legal and technical adoption issues and remedies for blockchain-enabled smart contracts". Journal of Information Technology. 35 (4): 337–360. doi:10.1177/0268396220924669. ISSN 0268-3962. S2CID 225409384.

25. Filatova, Nataliia (1 September 2020). "Smart contracts from the contract law perspective: outlining new regulative strategies". International Journal of Law and Information Technology. 28 (3): 217–242. doi:10.1093/ijlit/eaaa015. ISSN 0967-0769.

26. Fries, Martin; P. Paal, Boris (2019). Smart Contracts (in German). Mohr Siebeck. ISBN 978-3-16-156911-1. JSTOR j.ctvn96h9r.

27. https://blockchainlab.com/pdf/Hyperledger%20Whitepaper.pdf

28. https://consensys.github.io/smart-contract-best-practices/general_philosophy/

29. https://dl.acm.org/doi/abs/10.1145/3391195

30. https://docs.solana.com/running-validator/validator-reqs

31. https://ethereum.org/en/developers/docs/nodes-and-clients/

32. https://wiki.hyperledger.org/pages/viewpage.action?pageId=2394127

33. https://www.computerworld.com/article/3191077/security/

34. Hyman Gayle M, Digesti, Matthew P New Nevada legislation recognizes blockchain and smart contract erminologies August 2017, Nevada Lawyer

35. Hyperledger – Open Source Blockchain Technologies. (n.d.). Hyperledger. Retrieved July 12, 2021, from https://www.hyperledger.org/

36. Cieplak, S Leefatt, 'Smart Contracts: A Smart Way To Automate Performance' (2017) 1 Georgia L & Tech Rev 417

37. Jansen, Marc; Hdhili, Farouk; Gouiaa, Ramy; Qasem, Ziyaad (2020). "Do Smart Contract Languages Need to Be Turing Complete?". Blockchain and Applications. Advances in Intelligent

Systems and Computing. Springer International Publishing. 1010: 19–26. doi: 10.1007/978-3-030-23813-1_3. ISBN 978-3-030-23812-4. S2CID 195656195. S2CID 195656195.

38. Jia, Zhifeng; Chen, Rui; Li, Jie (2019). "DeLottery: A Novel Decentralized Lottery System Based on Blockchain Technology". Proceedings of the 2019 2nd International Conference on Blockchain Technology and Applications. pp. 20–25. doi:10.1145/3376044.3376049. ISBN 9781450377430. S2CID 207880557.

39. Jörg F. Wittenberger (2002). Askemos a distributed settlement. Proceedings of International Conference on Advances in Infrastructure for e-Business, e-Education, e-Science, and e-Medicine on the Internet (S.S.G.R.R.), L'Aquila.

40. Layer 2: https://academy.moralis.io/blog/comparing-layer-2-ethereum-scaling-solutions, https://www.bcskill.com/index.php/archives/965.html, https://l2beat.com/faq/

41. Makhovsky, Andrei (December 22, 2017). "Belarus adopts crypto-currency law to woo foreign investors". Reuters.

42. Martin Möbius (2009). Erstellung eines Archivierungskonzepts für die Speicherung rückverfolgbarer Datenbestände im Askemos-System (Thesis). Hochschule Mittweida.

43. Mik, Eliza, Smart Contracts: A Requiem (December 7, 2019). Journal of Contract Law (2019) Volume 36 Part 1 at p. 72.

44. Morgan, Herbert Smith Freehills LLP-Charlie; Parker, Chris; Livingston, Dorothy; Naish, Vanessa; Tevendale, Craig (23 April 2021). "Arbitration of digital disputes in smart contracts and the release of the digital dispute resolution rules from the U.K. jurisdiction taskforce | Lexology". www.lexology.com. Retrieved 2021-04-25.

45. O. Goldreich, S. Micali, and A. Wigderson. Proofs that yield nothing but their validity or all languages in N.P. have zero-knowledge proof systems. Journal of the A.C.M., 38(3): 691–729, 1991.

46. Oranburg, Seth; Palagashvili, Liya (22 October 2018). "The Gig Economy, Smart Contracts, and Disruption of Traditional Work Arrangements". Search eLibrary. doi:10.2139/ssrn.3270867. S2CID 216803648. SSRN 3270867. Retrieved 25 January 2022.

47. Peck, M. (28 May 2016). "Ethereum's $150-Million Blockchain-Powered Fund Opens Just as Researchers Call For a Halt". IEEE Spectrum. Institute of Electrical and Electronics Engineers.

48. Perez, Daniel; Livshits, Benjamin (17 October 2020). "Smart Contract Vulnerabilities: Vulnerable Does Not Imply Exploited". arXiv:1902.06710 cs. C.R.

49. Praitheeshan, Purathani; Pan, Lei; Yu, Jiangshan; Liu, Joseph; Doss, R. (2019). "Security Analysis Methods on Ethereum Smart Contract Vulnerabilities: A Survey". arXiv:1908.08605 cs. C.R.

50. Ross, Rory (2015-09-12). "Smart Money: Blockchains Are the Future of the Internet". Newsweek. Retrieved 2016-05-27.

51. Sergey, Ilya; Nagaraj, Vaivaswatha; Johannsen, Jacob; Kumar, Amrit; Trunov, Anton; Hao, Ken Chan Guan (10 October 2019). "Safer smart contract programming with Scilla". Proceedings of the A.C.M. on Programming Languages. 3 (OOPSLA): 1–30. doi:10.1145/3360611. ISSN 2475-1421.

52. Snook, Chris J. (31 October 2017). "Blockchain and Artificial Intelligence Are Coming to Kill These 4 Small Business Verticals". Inc.com. Retrieved 25 January 2022.

53. Soloro, Kevin; Kanna, Randall; Hoover, David (December 2019). Hands-On Smart Contract evelopment With Solidity and Ethereum: From Fundamentals to Deployment. California, U.S.A.: O'Reilly. p. 73. ISBN 978-1-492-04526-7. Retrieved 1 November 2020.

54. Tyurin, A.V.; Tyuluandin, I.V.; Maltsev, V.S.; Kirilenko, I.A.; Berezun, D.A. (2019). "Overview of the Languages for Safe Smart Contract Programming". Proceedings of the Institute for System Programming of the RAS. 31 (3): 157–176. doi:10.15514/ispras-2019-31(3)-13. S2CID 203179644.

Appendix E: Data Governance Tools

INTRODUCTION

We will discuss ransomware, data risk assessment (DRA), and tools to review if data security and privacy controls.

RISK ASSESSMENT

DATA RISK ASSESSMENT

A data risk assessment (DRA) is used to review if data security and privacy controls are implemented effectively and meet the risk appetite across all security products and applications in scope. These controls aim to mitigate Operational risks such as noncompliance or privacy/data breach. A DRA is urgently needed to regularly assess how Operational risks arise from gaps and inconsistencies in controls applied by data security, identify management products, and privacy through data protection impact assessments. A DRA is foundational to successfully implementing data security governance (DSG).

OPERATIONAL RELEVANCE

A DRA enables the mitigation of operational risks that will create a variety of financial impacts. It focuses attention on which data risks should be prioritized against the operational risk appetite.

- By identifying gaps and inconsistencies in how existing data security, privacy, and IAM controls are deployed, it enables guidance for changes to controls or new products that might need to be deployed.

REQUIREMENTS

Data is a pervasive asset that evolves in different formats and data repositories across the ever-changing multicloud, hybrid cloud, and IT architectures.

- There is a critical need to connect data risks with operational and financial risks to achieve support from operational leaders so that data access requirements for project teams can be identified.
- The operational and financial risks that affect operational outcomes will drive operational leader support for prioritization of DRAs and recommended actions.
- Operational priorities mean that not every operational risk identified will be prioritized for mitigation given the budget and prioritization of operational outcomes. This operational prioritization will typically focus on a finance-based DRA (FinDRA) and the economic impact to the Operational to decide how large the security budget should be.
- It is relevant to establish how each data or privacy risk impacts each operational risk to drive the focus and prioritization for each stage of the DRA.
- Creating a data mapping and data flow path analysis enables the assessment of privileges provided to each user/machine account against the data in scope.

BARRIERS

To carry out a successful DRA, it is relevant to gain operational leader support to understand the Operational outcomes for each project or service, otherwise security controls could create conflicts with Operational team operations.

- A DRA will only be successful if it can identify all user accounts associated with each project or service and reason certain datasets are accessed with specific privileges.
- Data categorization and discovery across disparate storage repositories can be problematic due to various vendor products that already deploy proprietary data discovery tools.
- The variety and geographic distribution of endpoints creates problems identifying and analyzing user account access to data repositories.
- Identifying all data security, privacy, IAM, and application products that overlay the data flow from the data repository to the endpoints may require support from the Operational leaders.

RISKS ASSESSMENT

FINANCIAL DATA RISK ASSESSMENT (FINDRA)

A financial data risk assessment (FinDRA) prioritizes financial investment decisions to mitigate data security and privacy risks to a acceptable level to balance operational outcomes. FinDRA achieves this prioritization by leveraging infonomics to analyze the financial impacts of operational risks identified through both DSG and data security and privacy risk assessments.

FinDRA enables security and risk management (SECURITY) leaders to translate the language of data security and privacy risks into the language of operational risks and operational outcomes. Operational Impact FinDRA creates the basis to establish a budget for investment in data security, by focusing on how data security and privacy risks affect Operational outcomes in financial terms.

REQUIREMENTS

Organizations exploit various datasets, leading to prolific data growth and Operational risks. However, they rarely—if ever—analyze the financial impacts that can result from investment decisions.

- FinDRA creates an opportunity to understand how financial impacts may emerge from the opportunity costs, waste, and risks associated with each dataset.
- Organizations need to assess how data security and privacy risks associated with security incidents—such as data breaches, privacy enforcement, noncompliance, or even accidental processing—can impact a Operational financially. This assessment capability requires a process to translate the issues of data risks into the language of Operational and financial impacts.

BARRIERS

Most organizations continue to separate the decision processes and responsibilities for data monetization investments from the investment decisions associated with data security and privacy.

- SECURITY leaders are normally not included in Operational decisions to use data. Therefore, they do not have the opportunity to translate the impacts of disparate security and privacy risks into Operational outcomes.

- Operational leaders do not understand the language of data security and privacy risks and will frequently prioritize Operational access to data over data-security-led controls.

Privacy Impact Assessments (PIAs)

Privacy impact assessments (PIAs) enable organizations to identify and treat privacy risk. Typically conducted before implementing new processing activities and/or major changes, the PIA starts with a quick scan (looking at the process owner and description, types of data processed for specific purposes, and retention periods per purpose).

A full PIA adds legal grounds, potential impact on data subjects, and mitigating measures to ensure a controlled personal data processing environment. A rapidly shifting regulatory privacy landscape has mandated that organizations develop foundational insight into what personal data they process, reason, and how it is protected. Very few organizations have the means to demonstrate insight in and control over personal data across the various repositories and silo types, let alone how they're used—or intended to be used. This insight, however, is vital to proportionate and adequate deployment of privacy and security controls.

Operational Impact A PIA aids in regulatory compliance, improves control over personal data throughout the data life cycle, and helps determine authorization and access management. It collaterally assists in preventing (internal) data breaches and personal data misuse. It helps SECURITY leaders quantify risk to subjects and timely apply suitable mitigating controls. Conducting PIAs frequently and consistently provides a basis for responsible and transparent personal data management.

REQUIREMENTS

PIAs are one of the cornerstones of an effective privacy program. However, many organizations conduct PIAs manually, using spreadsheets and questionnaires. With increasing volumes and the need for repetition of PIAs, a manual approach becomes unmanageable. It also traps the skills needed to conduct PIAs with a few people rather than making them part of an organization's data-handling fabric.

- PIA automation tools allow for API-driven triggers to initiate the assessment process, collecting the needed information at every step and tracking it through a predefined workflow until a case is closed or flagged for remediation.

BARRIERS

Often considered a tedious task because of poorly conceived manual workflows, there is a certain PIA fatigue in organizations where this activity has been mandatory for a longer period. Operational partners' view of a checkbox mentality does not help the quality of the PIA. Others simply underestimate its relevance and position and do not complete accurate PIAs or fail to frequently keep them updated, making the initial attempt essentially an ultimately futile one.

Guidance

Appoint and mandate Operational process owners responsible for their respective personal data processing activities.

- Require PIAs to be conducted as a mandatory, frequently reiterated activity. Ensure to triage the necessity for PIAs in change processes and the introduction of new processing activities.
- Include the PIA's results—especially from large projects—in the corporate risk register for monitoring and follow-up.

- Extend the assessment's effectiveness to processing personal data carried out by service providers by demanding that they complete and periodically revise a full PIA.
- Either provide for a PIA model centrally (e.g., as an internal automated workflow process) or require it to be conducted as a manual exercise when a less mature procedure suffices.

FRAMEWORK TO BALANCE BUSINESS NEEDS AND RISKS

The opportunities to use data are growing exponentially, but so too are the business and financial risks. Security and risk management leaders should use the DSG framework to mitigate business risks caused by security threats, data residency, and privacy issues, according to Gartner.

Key Challenges

- Organizations face increasing risks of financial liabilities, as the number of data protection and privacy regulations grows internationally.
- The growing number of privacy incidents and data breaches due to hacking, malicious insiders, and accidental disclosures is destroying brands and customer trust, resulting in increased financial liabilities.
- Data is spreading across hybrid IT infrastructure on-premises and multicloud services, but businesses are failing to develop consistent and holistic data security and privacy policies that keep pace.
- Increasing numbers of data security, privacy and identity access management products are in use, but they do not integrate, do not share common policies, and have siloed coverage of data stores and security functionality.

RECOMMENDATIONS

Security and risk management leaders responsible for data security and privacy should:

- Use the DSG framework to prioritize and address the complex array of business risks that need to be mitigated.
  Investigate how prioritized business risks might emerge throughout the data management life cycle.
- Use continuous adaptive risk and trust assessment (CARTA) to select appropriate security policy rules and controls that will mitigate critical business risks.
- Review data security policy rules annually, and whenever business risks change, to identify and address any gaps or inconsistencies.

CISOs and security and risk management (SRM) leaders responsible for data security and privacy must commit to implementing a DSG framework suited to the growth and proliferation of data. DSG helps provide a balance between the business need to maximize competitive advantage and the need to develop appropriate security policies that mitigate the prioritized business risks.

These policies will allow the development of appropriate policy rules that can be orchestrated through the available selection of security products and their controls. DSG requires collaboration across the security and data and analytics teams, typically led by the CISO and the chief data officer (CDO). Collaborations are already forming between the teams of the CISO and the data protection (or privacy) officer (DPO), due to the strong overlap in requirements for data security and privacy. Data budget responsibility is also increasingly split across different roles, including the CIO, chief marketing officer (CMO), chief risk officer (CRO), and DPO. Collaboration between the CISO and CDO is essential to perform several crucial functions, including:

- Align governance processes across different roles.
- Align approaches for data classification and data life cycle management.

Data Intelligence and Governance Market, IDC Data Control Plane

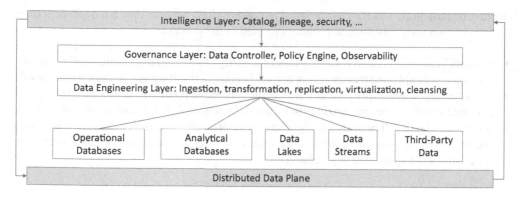

Source: Adapted from IDC

DATA CLASSIFICATION

Data classification is organizing information assets using an agreed-upon categorization, taxonomy, or ontology. The result is typically a large repository of metadata useful for making further decisions, or the application of a "tag" to an object to facilitate the use and governance of the data, including application of controls during its life cycle. Reason

This Is Relevant Data classification enables an effective and efficient prioritization for data governance programs that span value, security, access, usage, privacy, storage, ethics, quality, and retention. It is vital to security, privacy, and data governance programs. It also gives organizations the required knowledge about the sensitivity of their process data.

IMPACT

Data classification can be used to support a wide range of use cases, for example:

- Applying data security controls, for example, DLP and EDRM
- Privacy compliance
- Risk mitigation
- Master data and application data management
- Data stewardship
- Content and records management
- Data catalogs for operations and analytics.

REQUIREMENTS

The data classification approaches include categorization by data type, owner, regulation, or classification by data sensitivity or retention requirements. This enables organizations to focus on security, privacy, and analytics efforts on their relevant datasets.

- When properly designed and executed, classification serves as one of the foundations supporting the ethical processing of data throughout the organization.

BARRIERS

Data classification initiatives have often failed in organizations because they are dependent on manual efforts by users with insufficient training involved in the process.

- Classification efforts often revolve around a security-centric mindset, which means the purposes are not explained to users using natural language, resulting in low engagement levels.
- Today many vendors provide automated classification products, which can offer more accurate results while minimizing user efforts. However, it is relevant to note that, while automatic classification tools can significantly improve the amount of data classified, they are not 100% accurate, especially if the tools have been created using ML/AI algorithms where models require ongoing training.

PRIVACY MANAGEMENT TOOLS

Privacy management tools help organizations facilitate compliance insights and check processing activities against regulatory requirements. They bring structure to privacy processes and workflows, enhance insight into data flows and governance maturity, and monitor and track the privacy program's maturity progression.

IMPORTANCE

The increasing maturity of data protection legislation globally forces organizations to maintain awareness and control of personal data processing operations. Following the EU's GDPR, several countries have enacted or are finalizing similar laws. From state laws like the CCPA in the United States to national initiatives like Brazil's LGPD and India's PDPB, many requirements are similar to (but not the same as) GDPR. Managing compliance overviews manually is, thus, not impossible.

OPERATIONAL IMPACT

Privacy management tools allow Operational leaders to assume accountability when handling personal data, and enable transparency and control over those activities. They contain audit capabilities to demonstrate compliance especially across multiple jurisdictions. Point solutions are seeing more integration into suites to account for increasingly automated enablement of a privacy UX, vendor risk management, data intelligence inventories, etc.

The privacy landscape is becoming increasingly complex. Gartner estimates that by 2024, 75% of the world's population will have its personal information covered under modern privacy regulations. We calculate that by 2024, over 80% of organizations worldwide will face modern privacy and data protection requirements.

BARRIERS

After time, a sense of "good enough" can lead to delays in adopting privacy management tools, or worse, an absence of (automated) integration to reap the maximum benefit.

On the other hand, some already have point solutions for privacy UX components, data breach response, or impact assessments, and overlook other complementary capabilities in an integrated suite. Attempts to integrate loose components from various vendors often become disappointing.

- Finally, various organizations take a "wait-and-see" approach. The absence of immediate sanctions or investigations makes pressure seem to subside.

GUIDANCE

Incorporate the rapidly evolving privacy landscape demands into the organization's data strategy by developing a common baseline driven by applicable regulatory guidelines and privacy frameworks available.

- Maintain a focus on overarching capabilities relevant across the board, including PIAs, records of processing activities (RoPAs), consistent vendor risk management, and a people-centric privacy UX.
- Accept, adapt, and evolve with the new Operational challenges to privacy by leading with a cost-optimized set of privacy capabilities.

ENSURING PROTECTION OF YOUR DATA

Ensuring protection of your data and your customers' data is a never-ending challenge. Many security practitioners fail to understand some key gaps in the data security threat model.

ENCRYPTION COMPLEXITY

Most encryption is mis-applied, and quite frankly, doesn't do anything to protect your data. The protection measures that are most commonly used do NOTHING to protect you against modern hacks and breaches. For companies who have accepted that they will be attacked and breached, data-centric security can provide an effective counter-measure to attackers in your network.

MEASURE RISK

MEASURE RE-IDENTIFICATION RISK IN STRUCTURED DATA

Enhance your understanding of data privacy risk. Quasi-identifiers are partially identifying elements or combinations of data that may link to a single person or a very small group. Cloud DLP allows you to measure statistical properties such as k-anonymity and l-diversity, expanding your ability to understand and protect data privacy.

POPULAR FEATURES

- Automatic discovery, inspection, and classification.
- Flexible classification with pre-defined detectors focuses on quality, speed, and scale. Detectors are improving and expanding all the time.
- Simple ways to De-identify your data with redact, mask, tokenize, and transform text and images to help ensure data privacy.

RISK TOOLS

SUBJECT RIGHTS REQUESTS (SRRS)

Subject rights requests (SRRs) are a set of legal rights enabling individuals to make demands for clarity and in some instances change regarding their data and how it is used. Organizations handling this data must address these requests in a defined time frame. These rights come in three categories—informative, corrective, and restrictive. Their execution implicitly requires multiple capabilities of a modern privacy management program such as personal data discovery, automation, and mapping.

WHY THIS IS IMPORTANT

SRR management has evolved from anonymity to center-stage status in a few years due to the advancement in privacy legislation (such as the GDPR, CCPA, and LGPD), as well as increased consumer concern over handling their personal data. Today, over one billion individuals accounting for almost one-third of the global economy can exercise these rights freely.

SUMMARY

We discussed ransomware, data risk assessment (DRA), and tools to review if data security and privacy controls.

NOTES

1. https://techxplore.com/news/2022-03-homomorphic-encryption.html
2. https://go.chainalysis.com/rs/503-FAP-074/images/Crypto-Crime-Report-2022.pdf
3. https://www.zdnet.com/article/ransomware-as-a-service-negotiators-between-hackers-and-victims-are-now-in-high-demand/
4. https://arx.deidentifier.org/overview/privacy-criteria/
   IHS 2016 Update: The Complexities of Physician Supply and Demand: Projections from 2014 to 2025
5. https://www.aamc.org/download/458082/data/2016_complexities_of_supply_and_demand_projections.pdf
   Mckinsey & Company (August, 2016): How tech-enabled consumers are reordering the healthcare landscape. http://healthcare.mckinsey.com/how-tech-enabled-consumers-are-reordering-healthcarelandscape

Index

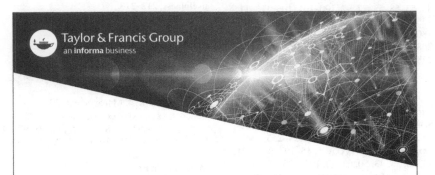

Printed in the United States
by Baker & Taylor Publisher Services